Gender Lessons

Teaching Gender

Volume 4

Series Editor
Patricia Leavy
USA

Scope
Teaching Gender publishes monographs, anthologies and reference books that deal centrally with gender and/or sexuality. The books are intended to be used in undergraduate and graduate classes across the disciplines. The series aims to promote social justice with an emphasis on feminist, multicultural and critical perspectives.

Please email queries to the series editor at pleavy7@aol.com

Gender Lessons

Patriarchy, Sextyping & Schools

Scott Richardson
Millersville University, Millersville, USA

SENSE PUBLISHERS
ROTTERDAM/BOSTON/TAIPEI

A C.I.P. record for this book is available from the Library of Congress.

ISBN: 978-94-6300-029-1 (paperback)
ISBN: 978-94-6300-030-7 (hardback)
ISBN: 978-94-6300-031-4 (e-book)

Published by: Sense Publishers,
P.O. Box 21858,
3001 AW Rotterdam,
The Netherlands
https://www.sensepublishers.com/

Cover art: Emily A. Pellini

Printed on acid-free paper

PRAISE FOR GENDER LESSONS: PATRIARCHY, SEXTYPING & SCHOOLS

"Read how kids and their teachers conspire to create the illusion that gender is uniform. In 'pledging the patriarchy' even the victors are victimized by the 'sextyping' schools accommodate and sometimes espouse. Read about teachers who sometimes teach gender lessons to their students a little too 'up close and personal.' No muckraker, Richardson reports what he learned from his resounding research, not always telling us what we're supposed to learn but allowing the facts themselves to teach. But if you haven't learned your lesson by chapter 6, you'll grasp it then. (Ah, the French, once again). Even if Richardson didn't have kids – he has two, Mali and Maria – you know he'd make a great Dad, because he is a great teacher: 'My hope is that we might fully recognize children as complex individuals—that we go beyond any biological assignment, and resist the pressure to stereotype (sextype) how boys and girls are "supposed to act".' Scott Richardson understands. Read for yourself." **William F. Pinar, Ph.D., Professor and Canada Research Chair, University of British Columbia, Vancouver, Canada**

"In the 1970s, feminists fought to reform sexist school curricula and challenged taken-for-granted tracking of boys and girls. Forty years later, drawing from personal experiences and insightful research in schools, Scott Richardson shows us that the job is far from finished. Informal interactions and stubborn sexist beliefs about gender difference still press girls and boys in primary, middle and high schools into different—and highly constraining—gender boxes. Teachers, parents, and anyone who cares about taking the next steps toward gender equality in schools will find in Gender Lessons a useful and hopeful map to a better future for our kids." **Michael A. Messner, Ph.D., Professor of Sociology and Gender Studies at the University of California, Berkeley and author of *Some Men: Feminist Allies and the Movement to End Violence Against Women***

"Dr. Richardson has done an excellent job providing an accessible and scholarly analysis of the ways in which gender is taught and reproduced in school settings. His style of combining personal narratives with data from his team's detailed observations in schools give readers an engaging entry point to think carefully about what he calls sextyping. He provides many examples that describe and problematize everyday practices in average K-12 schools and classrooms. These examples are familiar to anyone working in K-12 schools, but his analysis offers a new lens for many that can expose the frustrating and often heartbreaking nature of these taken-for-granted cultural norms. This book is unique in that it includes data from elementary, middle, and high schools from both students' and teachers' perspectives. His writing is provocative, engaging, and contributes to an important body of research that can help parents, educators, and policy makers think differently about what effective and inclusive schools look like."
Elizabeth J. Meyer, Ph.D., Assistant Professor of Education at California Polytechnic State University and author of *Gender and Sexual Diversity in Schools*

For Yara

TABLE OF CONTENTS

FOREWORD

In August before I started junior high school, I bought supplies I had not needed in elementary school. For my notebook I knew I had to get a pencil case. I liked the large one with bright colors rather than the smaller white one. "Those are the ones the girls buy," the store manager told my mother. So I put it back on the shelf. I also learned in the first week of junior high that the popular boys carried their books under one arm. I thought it made more sense to use both arms to carry the stack in front of my body. My arm hurt when I lugged four large textbooks on one side. But only girls carried their books in front, my best friend told me. That settled it—I lived with sore arms rather than risk social suicide.

Most of us learn early on what is and is not expected of boys and girls. The lessons come from many teachers—parents, friends, television stars, favorite musicians, the church…and from our school teachers. What we learn in classrooms usually reinforces what we already picked up outside the school when we were very young.

So the teachers you will meet in this book did not cause what Scott Richardson calls "sextyping." When a first grade teacher told the boys to wear cowboy hats and the girls to put on tiaras for a concert, she did what her community expected. Men and women differ, and the sooner our kids know it, the better. This isn't discrimination; it's reality. "Sounds like you live in a different world," one teacher told Scott when he questioned that view of life.

But if the teachers in this book did not cause sextyping, they certainly did not challenge it…or even talk about it. They accepted and often reinforced what we academics say is "constructed"—a view that gender is a performance. It is not innate, genetic, or inborn. Very few teachers wanted to be what the great sociologist David Riesman once called a "countervailing force"—the daring idea that educators should occasionally question what others take for granted. In fact, they celebrated the labeling and stereotyping that would, in their opinion, prepare the young to be happy heterosexual adults.

Several teachers agreed with Scott's view that separate is never equal, but they were a small group who met together, voluntarily, each morning. Even when Scott joined them, they only talked about sextyping after he raised the issue, and the very best conversation took place outside school, fueled by mimosas. There are few spaces in most schools for discussion of issues that aren't linked to the agenda of higher test scores. The vignettes in this book that make us cringe can happen so often because the classroom doors are closed.

But Scott got in. It wasn't easy—he had to pretend he was studying academic success when in fact he knew from the start that he wanted to extend the extraordinary work of his first book, EleMENtary School. It wasn't funded —Scott is a countervailing force because he is an ethnographer—a close observer who spends months in schools—in an age when scholarship without statistics is out of fashion. He stands apart by virtue of how he acts as well as what he believes.

An astute observer of early 19th century America, Alexis deTocqueville, said that "the majority lives in the perpetual practice of self-applause, and there are certain truths which the Americans can only learn from strangers or from experience." In this book we have the experience of a savvy stranger in a school district that is all too American.

Robert L. Hampel
School of Education, University of Delaware
Author, *Paul Diederich and the Progressive American High School* (2014)

ACKNOWLEDGEMENTS

Ethnographic work of this kind requires years in the field, constant processing of ideas with anyone who would listen, and endless lonely hours, blurry eyed, behind the glow of a computer. For me, it also required squatting in bars, coffee shops and anywhere I could find an electrical outlet. This work survived multiple computer crashes and my losing the only copy of the manuscript on a bus in Reykjavík. Luckily, I had a supportive team of people who kept me going.

My dedicated and wicked smart research assistants are amazing. Thank you to Khoan Ly, Sabrina Hensel, Samantha Lang, Brandon Leinbach, Kortney Gipe, and Jenna Bisbing.

I was gifted with a talented core of readers who provided invaluable advice. I greatly owe Yara Graupera, Elizabeth Soslau, Angela Wilson Kost, and Robert L. Hampel for giving me critical feedback from start to finish. Thanks also to Edwin Minguela, Mel Cleveland, Cajetan Berger, Edward Woestman, Savannah Rosensteel, Brent Schrader, Jessica Heindel, Dagmar Snowadzky, Dana Morrison Simone, Lindsay Eisenhut, Maria Cristina Bucur, Robert Jones, and Khristina Schultz.

I work with great colleagues in the Educational Foundations Department at Millersville University, to whom I owe significant thanks. In particular, Thomas Neuville for engaging in any half-baked idea at any time, Ojoma Edeh Herr for providing me with new writing spaces, Tiffany Wright for allowing me to force impromptu readings on her, and John Ward for always playing devil's advocate.

Thank you Patricia Leavy, a gifted editor with vision, generosity, and insight who has given my work a great home in the *Teaching Gender Series*.

Most of all, I am thankful to my family—all of you—for listening, reading, editing, challenging and questioning. It is you who provide me with deep inspiration.

…Mali and Maria, thanks for letting me be your dad.

TO AN EDUCATIONAL SYSTEM ATTEMPTING TO PREPACKAGE THE HUMAN CONDITION

When I was in the second grade,
the collars on my dresses were fastened like nooses around necks
to fit the mold of a woman
and to protect the boys from distractions.

Boys will be boys, so the girls need to cover up and shut up.

I wondered what rules I could depend on when I couldn't breathe
in this packaging you trapped me in,
yet your tune remains unchanged:

My gender is a lifeline carved into my hand
that will determine what I can and can't do
and if I am not a white boy basking in the hyper-masculine,
I cannot be equal.

My option has been preselected
predetermined by what's "down there"
(because god forbid we learn about our own organs and hormones
and how to safely engage them without a trial by pregnancy).

In history, you reduce us to footnotes
and contextualize our existence to that of a man.
I want to be complete on my own
but you say that makes me the sick one
for wanting to leave this box.

In math and science, you blame my vagina if I don't know the answer
when you should probably check your lesson plan
because while you keep insisting that there are only two options,
I know boys who are sensitive and demure

and girls who are calculating and adventurous
and kids who don't fit into your pronouns.

Your prescription is conformity,
but if students are committing suicide
because they couldn't fit,
Then these boxes are nothing more than coffins.

We are not the sick ones.
An education system with a fatality rate
is the one that needs a cure.

It starts in the classroom.
It starts with opening your eyes and realizing
you have more than just "boys" and "girls."
you have essays and poems
movement, energy, opinions
dirt and charcoal
paintings breaking out of their frames
touchdowns and scores of
symphonic melodies crafted by laughter.

You have students.
You have us.

—Nicole Weerbrouck

FIELD NOTE

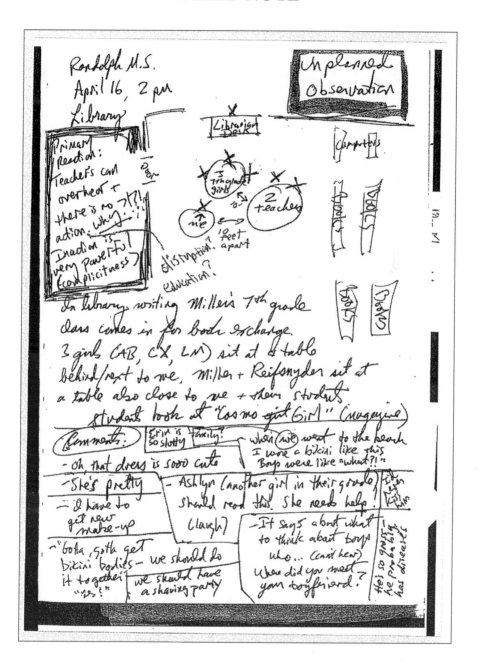

xvii

INTRODUCTION

This book is about how schools sextype and institutionalize gender. I explore how schools, particularly Monroe Valley, a suburban school district, explicitly and implicitly *teach* girls to perform femininity and boys to perform masculinity.

I am not the first person to write about how schools establish specific cultural roles and expectations for kids. There are many important books in this field. I am simply providing another example so that we may be opened to more conversations. This research employs ethnographic/narrative methodologies; makes sense of data by pulling from theories grounded in curriculum inquiry, sociology, philosophy, and gender studies; and creates narratives by weaving together conversations, observations, and interviews. In some cases, particularly when I use student voices, I employ composite non-fiction[2] so that I can offer more anonymity. Blended research methodology such as this may make it difficult for some readers to "trust" the researcher because the tone is less "research technical."[3] Traditional academics argue that work like this may not be taken seriously. To a large extent, I am not concerned about traditionalists, or about how traditional academic paradigms attempt to define and confine (essentially creating a monopoly) how inquiry needs to happen. As a writer, I chose this blended path, and work hard to create a narrative tone because I view it as important to connect with a broader audience (teachers, parents, students, academics, and so on) and engage them in their own sense-making processes.

This book is chock-full of examples detailing how gender is taught in schools. I am afraid that so many examples might make reading this work become tedious. I hear voices in my head, "Alright, alright, Scott, we get it." But the dozens of examples I provide here represent only a fraction of what I observed. I considered scaling back how many examples I should provide, but resisted because 1) the institutionalization of gender is a conversation rarely held, 2) readers have a better chance at connecting with certain stories and make sense of their own (or their students'/kids' school experiences), 3) few works have catalogued daily school happenings based in sextyping, and 4) gender is so incredibly pervasive…it is everywhere, in everything.

My hope is that we might fully recognize children as complex individuals—that we go beyond any biological assignment, and resist the pressure to stereotype (sextype) how boys and girls are "supposed to act." It is also my hope to *really* recognize that "racism, sexism, and elitism all have concrete institutional locations,"[4] and that it is our duty to radically reimagine these spaces.

NOTES

[1] Some examples: C. J. Pascoe, Dude You're a Fag: Masculinity and Sexuality in High School (Berkeley, CA: University of California Press, 2007); Lois Weis, ed., Class, Race, & Gender in American Education (New York, NY: SUNY Press, 1988); Judith Kleinfeld & Suzanne Yerian, eds., Gender Tales: Tensions in the Schools (New York, NY: St. Martin's Press, 1995); Emma Renold, Girls, Boys and Junior Sexualities: Exploring Children's Gender and Sexual Relations in the Primary School (New York, NY: Routledge, 2005); Peggy Orenstein, Schoolgirls: Young Women, Self-Esteem, and the Confidence Gap (New York, NY: Anchor Books, 1994); Barrie Thorne, Gender Play: Girls and Boys in School (New Brunswick, NJ: Rutgers University Press; 1993); Sarah A. Chase, Perfectly Prep: Gender Extremes at a New England Prep School (New York, NY: Oxford University Press; 2008).

[2] Theodore R. Sizer, Horace's Compromise: The Dilemma of the American High School (Boston, MA: Mariner Books; 1984).

[3] Also, the methods section of this book (Chapter 2, "Getting Into It") details how I gleaned information—how I came to know what I knew. This allows me to speak on behalf of participants in the study (e.g., how a student felt in a specific circumstance, or how a teacher interprets school policy, and so on) throughout the rest of the work without having to qualify every instance along the way. I find this technique useful and important for many reasons, but most importantly so that I do not continue to disrupt the powerful narrative of participants' experiences. For a good example of a work that is similar in nature, see: Tracey Kidder, Among School (Boston, MA: Houghton Mifflin Harcourt, 1989).

[4] Patricia Hill Collins, "Toward a New Vision: Race, Class, and Gender as Categories of Analysis and Connection," in Privilege: A Reader, eds. Michael Kimmel and Abby Ferber (Boulder, CO: Westview Press, 2010), 237.

DEAR MRS. BALDWIN, I'M CONCERNED

The word on the street, or at least in academic circles, is that by now it is well understood that gender is a social construct. Babies are born *sexed* with genitalia and often, before they open their eyes, they are swaddled in blue or pink. Bam! *Gendered.* "Baby banners announcing, 'It's a boy!' or 'It's a girl!' should read, 'I'm ascribing this baby boyhood' or 'I'm socially constructing this baby as a girl.'[1] Family members, teachers, communities, media, and more all work to continue to impose gender on individuals from birth through adulthood, and even beyond death.

"Grandpa was such a gentleman. He never raised a hand to those kids unless one of his boys was disrespecting a woman."

"She was so sweet. Jane was a great neighbor. Even into her eighties you could tell she used to turn a lot of heads. And she was always so put together…never left the house without her high heels."

A coffee shop near my house is a hot spot for stay at home moms. Toting their small children to brunch in bucket seats, strollers, and swaddles, they connect with one another chatting about money, school, husbands, parenting, sex, vacations, among other things. They fawn over each other's kids. One day I was watching a group of four moms, likely in their lower thirties, sipping lattes and going through the usual topics.

"Bill's applying for that new job at the courthouse…"

"Lexi hasn't pooped in a day, I'm going to call the pediatrician or I'm going to stuff her full of applesauce and prunes…"

"I just don't like the beach as much anymore, I think we'll try a ski resort this year…"

Interrupting, a friend of theirs, smiling from ear to ear, walked through the door. She was carrying her newborn, and it was evident that the rest of the moms have not yet met this kid.

"Oh my goodness! He's so handsome!" one mom exclaimed.

1

Another threw her arms around her friend, "You are so lucky to have such a cute little guy! He's going to be a lady-killer!"

"Oh, look at those eyes…you're flirting with me, aren't you?"

I thought about joining the conversation just to see what would happen, "You are one sexy baby…give me a call later." Surely, I would have been told off. But is it not absurd to sexualize an infant? To immediately bathe a two week-old in heteronormativity? And what if a group of dads did this around a newborn daughter?

"I bet she is going to date lots of men when she's a teenager."

"She is so hot!"

"Your daughter is giving me eyes…"

Girls too are gendered at birth, but differently. Boys are expected to hit the ground running, looking for the next girl to conquer. Girls are expected to be adorable little princesses, with their sexuality guarded by their fathers. From, "Oh, you're daddy's little girl…" to purity rings, daddy-daughter dances, the omnipresent threat of a boyfriend having to deal with dad if he took things too far (in my teenage years, a father once told me, "Don't make me have a talk with you behind the shed.") to fathers giving their daughters away at weddings.

Gender is continually constructed and imposed on each of us. Westernized heteronormative scripts are practically handed to us on day one. And the people in our lives (acting as producers, directors, and audience members) will continue to make sure we stick to the script: no improvising allowed; be your character, play your gendered performance. These scripts and performances *do* serve a perceived important purpose. They allow us to make quick sense of who one is/ should be and what we can expect of them depending if they are a man or woman. It is an unfair act of generalization that cues us to interact with each other in particular ways. But it does something else too. It helps to maintain what bell hooks calls:

"white supremacist capitalist patriarchy"—"the interlocking systems of domination that define our reality" (as quoted in Jhally, 1997). "White," "supremacist," and "capitalist" are adjectives modifying "patriarchy," the noun, which she defines as, "a political-social system that insists that males are inherently dominating, superior to everything and everyone deemed weak, especially females, and endowed with the right to dominate and rule over the weak and to maintain that dominance through various forms of psychological terrorism and violence" (hooks, 2004, p. 18). This is strong wording. It may be difficult to "see" psychological terrorism and violence in most of our everyday lives because patriarchy does not always (need to) explicitly employ it. What this means to me is that psychological terrorism and violence is often implicitly present, and ready to be unleashed if white men begin to lose their dominant status in our society.[2]

White supremacist capitalist patriarchy is both a long held American tradition (like baseball and apple pie) and enemy number one (that is, if we desire progress). Our gendering process does nothing but uphold and seriously defend this system of deep inequality. Related and just as important to recognize, I believe, is my claim that by teaching discreet performances of femininity and masculinity, and by not reimagining new genders and rendering them available to youth, *we are limiting our children's capabilities to be fully human*. It is simple: if we were to teach *all* of our children how to perform, enact, and own the great range of human traits—regardless of whether they are/used to be considered "masculine" and "feminine"—their potential to become more whole, well-rounded, and relatable would be exponentially greater. They would grow to better understand each other as individuals and produce a society that might be ready to take on, or starve, the white supremacist capitalist patriarchy in older generations. Our kids deserve the chance to be fully human, to become self-determined and self-actualized without the imposing boundaries of gendered performances. They deserve to challenge white supremacist capitalist patriarchy. But we have to teach them differently, now.

Though this book describes the institutionalization of gender, it is also a call for deinstitutionalization. There is no need for children to learn gender in a binary (male/female) and static manner. Society should be more nuanced by now, and demand that our schools recognize and actively teach about a flexible and ever evolving spectrum of gender. Enough, "boys and girls, line up," already. I know this is a tall order.

It would mean that teachers, administrators and others who work in schools must be open to, and receive, an education of their own. Many adults undoubtedly want what is best for children, but fail to see that by categorizing and enforcing "girl" and "boy" expectations, they work to limit kids to certain gendered performances.[3] These performances, then, become difficult to break and are expected of us over a lifetime. So, deinstitutionalizing gender for kids at an early age is important. This does seem like a utopic dream, but I do not see any reasonable excuse for leaving deinstitutionalization unexplored, especially since we already have a wide reaching publicly funded mechanism in place that could do this work: schools.

My philosophical positioning has been influenced by many factors: my experiences growing up as a boy and man, my work as a male elementary school teacher in a perceived "feminized" context, and by making general observations about gender relations in this country.[4] The status of women, particularly women of color, in this country is quite unimaginable. I am equally concerned about this "remasculinization" movement[5] that is being wielded, as if men are really suffering from the same economic and social disparities as women. Women are steadily, for the first time in American history, graduating at higher rates than men from all levels of education, from high school, bachelors, masters, and doctoral programs.[6] However, women are still paid $0.77 to every $1.00 a man makes for the same job.[7] Obviously, we do not live in a meritocracy in the U.S. Actual achievement is of little concern if it is by women. Also, there is the on-going epidemic of sexual harassment and assault that victimizes women mostly, but hurts men too. I could go on, and on, but the three extremely important phenomena that I theorize about and inspire me the most for this work are:

1. the relatively ignored socialization process that happens in and outside of our schools;
2. my undergraduate students, many of them fresh out of high school, who have learned—and perform well—stereotypical gendered behaviors that interfere with their education;
3. the deep worry I have for my own children in this gendered world.

GENDER SOCIALIZATION

In graduate school, when I first became interested in gender, I sought the help of a sociologist. She was well known for her work, and I needed to conceptualize "masculinity" and "femininity." We met at her office, and I sat nervously twitching in the uncomfortable wooden chair that was for visiting students. I only knew her by reputation, but I definitely did not want to seem dumb. I was still in the "imposter phase," wondering if I was good enough to be a graduate student and academic.

"So, what is it that you want my help with?"

I do not remember exactly what I said, but it was word soup; a jumble of things.

"I'm not really sure I understand. What exactly are you researching?"

After serving up more word soup, finally, I asked, "Has 'masculinity' and 'femininity' been defined? And if so, how?"

She smiled and pointed to a collection of rap CDs on her table. "Are those masculine or feminine?"

"I feel like this is a trick."

"It's not a trick, just tell me. When you look at those, do you think they are masculine or feminine?"

"Masculine."

"Why?"

"I don't know. I think about rap music, and most of the artists are men. I guess I know more men who listen to rap."

"OK, that's good. It's related to your reason. But just visually, tell me, what do you see?"

"Ummm...the labels are high contrast, lots of sharp lines, bold black and white shapes."

"Ok, good. How about that plant over there?" She pointed toward her window.

"Feminine."

"Why?"

"It has tiny flowers, it's green...I think of nurturing."

She smiled at me and said, "Do you need a definition of 'masculine' and 'feminine' after all?"

We parted ways with her saying, "Don't worry about it, everyone knows what 'masculine' and 'feminine' is, and sometimes they give words to it, but most times, we just know.

I was startled that this person, a social scientist, who lives in the world of academia, when given the opportunity to exhaustively define and ascribe meaning to constructs was just so nonchalant about it.

In the following months, I thought about it more, and did my own scouring of academic literature but remained without any solid definition. It was only after reading R. W. Connell's work on masculinity that I finally "gave in." Gender was not to be defined outside of the likes of silly internet blogs, YouTube videos ("Shit White Girls Say") and "young women's magazine" polls ("Quiz! Are You a Real Lady?").

> Connell's model asserts that there are a variety of masculinities, which makes sense only in hierarchical and contested relations with one another. R. W. Connell argues that men enact and embody different configurations of masculinity depending on their positions within a social hierarchy of power. *Hegemonic masculinity*, the type of gender practice that, in a given space and time, supports gender inequality, is at the top of this hierarchy. *Complicit masculinity*, describes men who benefit from hegemonic masculinity but do not enact it; *subordinated masculinity* describes men who are oppressed by definitions of hegemonic masculinity, primarily gay men; *marginalized masculinity* describes men who may be positioned powerfully in terms of gender but not in terms of class or race.[8]

Connell is careful to point out that masculinity is also flexible and "inherently relational" with "femininity." "'Masculinity' does not exist except in contrast and relation with 'femininity'."[9] "Masculinity," or femininity, "to the extent the term can be briefly defined at all, is simultaneously a place in gender relations, the practices through which men and women engage that place in gender, and the effects of these practices in bodily experience, personality and culture."[10]

So, yes, there is no one definition of "masculinity" or "femininity." This leaves us with just "knowing," or "sensing," by tapping into our cultural understandings of these terms, from moment to moment, situation to situation. While these constructs of "masculinity" and "femininity" are difficult to put into exact words, "as a society we have little trouble in recognizing it."[11] And we certainly have little trouble creating it. Practically everything around us has some sort of gendered meaning—from concrete materials like CDs and plants to abstract concepts like care and problem solving. Genres, subject matter, and interests also get gendered. Since forever women have been considered deficient in science, technology, engineering, and math (the "STEM" fields). Of course, there are no good reasons for the absence of women in these fields, and only now are we really taking this problem seriously.

We map on gendered meanings to everything, and we have expectations of how one should interact or engage with our world, accordingly. Even if we try to cancel out, or ignore, gendered meanings others ascribe, or we are conscious to not create performances that reify stereotypical "girl" and "boy" culture, we still end up feeling the pressure to conform/perform for two primary reasons. The first is social/economic, and the other is environmental.

Let's pretend that a stereotypical hypermasculine man uncharacteristically begins to perform femininity—wears a little bit of make-up or is openly emotional—or a stereotypical hyperfeminine woman uncharacteristically begins to perform masculinity—develops an interest in basketball or buys a Harley—their friends and family might express confusion. Perhaps it would be so confusing that their friends and family might not know how to interact or continue in their relationships in a comfortable manner. Employers might also find these transitions confusing and downright unwelcomed. This might have direct impact on their ability to support their employee's work. There are many examples that could be made, but here is an easy one: In the restaurant business (unless they are progressive or openly affirming) it would be hard to imagine that an androgynous person (despite how competent they might be) would be rewarded a job waiting on tables over a sweet, smiling, passive and pretty woman or funny nice guy. In sum, those who break gender rules, or are "border crossers,"[12] will suffer social and economic consequences for simply being who they are. On a personal note, I often wonder what might happen if I wore a skirt to class. How would my college students react? How about my colleagues? What about the dean?! I have not been brave enough, yet, because things could drastically change for me. I am a newer faculty member, and would like a long successful career—and this simple act might have deep professional (economic) and social repercussions. Perhaps I would be denied tenure and promotion. I should point out that I have no real inclination to wear a skirt, but that the option is not even really available keeps me from sincerely considering it. Who knows, maybe it is something I might like and identify with. How awful is it that the perceptions of others, and the threat of unnecessary consequences, keep us in check, restrict our sense of autonomy, and disallows our potential selves?

We have very little control over most of our environment. Sure, we can turn off the television, avoid the internet, draw the curtains, and turn out the lights, but that will likely lead to a lonely and uninformed life. Living out there and connected, however, means we are bombarded by lessons that try to convince us that the heteronormative gendered binary is completely normal and essential. These lessons are tethered to capitalism. For example:

Preteen girls can be pretty if they convince their parents to purchase certain clothes, make-up, and so on.

Little boys can be brave and just all-around awesome if their parents buy them play swords and shields.

Men can be sexy and irresistible with the right kind of shaving cream.

Women can be beautiful and apparently super flexible in yoga pants, if they just buy the right tampon.

Whether it is the purchase of products, entertainment, education, or something else, there is practically always a gendered/sexualized message that accompanies the specifications of what is being sold. After being so indoctrinated, it is almost absurd to imagine a commercial that would be straightforward and told the truth:

"The use of this make-up will result in a fight between you and your parents, and possibly your school. But these clothes are good, because you need to not be naked in public."

"These play swords and shields will affirm that secret you've kept to yourself—yes, in-deed your son is an asshole. You'll wish just once he would listen to your plea, 'No play fighting in the house.'"

"Shaving cream can be used in conjunction with a razor to shave any hair you desire. Go for it."

"This tampon will absorb your menstrual bleeding while you are doing any human activity, including yoga if that's your thing."

Capitalism, marketing specifically, sends strong cultural messages about how masculinity and femininity should look and how we, the consumers of products and gender, should embody it. Marketing ploys and other phenomena are providing environmental stimuli and reinforcing a binary gendered system teaching that we should fit in it on one side or the other. Consider this (short!) list:

- pink and purple versus all other colors
- pink and blue aisles in toy stores
- "boy" and "girl" names
- the phrase "you guys" to categorize *all* groups of people—old lady knitting clubs, Girl Scouts, mixed gender middle-agers, etc.— devalues others who might identify as women/feminine (working to make them "invisible,") or gendered in other ways. "This seemingly innocent phrase may be operating like a computer virus, worming its way into our memory files and erasing our sense of why we worry about sexism in language to begin with."[13]
- differently cut clothing (e.g., low rise jeans, long cut swim trunks, swimsuits for girls/women—99% of which would be "inappropriate" cuts for any other place, like schools that worry— perhaps unnecessarily?—about butt cheeks, etc.)
- "Mother's Day" and "Father's Day"
- "boy" and "girl" bathrooms (I use bathrooms for very specific biologically driven reasons...I wonder, what else happens in women's bathrooms that they must be separated?)
- TV channels (e.g., Lifetime for Women, Spike TV)
- "chick flicks"
- boy bands
- hair accessories
- select spas or massage parlors (including seedy ones)

- religious practices (think: different seating areas in the synagogue, women cannot become Catholic priests, roles and responsibilities differ according to denomination)
- greeting cards
- strip clubs (most cater to men, some do not allow female patrons, and male strip clubs are few and far between)
- man caves
- locker rooms (that are social/non-private, but are driven by gender)
- names of businesses ("Five Guys," "Pep Boys," "Kirchner & Sons Refrigeration," "Hooters," and "Dirty Dicks")
- representation in certain careers
- representations of "masculine" and "feminine" media—of every kind imaginable
- mud flaps with Playboy symbols or those tacky side profiles of curvaceous women sitting ummm…sexy I suppose?
- athletics (male and female teams, some exclusively gendered like football…some sports, like cheerleading, serve to sexualize women)
- recreational events (e.g., "girls night out" and "ladies night" at the bar)
- overheard or random jokes about sex
- general beliefs held by people that men and women have different capabilities (that men are more technologically capable, while women are more capable at caring).
- supposed humor like, the old man to the fourteen year old, "So, do you have a girlfriend yet?"
- men's body wash
- the criminalization of women's nipples[14]
- street and work harassment
- "mancations"
- Girl Scouts and Boy Scouts
- terms like, "human kind"
- phrases like, "man up"
- "selfie" culture and sexting
- men approaching women in social situations asking, "Do you have a boyfriend?"
- manscaping and Brazilian bikini waxes

No wonder we do not fully recognize the pressure we have been under to perform gender, or how we personally uphold patriarchy by being heedlessly complicit. To a certain degree we are all Truman Burbank in the movie, *The Truman Show*.[15] We recognize that something might not be exactly right. We experience some discontent. But, until suspicion and discontent turns personal, there is seemingly nothing much to complain about—it is just life. It is just how life is supposed to be.

My grandmother is sweet, thoughtful, and is always learning. Books and documentaries are a natural part of her daily diet. On occasion, because she is curious, she asks, "What are you up to?" With this question anxiety rushes over me and I remind myself that despite her inquisitive disposition, she also comes from a different era. I respond as if I'm a fifteen year old who just stole a six-pack of beer, a car, and got a tattoo of my girlfriend's name on my bicep. I tiptoe around an answer, "You know, nothing much." If she presses, I submit some real answers, but with the understanding that they will be met with criticism. I tell her I am writing about gender, which is almost always true. I will go into a few specific details, but then try to change the subject. More times than not, however, she does not let it go. "I don't understand what there's to write about," she would say. Or, "That's just the way the world is. Men and women are different. They are meant to do different things." I have tried in the past to talk about how we are socialized to be masculine and feminine and when we assume these roles, inequality ensues. On occasion, she agrees, "That's true, men never want to help out around the house." But more times than not, she thinks I am making a big deal out of nothing. She does not understand gender as multiple, flexible, constructed, or imposed. It is simple reality. My grandma is not alone.

MY STUDENTS

An important debate has endured the test of time in America: Should schools model themselves after society or should society model itself after schools? Meaning, should schools "get students ready" to "fit" the current conditions (economic, social, religious, etc.) of society?

Or should society look to schools to reimagine the future—for new and better ways that society should function. Undoubtedly, regardless of which side you are on, we can agree that practically, both happen. Sometimes schools push change and bring innovation to society, and other times schools spit out "products" who are expected to play certain roles. In my observation, however, when it comes to gender, high schoolers are graduating with few to no skills that allow them to critically think about gender, their individual performances, or society's impact (like the above list) on gender construction. Take, for example, the undergraduates that I teach.

I teach students who want to be elementary school teachers. Recently, I had my most challenging group of students of all-time.

As a teacher, I try to practice democratic pedagogical approaches. I want to build a learning community where students take care of one another. For several years now, I have been practicing a model of "open syllabus education" (OSE)—developed with a few innovative colleagues—that invites students to develop their courses with my guidance. The first day of class is usually very exciting. The great majority of students have never participated in K-12 or post-secondary courses that actively enlist their help, or empower them to "own" their education. Therefore, during our first class session, students usually experience a range of confusion, worry, and enlightenment. I love to watch them grapple with my sixteen page document of provocations (my invitation to a democratic class). I ask questions like:

- You may ask, "How can we (students) participate in designing a curriculum well if we are not familiar with the academic matter of the class? Is it not primarily, if not solely, the role of the teacher, who is considered to be very knowledgeable in this academic field and knows better what should be learned?"
- What would be the ideal practice for your learning and professional development: having grades or not having grades and if having grades, what kind of grades and how should grading be organized for you to make it highly beneficial and minimally (or not) harmful?
- How are we going to make organizational, curricular, instructional, and conflict-resolution decisions and reflect on their consequences

in our class? Should we try to do "democratic decision making" in our class? What does that mean?

• Should our community transcend the classroom? Meaning, do we become involved in each other beyond class? What does this look like?

Students are quick to see that none of these questions have any one answer. They discuss, argue, push back, wonder, and try to make sense of this new structure. Students do not have to accept my invitation to an OSE class; they can simply ask for a regular (closed) syllabus that has their entire semester planned for them. However, my classes always accept this democratic approach and report, "it's a unique opportunity to try to learn differently."

This one class, however, used it as a unique opportunity to bully one another.

"I like this idea," said Samantha, a student who I met just minutes before. She sat in the back, proper, and forthright. "But, it's not going to work."

"Why not?" I asked.

"Because this class is all girls."

Confused, I pressed on, "So, what difference does that make?"

"Girls are bitches," she said.

I needed a moment to recover, but Michelle, sitting across the room agreed, "Girls can't be trusted with getting along and making decisions with each other. She's right. We're all bitches."

The class, shook their heads and sharpened their eyes, and produced a chorus of, "yup, that's true," and "I agree."

"Whoa! Hold on a second!" I responded. I hoped they were kidding, but observing their serious demeanor, I was moved to spring to their defense.

"I can't believe what I'm hearing. Are you telling me that it is impossible for girls to get along? For them to be in a productive learning community together? To take care of one another?"

"It's not impossible, but it's not likely…it's just the way we are," said Samantha, now leaning back and talking with a sly smile.

I spent the next hour trying to understand why they believed that girls were inherently "bitches." Needless to say, they did not have any good reasons or evidence. They continued, like my grandma, "Girls are just that way."

It was the oddest first class I ever had, and the semester went downhill from there. This group of thirty women, nineteen to twenty-three years in age, made life miserable for one another. They used the democratic classroom to make bad decisions for one another. They would listen intently to what their peers expressed they needed, and then vote for the opposite. The class formed factions—the cool and pretty; the nerdy and serious; the emotional; the conservative religious; and so on. Students scrambled to sit with their factions prior to every class session. If one came late to class, and could not find a seat next to their "friends," horror would overwhelm them. How dare they sit with another group of people who are moderately different than themselves?!

Worst of all, they engaged in deeply aggressive behaviors. Some were quite explicit—for example, they took to real-time cyber-bullying during class. They foolishly followed me on Twitter and then used this platform to trash one another.

"Ppl are so retarded. Like anyone gives a fuck about your opinion. #shutupbitch"

"Every time she opens her mouth I wanna slap her."

"Your presentation @studentname was the shit, ignore those haters. They wish they could be us."

"I can't even. This class has so many sluts."

Implicitly aggressive behaviors, microaggressions, were just as bad, but more difficult for me to detect. When certain students in opposing factions spoke in class, eye rolling, deep sighs, turning away, and rebuttals that dug at their belief system, ensued. A look, ever-so-slight could, enrage another student for the rest of class.

Other professors who had these students in their classes were experiencing the same problem. So, we staged an intervention. We showed the film *Bully*[16] and afterward, talked about their behaviors. We told them, "enough is enough!" Students sobbed and some even confessed that they were acting terribly.

We believed this would reign them in. And for a week or so, it did. But by the end of the semester, they were all back in it—fighting it out, being terrible people. As one final attempt to help them make sense of their actions, I invited a good colleague and friend of mine, Elizabeth, and the associate provost at my university, Jeff, to my last class session of the semester. I asked them to sit up in the front of the classroom and directed my students to be quiet. I told my students that they were not allowed to ask questions or interrupt at all, and said:

> Teaching is tough. And sometimes you have really difficult situations. In the future, if you ever get a job teaching—which at this point, I kinda hope you don't—you should seek out good colleagues that can help give you feedback. That you can lean-on. That you trust will be honest. So, before you, I have invited two really great people to come in to talk to me. I'm going to tell them about my trouble teaching you, and they'll give me feedback. The point of this exercise is for you to 1) listen to how professionals can help each other improve their practice/what good mentorship looks like and 2) to inform you, again, about your unprofessional behavior. This semester has been hell for me. I cannot believe that people who want to be teachers, who want to enter relationships of care in a classroom, would take to bullying. Let's begin…

Then, I turned to Elizabeth and Jeff and we held an hour long conversation about my students' behaviors, my possible failures as their instructor, and what we desired in teachers.

As you can imagine, my students were stunned. They sat in disbelief that I would be so honest. That my colleagues were involved, that others were talking about them, made it even more "real." When the class was over, Elizabeth and Jeff reported that it was one of the most unique experiences they had in a college classroom. That held true for me too. I thought that for sure, my students would reflect a little bit and try to make sense of everything. I should not have been so optimistic. The next day, several came to my office fretting over whether I actually meant that they "shouldn't be teachers." We talked a bit, and right before they left, they frankly told me, "But Dr. Richardson, you knew this was going to happen. It's your fault too. We told you that it wasn't going to work because girls are bitches."

These girls were addicted to being mean. They were addicted to the idea of what it meant to be a girl. They saw no way out of it. It was clear that their high schools, and perhaps none of their schooling before that, challenged what it meant to be a girl—or better yet, a person. What a gift it would have been if they were taught and learned that they did not have to be this way. I wondered, what was the institutionalization process like for these students?

MY KIDS

I have two children, Mali and Maria. At the time of this writing they are nine and eight. They, like most siblings, are very different from one another, but share some core qualities. They are kind, wild, smart, silly, generous, eccentric, self-determined, hilarious, and witty. They are crazy about animals (particularly dogs) and have deeply adventurous spirits. As they have gotten older, they have begun to share interests in horseback riding, rock wall climbing, zip lining, exploring nature, and traveling to new places. They are naturally curious and desire to learn about the world around them.

They are different in some obvious ways: Mali is an old soul and deeply sensitive (like me), whereas Maria is a space cadet and "sour patch kid" (like my partner, Yara)—sweet one moment, sour the next. Mali's mind is that of a sociologist, while Maria's is of a philosopher. They look vastly different, too. Mali has always been tall and strong. She has deep dark brown eyes and hair. She rarely cares about what she looks like, and dresses for complete comfort. Maria has blue eyes, blonde hair and is on the shorter side. Occasionally she cares what she looks like, but is content to wear the same outfit for a week (or as long as we let her get away with it). Yara and I often reflect how challenging it has been at times to parent kids who are so similar and dissimilar to us, but ultimately feel blessed and amazed at how they are also their own unique selves—truly perfect in every single way.

Mali has been known to spend hours at night, lying in bed, thinking about the social interactions she encountered, examining adult conversations overheard, and wondering...just wondering...about everything she observed throughout the day. Mali's mind is almost always switched "on," and is constantly at work trying to make sense of all she has experienced. Most of all, she attempts to understand why people feel the way they do. Then, in her own nine year old way, she advocates for their needs. Mali cannot help but to care.

Once, we took the kids to a pig catching contest at a local fair—not something we typically do—and instead of running after the terrified greased up hog like the dozens of other children, she ran behind the pack and helped those who had fallen in the mud during the chase. These kids were strangers. Kids she knows are lucky to have a such a solid friend in her. She will forever stand by their side, and stick up for them.

Mali is also concerned about "right" and "wrong." She is interested in social justice, and believes that her contributions can help create change. She has been known to organize yard sales that benefit people experiencing poverty and animal shelters. This usually consisted of her setting up a table in our front yard with old toys, things she found around the house, and little pieces of artwork that she produced. Around election time, she pays attention to political advertisements, and asks whom we are going to vote for, and why. Most recently, she has become interested in political protests.

Mali is a kid who never wants to disappoint. In fact, Yara and I often wish she were just a little naughty, selfish, or would tune out the adult world; that is, we desire her to be a carefree kid. Last year she—the kid who never does anything wrong—worried for two full months that she might have been "accidently bad," possibly resulting in Santa Claus to skip over our house…or even worse, just visiting her sister.

Mali is wildly creative and has big ideas. By the looks of it, she has been managing an artist cooperative out of her bedroom. It is an explosion of yarn, paints, scrap material she's pulled from our trash, odd knick knacks, books, glue, modeling clay, and so on. She has twine strung between her windows and the ceiling fan so she could hang bed sheets and make hideaway spaces to work in. She has random sketches and paintings taped to her wall, pieces she has knitted strewn across the floor, and dozens of journals and sketch pads filled with her ideas all over her desk, bed, and elsewhere. Dare we attempt to help her "clean up," she accuses us of trying to get rid of her stuff. Her world is a creative one, and she feels secure being immersed in art.

Besides art, she has a wide spectrum of interests which include reading, writing, theatre, anything science related, Teenage Mutant

Ninja Turtles, outer space, the sea, theatre, climbing trees, wrestling, super corny jokes, spending time with her family (during the school week she pines for the weekend) and anything that has to do with our dog, Mia, our "schweenie" – go ahead, look it up. Mia is an odd looking dog with an underbite whose favorite activity is to sit close and breathe in your face. Besides this quirk, she is a sweet dog and an old soul, just like Mali. If Mali is feeling "mixed up," frustrated, or like she just needs a friend, we'll find her snuggling with Mia on her bed, or lying together under the warmth of the sun in our backyard. They get one another.

Droves of kids love Mali because she is so kind. And while Mali has a few close friends, she actually prefers to be around adults most of the time. Recently, I took a group of thirteen undergraduate students, and Mali, to Northern Ireland on study abroad. We motored around the country, shoved into a medium sized van. We were always on the move, staying in new locations, and kept an exhausting schedule. She was constantly, at all times, with my students—which for college kids on a trip overseas, could have been annoying. Instead, she and my students stayed up late, night after night, playing games like spoons, Catchphrase, and bullshit—which Mali refused to say because she deemed it "bad" so she called, "bullship!" They also built forts with blankets in the shared living spaces of the houses we rented, and baked cookies and Rice Krispie treats so they had late night snacks after the pub. She bunked with students in their rooms and giggled with them until the early morning hours. She and my students explored beaches, castles, schools, and cities together. I was so deeply moved that my students treated her so well, and I thanked them for this at the end of the trip. They, however, were confused and told me, "Well, she's awesome!" "We love her!" and "She's like one of us!" She had made thirteen genuine friends. It is extraordinary that a nine year old would make friends with college students, but it is not all that extraordinary for Mali. People of all ages think the world of her.

Mali is self-determined. She knows who she is and does not care about what other nine year olds deem "normal." She's happy to be her. She voices how lucky she is to have the life she has. How remarkable. When I tuck her in bed at night, I will often take a few moments to snuggle. I burrow my head into her shoulder and tell her all the great things she is and tell her I love her. Often she will respond, "I know, I rock…I'm awesome." I hope she knows this always.

As for Maria, our space cadet/sour patch kid, she epitomizes randomness. Maria is, for the most part, predictably unpredictable. She lives in her head for large swaths of the day, and only engages with people and her environment when it interests her. She can lose herself in any context and under any condition. This means that we have to continually keep watch of her. What is interesting is that when she wants to engage, she is wickedly perceptive. For example, we spent this past summer in Paris—a city that was new to us—so navigating the busy streets of the city with Maria proved quite stressful. Wherever we walked Maria would slip her hand out of ours so she could chase pigeons, run up flights of stairs, point and announce that certain statues were "naked," and pause to look at random things—a leaf, a jagged brick in the wall of a building, a dog in a store window, or just the sunlight trickling through trees. She was rarely where we wanted her to be: holding a hand, next to our side. However, on occasions in which we got ourselves lost, Maria would tune-in and lead us back to our apartment. This also happened once in the Louvre. Maria and I spent a few hours in the museum and I became completely turned around. She took my hand and marched me twenty or so minutes through hallways, up and down stairwells, winding through exhibits, and exactly to the exit in which I was hoping for, announcing, "See Daddy. It's just right there."

Her ability to tune-out provides her with resilience. Anything she does not care about simply does not exist in her world. Recently, I took her to an academic conference and she sat through seven hours of boring talks with only a Kindle and pad of paper. She did not complain once. Instead, she read, drew, and spun herself in circles looking at the ceiling.

Maria rarely minds being tuned-out. However, every now and again it does result in her missing out on some things—for example, ideas shared during important family conversations, what day of the week it is (she wakes up most days by saying, "Is today the weekend?"), and simply observing what's going on (like that time she mistook a large bat flying around her bedroom as a moth). She will probably call bandanas, "damn-banas," and easels, "weasels," for the rest of her life because every time Yara and I correct her she simply looks right through us, then says, "Whatever, I don't care, sometimes you say wrong things…I can say it however I want."

From early on, Maria has had a special affinity for animals. When she was just a toddler, she played "guinea pig" for hours every day. She used her crib as a crate, and begged us to come pet, and feed her through the rails. She eventually became a "puppy" and this lasted for several years of her life. There were many family dinners in which Maria simply barked responses, licked her paws, and ate off her plate like a dog. If we misinterpreted the meanings behind her barks, she became angry, clenched her teeth, and would give us a growl. It was only when we got our second dog, Zoe, a Chihuahua/Jack Russell mix, did Maria feel that she could graduate to "puppy trainer." She's often found dragging Zoe around the house, sternly giving orders, or crushing her in her arms snuggled on a chair. Maria loves roughly.

Though Maria also has deep interests in reading, drawing, towers and tall buildings, geography, history, and goofing around, dogs (particularly Zoe) dominate her mind. She has told us that she will either live in San Francisco or with us when she gets older and will be the owner/manager of a "dog hotel." For now, however, she spends a lot of time setting up imaginary spaces—most of them homemade using cardboard and other scrap materials—for dozens of plastic miniature dogs. She creates dog yoga studios, housing communities, airports, restaurants, new foreign lands, and so on. The dogs are situated within these sophisticated pretend worlds with jobs, families, social lives, and interests.

Maria takes everything a little personally. For instance, whenever someone burps, she feels it was directed at her—and so she burps in retaliation. How she has come to thinking and doing this, we will never know. In large groups, she will often accuse Yara and I of not listening to her, which I think might be a typical second kid complaint, but it occasionally results in her claiming, "You don't love me." When it is just her and an adult, however, she gets super trippy and asks weird questions like, "Is today tomorrow?" "If we get one more dog would it be more than other people?" "Can I have a dollar? Because, hey, I have two eyes and I can see it." Once I overheard her ask Yara, "Mommy, would you rather have a normal husband, or a husband with a human body and a Shar Pei head?"

Maria loves to put on a show, to make people laugh, particularly her big sister. She is bold with her jokes, and if you are lucky enough to meet her—you could be the butt of one. She often makes fun of doctors, wait staff, and other strangers she does not know. She likes teasing her family too. To play a joke on us, she secretly convinced her grandmother to wrap up a toilet plunger and give it to her as a Christmas gift.

Maria is incredibly loving toward her friends and her family, but she never really wants to be obvious about it. When I drop her off at school, I yell out, "I love you," and she responds, "I love you, but not more than I love Zoe." When I tuck her in bed at night, I begin to say sweet things and attempt to snuggle for a bit, but she pushes me away, stiff-armed, and says, "Ok, I know, you love me, I'm special, blah, blah, blah. Can you get out now?" and "Good night, jerk." Blissful.

I love Mali and Maria for who they are. And Yara and I have worked hard to not dictate who they must be. We want them to develop their own interests, explore life, and express themselves in ways that make sense to them. Of course, we offer guidance and security, but we love learning who they are outside of us. We understand Mali and Maria as brilliant, complex, real, and uncompromised beings. And perhaps, it is our collective societal responsibility to try to understand people, all people, in these ways. It is how I want everyone to understand Mali and Maria. I think they deserve it.

Tragically, though, when Mali and Maria go to school they become simplified. Teachers, and others at the school, make assumptions and quickly ascribe them to being "like" others—most notably, other girls. Not only does this violate Mali and Maria's sense of individuality, it violates the other girls too. And the boys for that matter, because they too become primarily recognized as something other than what it is girls are.

Of course, this kind of simplification might be perceived "normal" because this is what is done in the "real world." And it is true—I do understand that the vast majority of people in our society "makes sense" by generalizing, categorizing, and placing people in boxes. Maybe people simplify because it is what they can do most immediately. Yes, maybe it is about efficiency—I am trying to convince myself here. But, always? And is this fair? Should we not *try* differently? Aren't you…well, you?

Sure, your race, gender, sexual orientation, the job you hold, car you drive, type of food you eat, and everything and anything about you provides some pieces to the puzzle about who you are, but should it not be up to you as to how those puzzle pieces are shaped? And what the whole puzzle looks like when pieces lock into place? And should we not honor each piece as it is important to itself, but also to the whole? That one piece of the puzzle (one identifier) should not overshadow or distract us from the whole (from who you are)? I guess I am wondering, should your identity be how you perceive and define yourself, not how others (simply) see you?

Though we still do it, perhaps more secretly, it is at least publicly recognized taboo to generalize and stereotype by race, ethnic background, disability, religion, and other areas of difference. But every day I encounter vivid moments of gender differentiation on display. Recently I walked by a restaurant and noticed a sign in the window, attempting to be funny, that read, "Caution! Blondes at Work!" I often overhear people saying things like, "Boys will be boys," "Behind every good man there's a woman," and "Women, you can't live with them, you can't live without them." And people generally agree, "Men aren't sensitive" and "Women are 'catty' in groups." Why is this acceptable? Imagine this:

"Caution! Blacks at Work!"
"Christians will be Christians."
"Behind every good disabled person there's a non-disabled person."
"Hispanics, you can't live with them, you can't live without them."
"Jews aren't sensitive."
"Tall people are catty in groups."

These sentiments, if shared aloud, would be recognized as discriminatory or flat out crazy. We would not accept the "logic" behind these statements. We would probably even challenge them! I know I would walk into a restaurant and complain if they hung a sign that was racist, xenophobic, or bashed religion.

But in our society and in our schools we make assumptions, create generalizations, uphold stereotypes, design experiences, and hold different expectations about how girls and boys, women and men, just "are" and should be. I am calling this act of gender discrimination facilitated by stereotyping, "sextyping."

Sextyping

I believe in the revitalization, redefinition, and stylization of the term "sextyping." There have been several instances when researchers employed the term "sex-typing" (note the hyphen).[17] However, this term was never clearly established and became loosely understood as both an assumption making process as well as an adherence to certain gendered performances—much like "gender typing" (note the space). Gender typing has been defined as a process by which children develop gender identity by acquiring "the motives, values, and patterns of behavior that their culture considers appropriate for members of their biological sex."[18] Sextyping, as I mean it, is not something acquired, but rather something that is done to someone else. Sextyping is the act of stereotyping what an individual's preferences, likes/dislikes, interests, abilities, and so on, are according to how the individual is (assumed) sexed within the traditional male/female binary. I propose "sextyping" because the words "sexist" and "sexism" conjures up the kind of defensiveness that is mostly unhelpful. Responses to "you're being sexist" commonly result in anger, frustration, or shallow deflections that the accuser must be some sort of crazy, unrealistic hippie or feminist. And "stereotyping" simply lacks punch. "Stereotyping" must also be strung along with several other words—e.g., "you're stereotyping what color balloon that boy might want." Sextyping gets to the point.

In my opinion, people sextype more frequently and openly than participate in any other form of discrimination. We especially sextype children. I argue that sextyping is made possible in part by patrolling the borders[19] of what we collectively know as "femininity" and "masculinity." If children, especially boys, violate these borders, adults become unnerved, even actively concerned. Some adults worry about how border crossing children might grow up. Children have a difficult time with border crossers as well, but only as much as they have learned to be concerned. Often on the playground one can hear boys ridiculing other boys by calling them "girls" (the worst insult for a boy) for getting upset, asking for help, or by engaging in a so-called feminine activity. And girls patrol the borders in the same way—by ridiculing other girls who dress "too boy," play mostly with boys, and so on. Boys and girls will blatantly tell the opposite sex, "You can't like…because you're a…" I am not blaming children here for their sextyping—I am blaming adults! Adults have socialized our youth to understand gender as binary and to patrol borders, to sextype. Adults have taught children to be "boy" and "girl" before "kid" or "human" and that it is part of their responsibility as part of their sex/gender to ensure conformity. There is a moment of leniency when girls are allowed to be "tomboys." In fact, many parents and teachers find girls performing masculinity "cute" as long as it does not persist deep into adolescence. As I see it, these performances are accepted because they, "pay homage to patriarchy." Boys, however, are rarely praised for acting feminine because it is a "violation of patriarchy."[20] Yes, it is all about honoring and defending patriarchy. I once heard Ruby Bridges say, "Racism is a grown-up disease and we must stop using our children to spread it."[21] I loved this, partly because I think you can substitute "racism" with many things and it still works—"elitism," "xenophobia," "homophobia," "hate," and yes, "sextyping."

I do not agree with adults who sextype others, particularly children. However, I understand that when they were children their families, neighborhoods, media, and schools sextyped them. Additionally, I understand that since gender is predominantly performed without devoting safe space to deconstruct it in our daily adult lives, [22] then the tradition of sextyping simply carries on. It is what feels and appears natural. And "what appears 'natural' acquires the status of being fixed."[23] However, I expect more from schools. Schools, I believe, should be places where they disrupt the fixed, the status quo, and (re) imagine and grow a society that is better than what generations before us worked to reproduce or maintain. That is, schools should be a site of new ideas, social reorganization, and social mobility—not social reproduction.

Schools, however, have a lot of work to do. Looking at my kids' brief educational history there are several eyebrow raising moments:

Blocks for Boys; Dolls for Girls

At the end of almost every day of kindergarten, I walked into Maria's classroom to find "free time." During this time boys played (almost exclusively) with boys, and girls with girls. Boys played with blocks, cars, and puzzles while girls played dress-up, with dolls, and quiet board games. Of course, at times, there were exceptions, but this was the general scene. Maria mostly played by herself because what she really wanted to do did not fit the culture of the room. She sensed it. I doubt she was told she could not do one thing or another, but at the same time I am sure it was not made apparent that she could be her. In an environment like school—one that is controlled, contrived, and imposes adult authority—kids need active permission to take risks, to be as they desire. Otherwise, they end up performing a version of what they perceive is "correct." There was very little/no effort on the teacher's part to encourage or insist that kids must take turns playing with everything available to them.

Buzz Lightyear Pencil Box Fiasco

When Mali and her classmates first began experimenting with pre-writing the teacher decided to buy all of the students pencil boxes to stay organized. This was a nice gesture as she bought these with her own money. However, one day while I was in her classroom I noticed that Mali was given a pink puffy snail pencil box while many of the other students had Buzz Lightyear boxes. Then I noticed it was only the boys with Buzz Lightyear boxes. Mali had for at least two years of her life obsessed about outer space, so, of course, she liked Buzz Lightyear.

I asked Mali why she did not have one of these pencil boxes. She said, "Because the teacher said they were for the boys."

I responded, "Well, did you ask for one?"

"No, because Ms. Markle said they were for the boys."

"Oh. Did you want a Buzz Lightyear pencil box?"

"Yes. But daddy, they were only for the boys."

"Want me to help you ask if you can have one?"

"Um…," she said nervously, "Okay, but you have to talk."

So the next day, I could not find the teacher when I dropped Mali off, but I left a note on her desk. It was a nice note explaining that perhaps she did not know (and of course, she did) but Mali loved space and was bummed about not getting a Buzz Lightyear pencil box. I asked, "Could she have one?"

I saw the teacher at the end of the day and she apologized by saying, in front of Mali, that she knows "Mali likes boy stuff, so she'll do better by including her in boy things."

I responded, "I think you have it wrong…there isn't boy stuff, boy things or girl stuff, and girls things, there's just stuff and things! How is being an astronaut/space explorer male or female? It's just cool."

The teacher gave me a blank stare and apologized again.

Over the next several weeks Mali would inform me when the teacher made an effort of letting her know she can do boy things. I imagined her announcing to the class, "Let Mali play with the blocks…remember, she likes to play with boy toys too."

I wondered, how might this damage Mali?

Patriotic Princesses

Near the end of her first grade year Mali asked me, "Daddy, are you going to go to my patriotic concert?"

"Sure!"

"I don't want to be in the concert though."

"Why?"

"Well…the girls have to wear tiaras."

"Why's that?"

"I don't know. Mrs. Baldwin just said girls have to wear tiaras and boys have to wear cowboy hats."

"Oh…well…what do you want to wear?"

"Cowboy hat. I wanted to wear the one I got when we went to Texas."

"Want me to ask Mrs. Baldwin?"

"No!"

"Why not?"

"Just because…I don't want you to…It's just the way it is."

It was evident to me that Mali, at the ripe age of just-turned seven, figured out that adults dictated the rules of gender and that children should not challenge this position of authority. Just a few years earlier, during the Buzz Lightyear pencil box fiasco, she was less comfortable with teachers imposing strict gender roles.

Despite Mali's plea, I discussed this issue with my partner and we decided to secretly email the teacher something like:

Dear Angela,

Hi! Hope you had a restful weekend. I'm emailing today with something that came up…Remember, gender, sexuality and schooling is what I'm always thinking about and I'm a geek… so don't take this personally! ☺ Mali told us about the patriotic concert and that for this performance the girls are expected to wear tiaras and the boys to wear cowboy hats. She REALLY wants to wear a cowboy hat! (We were just in San Antonio and she bought one!) We told her that maybe she should ask you about it, but she was terrified at that suggestion! I think for two reasons…1) she thought since you already assigned roles it would be a "violation" of your authority and 2) if she were the only girl to switch, there might be some peer jeering. So…she doesn't want anything to be done now—and that's fine with us too. I just wanted to let you know of her feelings. And for future events with other kids, maybe you can offer (and encourage student) choice? Or pick items that aren't so polar opposite? Or *even better* you could just have all students wear the same thing (tiaras one year, cowboy hats the next)!

Thanks! See you at the concert!

Scott

Mrs. Baldwin was a perfectly nice person. She strove to be the penultimate professional—and in my experience, worked hard to do the little things "right". Of the dozen or so emails I had sent her prior to this one she answered them immediately. This time, however, it took her three days to issue a response. And her email carried a different tone—concise, formal, and defensive:

Dear Dr. Richardson,
I understand your concern and am willing to allow Mali to have a cowboy hat.
If you have any further questions, please feel free to contact me or my principal (copied on this email).
As always, I appreciate your communication.

Sincerely,
Mrs. Baldwin

Obviously, Mrs. Baldwin problematized me and my email. It is also completely possible that she never really fully thought about how the decisions she makes in school provide cultural meanings (in this case gender). Or if she has thought about it that she believes it is completely appropriate for the girls to learn how to be the kind of girls she understands to be correct, and boys to learn how to be the kind of boys she understands to be correct. Regardless, my simple provocation made *me* the issue not *gender,* or Mali's desires.

Daddy & Daughter Sweetheart Dance

Around Valentine's Day, my children came home with a "Daddy & Daughter Sweetheart Dance" flyer. It announced that all elementary aged girls, for $25, could bring a date—their dad, or another male over the age of 15—to a special "night of love." I thought about going, just to see what it was all about, but I backed out. Really, I could not bring myself to subjecting one of my daughters to an event so steeped in heterosexualized grooming. The "daddy-daughter dance" has long been ritualized at weddings, which compliments the father "giving the daughter away"—to be owned and/or deflowered—and this elementary school's effort was an early (perhaps subconscious) attempt at introducing girls to being their "dad's." Masked in sweetness, I found the line between "cute" and "romantic" to be a blurred one at best. Then, of course, was the problem that it did not allow boys to the dance. Nor did it allow girls the option to bring anyone female. (Sorry kids, the "Two Moms-or-Two Dads-or-Single Mom-or-Parentless-or-Otherwise & Kid Sweetheart Dance" has yet been invented or deemed important).

Mardi Gras Parade in the 2ⁿᵈ Grade Hallway

Edgewater Elementary proudly celebrates a diverse collection of American holidays. This includes, "Fat Tuesday." This past Fat Tuesday, I waited for Mali and Maria on the sidewalk moments before dismissal. When the bell rang a flood of kids exited the building. Maria smiled and walked proudly toward me, showing off her newly acquired Mardi Gras beads. She looped her thumbs under the beads, lifted them up toward me and said, "Look Daddy! I got beads from the parade!"

I asked, "What parade?"

"The Mardi Gras parade!"

"Oh…hmmm…ummm…you were in a parade? That's how you got those beads?"

"Yup. Lots of older kids were on the side and we walked down the hall. We had to yell, 'Hey Mister, throw me some beads!' Then they would throw us beads."

Of course, we know how beads are acquired during Mardi Gras in New Orleans. The teaching of, "Hey Mister…" is particularly disturbing. This is another example of grooming, particularly female students, for performing successfully in a highly sexualized, heteronormative American culture. Just yuck.[24]

I could go on…but you get the idea, right?

Though *I* found these events troubling, they went on with no concern from other parents, teachers, or administrators. In fact, when I made small talk to the typical drop-off/pick-up parent crowd, I asked, "Wasn't it weird how…?" I consistently received blank stares or a troubling, "What do you mean? I thought it was cute." There is something to say here about the way people interpret and narrativize events. In reading these events, they seem crazy, but I wonder if you were working at my kids' school and witnessed these happenings if they would have raised any red flags? Would you even notice? By the way, I am completely aware that there are plenty of other acts of sextyping or sexualization that occurred, that I had likely missed, because I too have been socialized to see the binary as normal. It is difficult to break.

Given that my kids have knocked up against these so-called, "educational events," and I have had to struggle with understanding them, I wondered how teachers have allowed these things to happen. Did they not know who my kids were? I imagine that though you have not met my kids, I bet that with the limited information I shared about them here, if I were to swing by your house, drop them off, and say, "So…I'll be back in a few hours," that once you got over some initial shock, you would find some fun stuff to do. And I bet this stuff would be designed around their interests—that you would take into consideration of who they are. *Why was the school more concerned about sextyping (my) kids than designing instruction and an educational environment that honored their personalities?* This got me thinking…

Maybe these teachers were just too busy to get to know their students. But I wonder, is this excusable?

Maybe when these teachers were kids, they were so successfully sextyped, groomed, and socialized so that now they only understand the world as one that is perfectly gendered. But I wonder, as adults were they never exposed to thinking differently about gender (at least in their teacher preparation programs!)?

Maybe it is simply more efficient for these teachers to sextype. But do these teachers not see themselves as individuals, as complex human beings? That is, can they connect with the fact that even if they largely perform or identify feminine or masculine, that they also do not fit with others who identify similarly? And this could be true for their students too—that they should not make assumptions about them?

Maybe they would claim that the school inhibits them from challenging sextyping. Often teachers blame the school system, or claim that parents might "get upset," from enacting "progressive" practices. But I wonder, have they tried and been told "no?" And must they radically "challenge" stereotypes? Could they just not reinforce them? Yes, I understand that this is still a method of challenging, but maybe it is more discreet. And so what if it makes parents upset? *Is it their job to be non-discriminatory? Equitable? Fair? To realize the fullest potentials of their students? To offer an intellectual space that challenges the status quo? To not be OK with social reproduction—to want more for their students? To want a better world?*

I do not think I am being too unreasonable here. I think those who work in schools need to take upon themselves the moral and ethical responsibility to wonder about what is required of them so that students become self-actualizing and self-determining individuals. This will not happen if teachers and their schools institutionalize gender.

NOTES

[1] Scott Richardson, "Blurred Lines of a Different Kind: Sex, Media and Kids," in *Gender & Pop Culture: A Text-Reader*, eds. Adrienne Trier-Bieniek and Patricia Leavy. (Boston, MA: Sense Publishers, 2014).

[2] bell hooks, *Ain't I A Woman: Black Women and Feminism* (Boston, MA: South End Press, 1981).

[3] Judith Butler provides the most important conceptualization of gender as performance. See: Judith Butler, *Gender Trouble: Feminism and the Subversion of Identity* (New York, NY: Routledge, 2006).

[4] I also do this work because I am a feminist. David Tyack & Elisabeth Hansot said that the work of feminist researchers (particularly since the 1970s) hope to make schools a more equitable place for all children by studying three overlapping themes, "(1) patriarchy, which encompassed the whole of society as the unit of analysis and described universal male domination; (2) sex-role stereotyping, which stressed the individual's internalization of cultural gender roles; and (3) institutional sexism, which addressed the inequalities built into institutional structures and policies." See: David Tyack and Elizabeth Hansot, *Learning*

Together: A History of Coeducation in American Public Schools (New Haven, CT: Yale University Press, 1990), 250–251.

5   For example: Hanna Rosin, *The End of Men and the Rise of Women* (New York, NY: Riverhead); Christina Hoff Summers, *The War Against Boys: How Misguided Feminism Is Harming Our Young Men* (New York, NY: Simon & Schuster).

6   See: National Center for Education Statistics, "Degrees Conferred by Sex and Race," *Institute of Education Sciences*, accessed December 10, 2014, http://nces.ed.gov/fastfacts/display.asp?id=72; National Center for Education Statistics, "Public High School Four-Year On-Time Graduation Rates and Event Dropout Rates: School Years 2010–11 and 2011–12," *Institute of Education Sciences,* accessed December 10, 2014, http://nces.ed.gov/pubsearch/pubsinfo. asp?pubid=2014391; U.S. Census Bureau, "Degrees Earned by Level and Sex: 1960 to 2009," *Statistical Abstract of the United States*, accessed December 10m, 2014, https://www.census.gov/compendia/statab/2012/tables/12s0299. pdf; Richard J. Murnane and Stephen L. Hoffman, "Graduations on the Rise," *Education Next* (Fall, 2013); 59–65.

7   National Committee on Pay Equity, "Wage Gap Narrows Slightly but Statistically Unchanged," National Committee on Pay Equity, accessed December 14, 2014, http://www.pay-equity.org/

8   C. J. Pascoe, *Dude You're A Fag*, 7.

9   R. W. Connell, *Masculinities* (Berkeley, CA: University of California Press, 1995), 68.

10 Idid., 71.

11 Judith Halberstamm, *Female Masculinity* (Durham, NC: Duke University Press, 1998), 1.

12 Barrie Thorne, *Gender Play: Girls and Boys in Schools* (New Brunswick, NJ: Rutgers University Press, 1993). See also: Cecilia L. Ridgeway, "Framed Before We Know It: How Gender Shapes Social Relations," *Gender & Society,* 23 (2009): 145–150.

13 Audrey Bigler, "On Language: You Guys," in *Bitchfest: Ten Years of Cultural Criticism from the Pages of Bitch Magazine*, eds. Lisa Jervis and Andi Zeisler (New York, NY: Farrar, Straus and Giroux, 2006).

14 See: Lina Esco, Hunter Richards and Sarabeth Stroller, *Free the Nipple,* Film, Lina Esco (Paris, France: Bethsabee Mucho, 2014).

15 Andrew Niccol, *The Truman Show,* Film, Peter Weir (Universal City, CA: Universal Studios, 1998).

16 Cynthia Lowen and Lee Hirsch, *Bully*, Film, Lee Hirsch (New York, NY: The Bully Project, 2012).

17 See: Pauline Sears and David Feldman, "Teacher Interactions with Boys and with Girls," ed. Judith Stacey, *And Jill Came Tumbling After: Sexism in American Education* (New York, NY: Dell, 1974); Paul Musen, "Early Sex-Role Development," ed. David A. Goslin, *Handbook on Socialization Theory and Research* (Chicago, IL: Rand McNally and Co., 1965).

18 Carol K. Sigelman and Elizabeth A. Rider, *Life-Span: Human Development* (Belmont, CA: Wadsworth, 2011).

19 Thorne, *Gender Play.*

20 Richardson, "Blurred Lines of a Different Kind."

21 Ruby Bridges, "Untitled" (paper presented at the MLK Day Celebration Keynote Address, Millersville, Pennsylvania, February 6, 2013).

22 Scott Richardson, *eleMENtary School: (Hyper)Masculinity in a Feminized Context* (Boston, MA: Sense Publishers, 2012); bell hooks, *The Will to Change: Men, Masculinity, and Love* (New York, NY: Harper, 2004).

23 Madeline Grumet, *Bitter Milk: Women and Teaching* (Amherst, MA: University of Massachusetts, 1988), 46.

24 This was a tipping point for me. I was outraged, particularly after all of the other sexist, misogynist, gendered practices I kept quiet about. I had a meeting with the principal and addressed it by literally saying, "This mardi gras thing…what the fuck?!" She agreed it was ridiculous, but that she had a difficult time stopping the teacher who coordinates it every year. I pleaded for her to do her job as a supervisor.

GETTING INTO IT

My interest in the institutionalization of gender grew primarily out of concerns I have about the broad socialization process (in and out of schools), my undergraduates performances of stereotypical gender roles, and the impact schools have had and will have on my children.[1] But I have also noticed gender at play while teaching public school, supervising student teachers, and consulting several school districts. All of these experiences influenced me, in one way or another, to formally conduct research so that I can explore the process of how gender is institutionalized, including the problems of sextyping. I hoped, along the way that I might gain some insight about how to deinstitutionalize schools, or at least, make kids more resilient to schools' efforts of institutionalization.

Constructs and perceptions of gender are deeply impacted by a wealth of cultural factors, and I desired to study several urban and suburban school districts. However, I was unable to do this kind of comparative work. Urban school districts—short staffed, underfunded, and burdened by other concerns (namely, state testing)—were unable to invest energies in hosting a researcher like me.[2] One superintendent candidly told me, "If you're not here to help us raise proficiency rates on our tests, or decipher the state's new teacher evaluation system, we are uninterested. I mean, we are totally interested in gender equality, but you know what I mean…we just can't put that before pressing demands." Of course, I could (and wanted to) protest, "Gender equity isn't a pressing demand?!" However, I knew I would not change his mind. My work simply was not important enough to them.

Superintendents in three suburban school districts, however, with very little hesitation, agreed to have their schools participate in the study.[3] At the onset, I met with each of them and explained that I wanted to observe schools as they are and that if I told teachers, principals, and others that I was studying gender, they would likely change their behaviors. Therefore, we agreed it was appropriate for me to employ deception; only superintendents and my university knew the real focus of my work. I recruited teacher participants by sending emails stating that I wanted to study, "narratives of success…how teachers and students embodied achievement."[4] This reaped dozens of positive responses and soon I had forty-five different classrooms ready to be observed.

Each school district resided in different counties, and closely resembled my kids' school district. They were suburban districts that tilted rural. All three school districts, however, were experiencing a slight shift in demographics. Just a few years before, at least 95% of all students were White, and the great majority of them came from middle and upper class families. The school districts now ranged between 5,200 and 7,700 students with a combined average of 88% of whom were "White," 4% "African American," 4% "Latino," 2% "Asian," and 2% "Other." Approximately 32% of all students received free/reduced lunch. There are claims that "suburban schools are a major attraction to minority populations because of their reputation of providing significantly better educational opportunities than their urban counterparts."[5] There are also claims that this increase in diversity (ethnic, racial, and socioeconomic) brings new "challenges" to suburbs and their schools.[6] These so-called "challenges" are predominantly perceived because the influx of "new" cultures—their simple existence—threaten the dominant (White middle and upper class) culture. All three school districts and their communities, in my observation, worked tirelessly to uphold "whiteness." It was evidenced in the manner real estate was marketed and residents recruited friends to become their neighbors. The goal of many of these residents, particularly parents, was to maintain:

> sufficient social distance and geographical isolation to separate themselves from people of other classes, races, or ethnic groupings and to be in the proximity of others from their own social group. This separation becomes part of the social reproduction of the upper class; whether parents explicitly use such terms or not, elite children quickly learn that some people are 'our kind of people' and all others are not.[7]

Teachers dismissed the idea of culturally relevant pedagogy—to develop students academically, a willingness to nurture and support cultural competence, and the development of sociopolitical or critical consciousness,"[8]—as "not the job of the school," "absurd," and "going too far." A social studies teacher, claimed:

> This community's values have been here for a long time. I'm not 'against' being more culturally sensitive, but the dominant culture isn't urban.[9] I think, then, it is just difficult to say we have to do things different to accommodate just a few. Sometimes you get parents in here thinking it should be the same [as the urban school they moved from], but they made a decision to come here. I think it's on them to adapt.

While it is a limitation that rural and urban school districts were not included in this study, observing how gender was produced within these mostly middle and upper class Euro-centric schools is deeply important.[10] If we desire gender equity, then, we must hope that these suburban school districts—whose kids will likely grow up to own, control, and govern much of America—are actively studied, challenged, and ultimately changed.

METHODS

I was lucky to have three field research assistants—Sabrina, Khoan, and Samantha. Before doing any observations and interviews, we held meetings to design codes and observation tools, invent methods that would allow us to share data, and conduct literature reviews. Once we felt organized we began our work in schools. We spent September through November in all forty-five classrooms. It was a whirlwind. Each school was very hospitable. Then, out of the forty-five we selected nine classrooms that represented "the middle" of what we were observing, and followed them closely from November through June. These nine classrooms—three in each level (elementary, middle, and high school)—were chosen because we characterized them as "typical" of what we saw and believed they revealed how schools institutionalized gender for students on a consistent basis. This consistency, I believe, grounded students in what was thought, and expected to be, "normal."

Meaning, these contexts normalized the on-going institutionalization, and traditional performances, of heteronormativity and male/female roles. The "extreme" classrooms—those atypical because they were highly sexualized/gendered, "neutral," or operated under pedagogical dispositions that honored gender equity and social justice—provided a different, but equally valuable insight about how gender is at work within schools. Data in these extreme classrooms were collected quickly, and so we did not feel as though our energies needed to be employed in these settings for an entire year.

We chose our nine "middle," or "focus," classrooms—all from the same school district (Monroe Valley S.D.)—for three primary reasons: 1) theoretically, a lengthy and concentrated look into these classrooms would provide a deeper understanding of how gender becomes culture; 2) practically, we could organize our data to more easily and fairly represent "daily life," and; 3) logistically, our resources would not be spread too thin. Each classroom was observed approximately fifteen times after our initial visits. In each observation, lasting between one and three hours, we attempted to see a variety of procedures. Lengthy observations were crucial because I wanted to know what gendered messages manifested for children in elementary school within, and while transitioning between, different subjects, lunch, recess, specials, special activities, and so on. I understood that formal instructional time was just one kind of opportunity for gender to be institutionalized. Sitting in middle and high school classrooms for several hours at a time, allowed us to see how teachers' approaches to different "leveled" subject matter, content, and children varied. Though we drew generalities, and took note of the "extremes," from our forty-five initial classrooms, our nine focus classrooms gave us the opportunity to develop narrative case studies:

> Perhaps the simplest rule for method in qualitative casework is this: Place your best intellect into the thick of what is going on. The brain work obstensibly is observational, but, more basically, it is reflective...Qualitative case study [as is narrative and ethnographic work] is characterized by researchers spending extended time, on site, personally in contact with activities and

operations of the case, reflecting, revising meanings of what is going on.[11]

Framed within evolving understandings of experiences, our goal was to enter into productive spaces of narration by focusing "the social, cultural, and institutional narratives within individuals' experiences."[12] During each observation we used an electronic document that we created, prompting us to organize our notes within particular themes: Environment; Instructional Decisions; Informal Language; Language Between Adults; Body Language; Preferences; Literature (Self-Published); Literature/Materials (Curricular Programs); Complicity/Inaction; Other. At the end of each observation, the electronic document was immediately uploaded to our shared Gmail account so that the entire research team could access all notes. It was particularly helpful when two separate researchers, during the same observation, filled out this form independently. Beyond using this standard document, we also recorded notes in other ways that felt right to us. I often kept what I called "time studies." I used my phone as a stopwatch to record the "attention" (type/quantity/quality) given by teachers and to whom. Sabrina, a logical and straightforward thinker, often wrote the obvious. She was dutiful in scripting important conversations and keeping track of student interactions. Sabrina was particularly useful when baseline/descriptive data needed to be collected—she was the most reliable out of the four of us to make observations on her own. Khoan, who is quite philosophical, often spent most of her energy developing theories about what she saw. She wrote several explanations for each observation made, which challenged us to see differently and consider alternative explanations. Samantha had the most unique approach, which concerned me at first. She alternated between large periods of time quietly, intently, and deeply "looking," and making visual representations—sketching and diagramming—her observations and interpretations. It turned out that these representations were extremely helpful, especially during the post-coding writing process. During data analysis, we employed a "negotiated coding approach" allowing us to discuss our "codes to bring most coded messages into alignment."[13] This method of negotiated agreement helped move us beyond intercoder reliability and toward a "state of intersubjectivity, where raters discuss, present, and debate interpretations to determine whether agreement can be reached."[14] We constantly thought through possible and alternative explanations[15] and looked for emergent themes[16] in a manner that organized our ideas.

During the final month of school, I conducted interviews with the teachers of the nine focus classrooms, and several others—including those in other school districts—who I felt might understand how schools institutionalize gender. These additional interviewees held interesting positions and additional responsibilities in their schools— as coaches advisors, department heads, extracurricular programmers, and so on—throughout their lengthy careers. I was on edge about the interviews because the teachers did not know that I spent the year specifically thinking about gender in their classrooms. Toward the end of each interview, after I "interrogated" their answers to my questions and brought up observations I made of their teaching in the hope to get more answers about how they performed, cultivated, and imposed gender. I revealed what I was researching. Approximately half of the teachers reported that they held no grudge for being deceived. Many wanted me to share my findings and to contact them if I needed more help. The other half felt trapped and worried that my description of them would paint them as sexist, or favoring boys or girls. I do not think this was because they were concerned others might read this work, figure out who they were, and think poorly of them, but it just *hurt* them to think that they might have created inequitable environments. They all cared deeply about their students. Guilty feeling teachers would shift uneasily in their chairs, and say things that exposed deep concerns they probably have not shared often, "You don't think I care for the girls more, do you?" or "I don't know, I do have a different attitude with the boys, but it isn't because I want them to do better…what do you think?"

One group of teachers felt betrayed more than the others. Teachers at Williams Elementary School, who were all close friends, politely declined to answer any more questions post-interview and refused to participate in a proposed focus group that would read a draft of the manuscript and provide me with additional feedback. Ten months after the interviews were concluded, the superintendent reported that teachers at this building felt "extremely uncomfortable," however, he did not specify what this meant. Since none of the teachers withdrew from the study and the principal did not contact me, I was unsure how to think about this report. So, though unnecessary, out of good faith to ease the concerns of the superintendent—and perhaps the elementary school participants—I destroyed their data, and the rest of the data collected in the school district, and promised to not include it in future publications. This loss of data was semi-insignificant as this school district did not house any of our "focus" classrooms. This data merely supported the conclusions and descriptions we made regarding Monroe Valley S.D.

It is important to reiterate that regardless of how teachers responded to the news of my deception, none asked me to discard data about them and their classrooms. They all felt that this work was important. Though generous, I wanted to be cautious. I never like deceiving people, and I hope to never write something that could bear some sort of personal or professional consequence. After all, these teachers desired to be helpful, and on all accounts they were well-intended and good people who did what they thought was best for their students. Yes, some did create inequitable environments and harmful narratives about masculinity and femininity, but they were not consciously out to damage or advance certain kids. Therefore, I utilized "light" composite nonfiction when necessary, if I felt that I would "out" a particular teacher and their classroom. This is not a methodological conflict for many reasons, but primarily because, "my purpose is not to tell their [teachers'] special stories, but to use aspects of their experience to make some useful general points."[17] I wanted my work to represent how the institutionalization of gender is commonly found in many classrooms, schools, and districts.

Throughout the research, I employed the lens of a curriculum theorist. Many perceive "curriculum" as an instructional program—a reading series, math set, science kit, and so on. But understanding curriculum in this narrow way limits the dynamic meaning of the term. "Curriculum" is derived from the Latin, "currere," which means the "running of a course." The curriculum is everything and anything that impacts the course of students' experiences. This includes programs and units of study, but it also includes things like the way the day is organized, the affect of the teacher, and the physical environment of the school. Adults, to some degree, impact all experiences students have in school.

Many studies by curriculum theorists seek to explore or expose one faction or kind of curriculum (e.g., the hidden, null, written, rhetorical, c/overt, operational, extra, formal, phantom, received, or intended).[18] I considered using some of these categories/ways of thinking as coding systems, to organize this text, explain findings, and so on. However, I did not find that it enhanced what I aimed to do: I wanted to narrate, to be descriptive. I wanted to be freed from the overwhelming burden of trying to explain how *all* observations/instances of institutionalization fit within discrete, yet intersecting, curricular categories.

I found it helpful to continually wonder about students' experiences, and whether or not they were the result of mindful or mindless adult decisions. I hypothesized that mindful experiences, those that were deliberately planned, mostly occurred during direct instruction with students. Whereas the less mindful, even mindless, experiences—but experiences that transmitted knowledge and culture nonetheless—happened mostly during informal times: transitions between classes, walking in the hallway, at lunch, and so on. Schools shape students' experiences during informal moments because they have made decisions about how they would control the environment. Schools choose how long recess is, the kind of play equipment available, and what classes will socialize on the playground together. They choose hallway policies, the physical design of the school, and rules and consequences. School boards, administrators, and teachers have some choice (and they are probably mindful about it at the time) about every aspect of the curriculum. Though they were likely mindful when making initial decisions, implementation often becomes "mindless." There is little intent to "teach" something to students, or transmit culture in a particular way in-between the bells or during "non-instructional time." What is interesting, however, is that these informal moments become deeply important for students. Students often report that they learned the most in school while at the cafeteria table with their friends, in a student club, or exchanging notes in the hallway.

I am interested in mindless and mindful decision making for a simple reason. If school districts, teachers, programs, policies are institutionalizing gender and they are doing so in a mindful manner, then this research becomes an interesting study of a culture that desires to replicate specific versions of masculinity and femininity for boys and girls. If they are mindlessly institutionalizing gender then this research becomes a way of wondering why, bringing consciousness to practice, and beginning the process of figuring out what schools actually do and desire.

MONROE VALLEY SCHOOL DISTRICT, U.S.A.

Community

Monroe Valley was a medium sized suburban school district. It encompassed two small towns located just within the east and northwest borders with many mini-mansions and developments sprinkled in-between. Farms consumed large pieces of land in the west and southwest, and a mid-sized city, Pierce, was approximately ten miles from the eastern district borderline. Pierce was a typical all-American midsized city. It was once known for industry and tourism, and acted as an economic hub for much of the Northeastern U.S. region. Then, things changed. It is now in an era of reinvention. Micropubs, galleries, chic boutiques, and organic based restaurants are claiming Pierce "hip." White people presently living in Pierce are either older residents who grew roots in the city many decades ago, or young hipsters—the "urban farmer" type.

Families in the Monroe Valley S. D. territory rarely visited Pierce. Horror stories of the "big city" were spun in the suburbs. Mostly tales of crime. Vague stories like, "My friend's aunt's sister knew someone who went to Pierce to buy a…and in the parking lot she was accosted by these two black guys…" tempered any ambition to go to the city. That is, unless it was "First Friday." During the first Friday of each month galleries swung open their doors offering wine and cheese, bands played in restaurants and parks, and special events were orchestrated for children. White people from the suburbs flocked to the city. The very next day, things went back to normal.

Besides feeling adventurous and artsy every once in a while, suburbanites did not *need* the city. They created markets of their very own with restaurants, movie theaters, shopping malls, and the like, making it unnecessary to travel far. If Monroe Valley families went beyond district borders for leisure, it was on vacation to a different state or nation.

Schools

The school district had six elementary schools, two middle schools, and one high school.[19] The high school was known for its International Baccalaureate program,[20] high achievement in athletics (basketball for girls, wrestling for boys) and success rate for getting kids into college. "A few students," the high school assistant principal told me, "slip through the cracks and just disappear after graduation. Most go to college, trade school, or begin working." Monroe Valley is considered a "good district" though teachers, and particularly parents, often lament that Jameson School District, an über wealthy district due north, scores "the best in the county" on state performance exams. The current superintendent of Monroe Valley, Kenneth Kreskil, was an ex-principal who departed from Jameson after a bitter argument. Teachers suspected that the hyper-standardization and unreasonable "pushing" they experienced from Kreskil was because he desired to topple Jameson. Competition like this, whether out of vengeance, elitism, or something else completely was not uncommon between the many suburban school districts in the county.

Teachers & Administrators

Monroe Valley School District teachers were an eclectic crew. Some teachers sustained entire careers at Monroe Valley. Others jumped around from school district to school district, sometimes all over the world. And others were fresh out of college. Although they were diverse in experiences, sad to say, they were not diverse in their pedagogical approaches. The current era of standardization crippled Monroe Valley teachers. No Child Left Behind (NCLB), Race to the Top, Common Core, standards based language arts and math programs, and district wide lesson templates all impacted the way teachers taught: the same. By looking at their lesson plans, the physical environment of their classroom, and their teaching strategies, there was no discernable way to spot veterans from rookie teachers. There were very few moments during the day when teachers found space to do something beyond or different from the test. Some teachers, tried to provide some "buffer"[21]—to destress students from the constant rat race of school— by employing humor. At the end of the day, as students lined up to go home, one elementary teacher sung silly songs she had written. A high school English teacher, Jay Mascenik, always wrote an incredibly corny joke of the day followed by a false agenda on the board. One morning it read:

Person 1: Someone said you sound like an owl?
Person 2: Who?

Agenda (super important!):
1. Review: How to make a perfect milkshake.
2. Might there be a man on the moon? Do you like R.E.M.?
3. Seriously, do you like R.E.M.? I do. Ask your parents. They're awesome.
4. The history of the Earth from 2012–2013.
5. Dance party!!!

In the hallway, between classes, a middle school teacher, Beth, would yell out random history facts to kids—particularly at kanoodling couples pressed against lockers. She was good friends with the music teacher who every now and again would bring an instrument into the hallway, lay down a hat for "donations," and play a tune. These small bits of fun were often appreciated by both teachers and students. It helped them to survive the boredom that the typical school day brought. These moments told me that hidden in these teachers' souls were people who wanted to make learning fun and engaging.

From the very beginning of my time in Monroe Valley, I made a general observation that holds true in most school districts I have observed or worked in: the elementary school teachers were caring individuals who desired to nurture young minds.[22] These teachers were mostly full of hope and believed that students, with the right counsel and educational opportunities, could be someone. These teachers were optimists. The middle school teachers, on the other hand, were mostly pessimists. There were several teachers who loved working with middle school aged children, but there were equally as many who desired to "play in the big leagues"—high school. High school teachers, not all, but certainly a good many, were cockier because they were the "gatekeepers"—they would help "make" or "break" students who would go off to college, or find a path that is suited for their talents and abilities. High school teachers thought it was odd when I told them that middle school teachers pined for their jobs, unless they were once teachers in a middle school. Most high school teachers jockeyed for the "best" classes—the AP and honors sections. Such assignments were a badge of honor demonstrating that they were, among their colleagues, the most knowledgeable in their field.

Mostly, elementary school teachers were interested in children, middle school teachers in procedures and control, and high school teachers in subject matter.

Administrators were bean counters and politicians, but they wanted desperately to be well liked and held in high-esteem. They were continuously trying to find ways they could talk about their accomplishments. In faculty meetings, they would brag about people they met at conferences, compliments received by the superintendent, and notices in the local newspaper. Most of their backgrounds consisted of teaching a few brief years and attending a diploma mill, receiving an Ed.D. (applied doctorate in educational leadership). For the most part, these administrators knew very little about instruction. Teachers deeply distrusted them. Administrative observations of teachers were almost instantaneously disregarded. "I'd like to see what they can do in the classroom…and then I'll take their comments seriously," and, "They only give a shit about student performance on test scores…they want their bonuses. So, I know that anything they have to say to me doesn't have anything to do with student learning," teachers would say. It was true, administrators were deeply concerned over their schools' test scores, and they received bonuses for meeting certain criteria. Scores were compared between schools. All wanted to be on the top.

Public Relations

Monroe Valley was a conscientious disseminator of information. They took great pride in keeping parents and the community "informed." They were extremely meaningful about what was conveyed, and how it broke to the public. One parent who recognized this deliberateness called it "propaganda." Jon Davenport, the principal at Randolph Middle School and Clark Kent lookalike, however publicly called it an "open platform of communication" which included personally taking to Twitter. Davenport tweeted throughout the day about academic or athletic achievements, early dismissals, faculty features, and special events. These tweets were always boastful and they read like a proactive PR campaign. Other on-line sources included principals' messages, teacher blogs, and school webpages.

In a closed door meeting, a top central administrator admitted that the school district makes an effort—to a fault, he believes—to never communicate the needs and challenges of the school district. He said:

> It is completely unreasonable that any school district wouldn't have their share of problems. I think it might worry parents who live in reality. Some of our students are continually getting suspended, are caught up in groups of kids that are making poor decisions, are failing in school, and we only communicate, 'Everything here at Monroe Valley is great!' Not only does it come off disingenuous, but it could also come off like, 'Monroe Valley is great...it is just your kid that is the fuck-up!'...It's certainly important to emphasize achievements, but I don't think much progress is made if we whitewash everything. It's important to reach out and ask for help, to include others that might have answers. I mean, I'm kind of astonished they let you in here to do this work...you know how many professors we turn away who want to do research or help us in some capacity? Tons.

School districts like Monroe Valley are known for espousing certain educational goals—though, these might be propaganda too. But to a certain degree, I suppose we should take these seriously, as the "official," "espoused," "premeditated," or "formal" curriculum—but as far as I am concerned, I cannot be sure if communication of this type is "mindful." It may be mindful on one hand because the messengers tried to put forward certain kinds of impressions, and have been to a degree "premeditated," however, I am skeptical that these messages *really* align with what happens, or what schools actually *do*. Take for example:

> *We ensure a physically safe and academically rigorous environment for all students at #MVSD #JRRMS #Proud* – Jon Davenport Tweet

I doubt *all* students feel safe, particularly those who find themselves in the "counter culture" or "minority"—kids who identify queer,[23] are not "white," and so on. I also doubt all students feel academically challenged. Surely there are students who go unchallenged most days, who sit in their classes bored to tears, who skip school altogether because they find it useless.

The "Principal's Message" or "Principal's Welcome" seems to be a fundamental component of school websites. Arguably, the principal's message is part of the unofficial curriculum since it is not a legally binding document or a formalized program of instruction. But that it is formalized in writing and issued to the public, I find it to be a decree of sorts, announcing, "this *is* our school." Principals, and other administrators, have a significant impact on the cultural climate of schools and one would think that their words would carry great weight. But again, in this age of standardization where No Child Left Behind and Common Core reign supreme, and the act of "public" institutions bowing to the needs of certain powerful political and cultural regimes (such as the Bill & Melinda Gates Foundation) is commonplace, I doubt "collaboration, critical thinking, and effective communicating," or "opportunities to explore, discover, and create" is happening to any consistent degree in most of our nation's schools. Additionally, I am skeptical that teachers can dedicate much energy to students and their needs (as claimed in the principal's message) after they work to align instruction to standards (with every lesson, every day), are constantly learning new canned standardized curricula designed, live in fear of administrative demands, and are continually testing the hell out of their students.

The staff at Fisk Elementary focuses on developing 21st century learners who are capable of such skills as collaboration, critical thinking, and effective communicating. This is accomplished by providing students the opportunities to explore, discover, and create. Along with a strong emphasis in the basic skill areas of language arts, math, science, and social studies, students are provided experiences in art, library, music and physical education. I look forward to meeting all of you as we work together to provide each child a safe, caring, and joyful place to grow and learn.

(Josie Fisk Elementary website, Jan. 2013)

Public messages not only attempt to inform the public, or try to project a certain vision about goals of the school district, but it provides some insight (mindful or not) about how the district may recognize, honor, or understand diversity. Meaning, we get a peek at the culture of the district. Most written messages are "void" of gender—which might be problematic...like being "color blind"—but, visual images, particularly those that picture people, are not. Monroe Valley chose to have, surprisingly very few, images on the district webpage. On the home page, there were seventy-eight possible links a visitor could choose. Seventy-five of these links (e.g., "Transportation," "Calendar," "Alumni," "Library," "About MV," and "New Hires") connected visitors with pages that did not have any visual images—only text. The three links included pictures of people; "Athletics," "Special Education," and "Career & Technical Services." "Athletics" featured one large picture of recent grads who "signed" to play for universities. These student athletes wore t-shirts, hats, and jackets signifying their new school. The athletes were separated by gender. Males constituted two rows, one standing broad chested, and the other kneeling. Females sat on the floor, legs crossed.

NOTES

[1] Researchers, in my view, cannot fully separate "self" from "work." Those who try to do so—usually so that they can claim "generalizability"—I find are extremely disingenuous. Lived experiences, and socialization as an academic, has a deep impact on how researchers see and represent data. The old saying "research is 'me-search,'" holds true. So, I do not avoid my biases and lenses, but rather

spend a lot of time trying to understand how I "know." "My responsibility as an ethnographer was not to forget my own story, but to know it well and to refer to it constantly to make sure that it was not blinding me to what I saw or focusing my attention on only some of what I saw." See: Penelope Eckert, *Jocks & Burnouts: Social Categories and Identity in the High School* (New York, NY: Teachers College Press, 1989), 27.

2 I have no empirical research to back up my theory, but I suspect that increased standardization has thwarted school districts' willingness to be open to a diverse range of research opportunities.

3 All school districts, schools, personnel, and students have been assigned pseudonyms. In some cases, I employ composite non-fiction, altering and blending details so that I can accurately capture emergent themes in the work and to further disguise the identities of those involved. Additionally, readers are often anxious about the generalizability or representational nature of narrative/ethnographic works like this. I think it is best addressed the way that Tobin, Hsueh, and Karasawa did in their groundbreaking work *Preschool in Three Cultures Revisited*: I "make no claim about the representativeness or typicality" of the three suburban school districts used in this study, "other than to say they are not atypical" (p. 8). See: Joseph Tobin, Yeh Hsueh and Mayumi Karasawa, *Preschool in Three Cultures Revisited: China, Japan, and the United States* (Chicago, IL: The University of Chicago Press, 2009).

4 This was a vaguely espoused research plan, but most teachers were simply happy to help and did not inquire much about my work. In fact, many teachers took to emailing me, even texting at times, to simply share stories for one reason or another.

5 Shelley B. Wepner, JoAnne G. Ferrara, Kristin N. Rainville, Diane W. Gomez, Diane E. Lang and Laura A. Bigouette, *Changing Suburbs, Changing Students: Helping School Leaders Face the Challenges* (Thousand Oaks, CA: Corwin, 2012).

6 Ibid.

7 Diana Kendall, "Class: Still Alive and Reproducing in the United States" in *Privilege: A Reader* eds. Michael Kimmel and Abby Ferber. (Boulder, CO: Westview Press, 2010), 148-149.

8 Gloria Ladson-Billings, "Toward a Theory of Culturally Relevant Pedagogy," *American Educational Research Journal* 32, no. 3. (Fall, 1995): 483.

9 Unfortunately, this teacher's use of "urban" meant "Latino," "African American," and "other" ethnicities/races.

10 bell hooks, *Ain't I a woman?*

11 Robert E. Stake, "Case Studies," eds. Norman K. Denzin and Yvonna S. Lincoln, *The Handbook of Qualitative Research, 2nd Ed.* (Thousand Oaks, CA: Sage, 2000), 445.

[12] D. Jean Clandinin and Jerry Rosiek, "Mapping a Landscape of Narrative Inquiry," ed. D. Jean Clandinin, *Handbook of Narrative Inquiry: Mapping a Methodology* (Thousand Oaks, CA: Sage, 2007), 42–43.

[13] Elizabeth Soslau, "Opportunities to Develop Adaptive Expertise During Supervisory Conferences," *Teaching and Teacher Education*, 28, no. 5 (July 2012): 773.

[14] Martin D. Lampert and Susan M. Ervin-Tripp, "Structured Coding for the Study of Language and Social Interaction," eds. Jane Edwards and Martin D. Lampert, *Talking Data: Transcription and Coding in Discourse Research* (Hillsdale, NJ: Lawrence Erlbaum Associates, 1993).

[15] Though I went in to this research looking for how schools institutionalized gender, I had to be open to the idea that maybe I was wrong.

[16] This method of coding and process of seeking emergent themes is consistent with the field of narrative inquiry. See: D. Jean Clandinin and F. Michael Connelly, *Narrative Inquiry Experience and Story in Qualitative Research* (San Francisco, CA: Josey-Bass, 2000).

[17] Theodore R. Sizer, *Horace's Compromise*, 8.

[18] See: William F. Pinar, *What is Curriculum Theory? 2nd Ed.* (New York, NY: Routledge, 2011); William F. Pinar, William M. Reynolds, Patrick Slattery, and Peter M. Taubman, *Understanding Curriculum* (New York, NY: Peter Lang, 2004).

[19] Students who attended Monroe Valley S. D. were no different than the thousands of students I have met and taught over my career. They were unique individuals with varied interests and experiences. That said, they predominantly shared white middle-class values. Young children, prior to attending kindergarten, were socialized by their families, communities, media, and environment at large to perform stereotypical masculinity and femininity.

[20] For information about the International Baccalaureate Program see: "The International Baccalaureate," accessed November 25, 2014, http://www.ibo.org/

[21] Alfie Kohn, "Fighting the Test: A Practical Guide to Rescuing Our Schools," *Phi Delta Kappan* 82, no. 5. (January, 2001): 349.

[22] There were only three male teachers in the elementary school. The two youngest (with 13 years of experience combined) reported that they were being "groomed" for administrative positions, even though they had little interest in this line of work. The third described himself as a "salty old dog" and told me that "administrators, parents, and district politics just gets in the way. I'm not shy about telling them to go to hell...but, I'm one of the few teachers left with a moral compass and guts."

[23] Most students in Monroe Valley S.D., like many of their generation, reclaimed and preferred the term "queer." Many find it less oppressive and appreciates that queer as "an identity category...has no interest in consolidating or even stabilizing itself and that 'queer' declines to reduce gender to sexuality." See:

Annamarie Jagose, *Queer Theory: An Introduction* (New York, NY: New York University Press, 1996), 132; William F. Pinar, *Educational Experience as Lived: Knowledge, History, Alterity* (New York, NY: Routledge, 2015), 170.

JOSIE FISK ELEMENTARY SCHOOL

An Anchoring

You must have been a beautiful baby
You must have been a beautiful child
When you were only starting to go to kindergarten
I bet you drove the little boys wild

—Bing Crosby[1]

"How would you describe your school?" I asked Marisa, a pensive looking second grader.

"Adorable."

I laughed, "adorable?"

"Uh-huh. Can I go jump-rope with my friends now?"

"Of course! See you later."

Marisa and I met for the first time during recess. We were introduced by a small group of girls, Jess, Ashley, Emma, and Gillian. These girls were "popular" and did not want to talk to me that day. We had many conversations prior, but they pawned me off on Marisa, a quiet girl I had been watching for quite some time.

Marisa had one frenemy—half-friend, half-enemy—in Dana, another quiet kid. They were in a deep and tangled love/hate relationship. Marisa and Dana lacked self-confidence, so they said terribly hurtful things to one another causing weeks of heartache. They were always on the "outside" of other groups at school. They definitely did not fit in with the "popular kids" and they knew it. They did, however, enjoy several of the boys, particularly nice ones who retained a childish sense of humor. The kind of boys who, at lunch, dipped their fingers into bar-b-que sauce and smeared it across their upper lips to don silly yet distinguished looking mustaches. They laughed and flashed smiles with large gaps where their baby teeth used to be. The boys gave these serious girls some comic relief throughout their otherwise stress filled days. It seemed that the boys could do something that Marisa and Dana could not do, and that they envied; they could "let go," be silly, act as kids should act. Marisa and Dana hovered around the boys during lunch, recess, and other informal times like in the hallway or at "free time." The boys liked Marisa and Dana because these two provided them with a giggling audience. However, the boys never really included the girls in their play. That was, except for Ian. Ian was an extraordinarily nice kid and tried to include Marisa and Dana in on any jokes. This meant he would chase them around and try to give them bar-b-que mustaches too.

Marisa was right, Josie Fisk Elementary School was adorable. It was located on the fringe of Bonstead, the small town located in the eastern part of the school district. The school was built in 1957, and went through several renovations. It maintained its old-school charm. Classrooms were spacious and bright thanks to the large crank windows that lined the length of each one. Some classrooms had relics of decades past. Ms. Ferguson, a fourth grade teacher proudly fought off the janitor from replacing her large wooden teacher desk with a new one. "This desk has been here forever," she explained to me. "Can you believe it was just going to be thrown out?! I love it! Look, I don't know how far this goes back, but there are eleven teachers' names carved on the inside of this drawer."

Josie Fisk Elementary School, named after the first public librarian in Bonstead, sat up on a small hill, pushed back and off the busy thoroughfare of Green Street. About one-third of all students were driven to school by their parents. Another one-third were piped in on school busses. These kids lived in the more "rural" parts of the school zone. The remaining children walked with their parents or rode their bikes. The crush of cars, busses, bikes and foot traffic made 8:25 a.m., the start of the school day, quite chaotic. But parents, teachers on duty, "safety patrol"—a group of fifth grade kids trained to help the younger kids cross streets and stay safe—and adult crossing guards made the transit run smoothly. The assistant principal, Rob Drake, stood outside with a walkie-talkie, and greeted parents.

Every now and again, a kid or two would be deep into play and not hear the bell signaling students to line-up and wait for their teachers.

Rob would make a lap around the school, and find these stragglers innocently playing on the playground or sitting among the trees of a small grove tucked into the deep pocket of a large field behind the school. This patch of trees, mostly mature red oak and pine, served in the evening hours as a spot for older kids who lived close by to meet up and make out. It was nicknamed "Grabby Grove" by several teachers years ago. Rob and the groundskeeper swept the area for random cans of cheap beer on Monday mornings. Rob told me,

> Every so often we even find underwear, usually girls', and condoms. I kind of wish there were more condoms. Maybe it's a reflection of our awful sex ed program in [Monroe] Valley. I'm sure our Fisk kids, especially our fifth and fourth graders know what happens back there. They probably have brothers and sisters who go back there and fool around. But I don't think the younger kids have much of an idea. I'm sorta mixed about how I feel about 'Grabby Grove'—shit, I hate that name. On one hand, it's a wonderland, a place for our little kids to climb trees and catch bugs. But, on the other hand...I don't know. It's just gross. I wish the district would just cut it all down some days.

The field, the bright yellows, reds, and blues of the playground equipment, the charming exterior architecture of the school, the old brick walkway from Green Street to the front of the building, the small vegetable garden on the west side of the building, and even Grabby Grove, made this place charming.

Parents loved this school, in part, because many of them attended Fisk as children. Families lived in this community for generations. Fisk holds fond memories, which are shared with their kids and other parents, especially around special school functions.

"I remember our basketball team was the shortest around...we were terrible, but old Coach Morlin made it so much fun. I think we lost twelve games and won one."

"Every April Fool's Day, the principal, Mr. Hayes, would play a trick on the teachers. My fifth grade teacher, this beautiful young woman, got it bad. I should say, I don't even know if this is true, but this is the story we all heard. Mr. Hayes sent her a bouquet of flowers and it was signed, 'Love, You Know Who.' So she thought it was this married man she had been flirting with for weeks. She went to his work and made a complete fool of herself."

"I loved our annual Christmas concert. Everyone got dressed up. Each class would do a short skit and song. I remember all of the old people, grandparents and their friends, would come and cheer us on. It was a wonderful way to celebrate the community."

This school was fiercely loved.

SCHOOL CLIMATE

Fisk Elementary was a symbolic fixture of the community. Many stores around town sold small wooden replicas of the school. They were a popular gift for alum and were displayed in many grandmas' living rooms. Parents slapped "Fisk Falcons" bumper stickers on their cars. For students, however, the school's charm, was only skin deep. They found themselves faced with typical problems; overbearing teachers, long lists of rules, and lots of tedious "work." Most students reported "liking" school but only because they got to be with their friends. Their most favorite times were recess—which was only fifteen minutes long—and specials like P.E., music, and art.

There was a definite sense of order to a regular school day that provided a mechanical, even prison-like, flow. Rob reminded me, "Kids need structure." The beginning of the day began ceremoniously in each class—they said the Pledge of Allegiance, completed morning jobs (water plants, check on classroom pets, sharpen pencils), took attendance, reported to the cafeteria who needed lunch that day, and went over the daily agenda that did not change that much from days prior. And during all of this, within the first fifteen minutes of being in their respective classrooms, students were expected to have completed a "Do Now."

Teachers were instructed by the principal, Sam Borders, to have a "Do Now"—a language arts prompt or math problem—written on the board at the start of each day. Upon entering their classroom, students were to find their seats and immediately get to work. Sam told me, "We can't waste a minute of instructional time, and the 'Do Now' gets kids in a working frame of mind." "Do Now" prompts were always aligned with state standards and modeled after questions students might find on the state standardized test.

Beyond having a *Student Code of Conduct,* the school had not established any school-wide rules. They did, however, have a slogan that hung in the hallways, on the main doors of the school, and in the office, "Be the Best You!" Slogans like this irk me. Throughout the year, I would witness the same kids "in trouble" and imagined their "best them" just was not "good enough." These "trouble kids" were mostly nice, and almost always male. Classroom teachers established their own sets of rules and displayed them on posters for their kids to reference throughout the day. Though rules varied from class to class, most had something to do with "respect." For example, "Respect your friends' personal space," "Respect school property," and simply, "Be respectful."

Students at Fisk displayed typical kid behaviors. Mostly, they got in trouble for talking, acting silly, not following instructions, and occasionally arguing. About every other week, one student was suspended for a serious infraction like vandalism or physically hurting another student. Most minor infractions did not warrant suspension, but resulted in a loss of recess and a call home to their parents. All misbehaviors were "written up" and the students reported to the assistant principal. He would determine consequences, and would refer students to the guidance counselor if he thought students displayed any social and emotional needs.

For every one girl, four boys were written up for misbehavior. However, teachers reported that boys were "easier to deal with." Girls were sent to the office for talking and having conflicts with other girls. Boys were sent to the office for aggressive behaviors and talking back. Throughout the year, we—my research team—witnessed twelve students at Fisk get "written up." For each of these incidents, we followed the students to Rob's office, and if referred, to the guidance counselor as well. Only one incident resulted in suspension.

Incident one. Two girls (Marisa and Dana) complained to the teacher that they were "bullying" each other.

Intervention. Rob closed his door, shook his head and said, as though he was lost for words, "I don't know what it is with you girls…There's always some kind of drama. I'm going to send you to Ms. Lanzalotto's (the guidance counselor) to work this out. Okay, ladies, get out of here.

Incident two. One boy, unprovoked, smacked an unpopular kid's head as he walked by his desk.

Intervention. Almost yelling, with intensity in his eyes, Rob got within inches of the boy's face and said, "You think it's cool to act like that?! You think you're a big man picking on other kids? You're going to miss recess all week, buddy. You're in with me. Do you understand?"

Incident three. Two boys physically fought during recess, resulting in one bloody nose, and one bloody knee.

Intervention. Rob said, "Boys, I'm very disappointed in you. You know this isn't the way to resolve your problems. You could have talked to your teacher, or to me, to help you. It's just unacceptable to fight like this at school. I'm going to have to suspend both of you.

Incident four. Two boys harassed an androgynous boy, yelling, "That's the wrong bathroom!" "Hey girl!" as he walked into the boys restroom.

Intervention. Rob calmly questioned, "You know this is no way to treat others, don't you?" The students shook their heads in fake remorse. "Get back to your classrooms, I don't want to see you in this office again."

Incident five. One girl stole a boy's pencil.

Intervention. "Why would you steal someone's pencil?" Rob asked. The girl responded, "Actually, it was mine. He took it from me the other day and never gave it back." Rob said, "Are you telling the truth?

If so, I'll go and talk to him." The girl responded, "I'm telling the truth." "Is there anything else bothering you?" Rob asked.

Incident six. One boy stole another boy's set of crayons.

Intervention. "Look," Rob said, "You know what you did was stupid. Don't do it again. Next time, it's a suspension."

Incident seven. Two boys took wads of toilet paper and stopped up a sink, flooding the restroom.

Intervention. Rob said, "Well, this is a clear case of vandalism. I'll be contacting your parents and then you'll be serving recess inside. Also, I want you to go down to the bathrooms right now, and make sure any traces of toilet paper are picked up."

Incident eight. One boy threw his worksheet on the floor and said, "I'm done. I'm not doing any of this stupid sh...anymore."

Intervention. Rob said, "Buddy, you need to do your work. And you need to respect your teacher."

Addressing misbehavior is an important task that takes careful consideration of who the student is—what their history is at the school, the kinds of relationships they have with staff and students, whether they are frequently in trouble, and the gravity of the incident. In the cases above, none of these students were "regulars." They were kids who rarely got in trouble. Though these eight incidents/interventions do not provide us with enough insight, they are representative of approaches we saw taken by both male and female administrators at other elementary schools.

Boys were 1) more likely to be threatened, spoken to in a harsh tone, and have their masculinity questioned (e.g., "You think you're a big man picking on other kids?"), or 2) completely dismissed because their misbehaviors represent "normal boy stuff" (as was the case of harassing the androgynous student). There seemed to be no middle ground where Rob (and other administrators) would talk about how the boys felt or what caused their misbehavior. Boys were rarely sent to the guidance counselor. Girls, on the other hand, were 1) often referred to the guidance counselor because of the perceived complexity of their "drama," or 2) would be asked about their feelings. Rob lamented seeing girls in his office for problems. He reported, "Girls just fight dirty. They are petty, sneaky, and will do all kinds of little things to hurt feelings. I used to try to talk it out more with them, but who has time for that? I just send them along [to the guidance counselor]."

Teachers agreed with administrators, perceiving that the cause of girls' misbehavior was due to tangled emotional strife, whereas boys just get "overheated" and "punch it out on the playground and be over it." Our observations confirmed that girls did engage in microaggressions and passive aggressive behaviors more than boys, however, it did not mean that boys' issues and feelings were actually resolved once they melted down or resorted to some sort of violence. Nor did it mean that their emotional strife was any less tangled than what the girls experienced. There was certainly an expectation for boys to "man-up" and get over anything bothering them. In this way, boys were shortchanged. They did not receive the opportunity to process their feelings, practice ways of talking about situations, or acquire language that might resolve issues before resorting to violence or blowing up. This is dangerous because among many reasons these boys, like the generations of boys before them, might grow up to be men who have lousy communication skills, have bottled up anger, and commit the majority of crimes in American society.

Girls fared better than boys because their problems were usually given more attention. However, the quality of attention was mediocre and focused on "repairing" or "replacing" girls' feelings. Adults would say things like, "Well, there's no reason to feel like…" and "That's just silly…that shouldn't be a big deal." Adults were also visibly exhausted when dealing with girls. They would sigh and not fully invest themselves into hearing the intricacies of girls' issues. I wondered if the girls believed, then, that they were just being "irrational" when they perceived half-hearted investment from the adults in the school.

Marisa and Dana were interesting to observe because they represented the perceived complexity of girls' relationships. Also, the manner in which Fisk adults intervened was closely representative of how most adults approached similar problems between girls.

"You said, you wanted to be next," Marisa sobbed and placed her head in her hands.

"Honey, I need you to take a nice deep breath," Becky Lanzalotto, the guidance counselor calmly said.

Dana sat across the table, hands in her lap looking startled and curious. She sat still, studying Marisa as though she was learning about what she looked like when she was upset. Dana could most definitely relate to Marisa's sadness.

These girls were young. Too young, I thought, to have, let alone untangle such sensitive and emotionally charged conflicts. Intellectually I know the capabilities of young children to be complex emotional creatures, but Marisa and Dana's interactions were overwhelming for me. They were frustrating for their classroom teacher and the guidance counselor. I could not help to think, however, that the adult expectations for girls' relationships to be complicated wore off, or primed, Dana and Marisa to behave like this.

Marisa looked up and tears ran down her cheeks and collected in the corners of her mouth. She said, "I want Dana to be my friend."

Nervously, glancing at Becky making sure she said the right thing, Dana responded, "I am your friend."

"What makes you think Dana isn't your friend?"

"All day she just keeps picking on me."

Dana, in a sharp change in tone, "I'm not picking on you! I wasn't even looking at you. I wasn't even paying attention to you."

Marisa felt wounded by this comment, that Dana was not even concerned about Marisa's presence, making her feel insignificant and that her concerns might have been an overreaction.

"I feel like you were picking on me, and it feels yucky."

Her choice of, "yucky," sounded out of place for me. It lacked the emotional charge the rest of her words represented.

Becky praised Marisa, "Great use of an I statement."

Dana, needing a bit of praise herself swiveled in her seat and glanced around the room. She searched for the large "I feel..." poster taped to Becky's closet door. At the top of the poster, it read, "I feel..."

and underneath it displayed a bank of words like, "happy," "sad," "worried," "anxious," "fearful," and "yucky."

"I feel yucky too, because I am *your* friend…but I feel like you aren't *my* friend because you aren't treating me nice."

"Oh, good I feel statement, Dana," Becky said, smiling, rubbing each girl on the back. "I'm really proud of you for talking with me. You both want to be friends. Can you be friends the rest of the day?"

Both silently nodded "yes."

"OK, give me a hug and back to class, you two."

This was a lame pseudo-clinical response to an emotionally charged and on-going situation. Marisa and Dana left and the guidance counselor sat back in her seat, looking exhausted and satisfied.

"I made that poster so that kids would have language. They don't know what kinds of words to use."

"They used those words, but did they mean it?" I asked.

"'I feel' statements are really helpful. After kids use 'I feel' statements whatever the problem was seems to stop. They usually don't have more to say."

I wondered if this "I feel" tactic was really a way to signal an end to a conversation—not a solution or plan to resolve future issues. The guidance counselor seemed to "give up" on Marisa and Dana—to put a band-aid on something really important, particularly to Marisa—and simply sent them away. We never understood Marisa's concern, why she made the statement, "You said, you wanted to be next."

I wondered what this taught the two girls. I wondered if subconsciously it told them that their problems are not worth really listening to, let alone solving. Maybe they learned that having emotions in general are just problematic.

Kids at Fisk seemed like they felt safe at school. Parents too, also trusted that the school was a safe place. In the beginning of the school year, the PTO pushed the administration to hire a safety consultant to assess the school grounds for areas that might be "weak spots" for outsiders who might want to enter the building. Also, these consultants would provide teachers with training so they knew how to act if there was a bomb threat or if a shooter had made their way into the school. Teachers thought this was "over reactive" and not helpful since the consultants instructed, "If a shooter makes their way into the school, there's not much to do. You and your students, if confronted, should try to throw things at them. Confuse them. Throw chairs, books, pencils, anything you can find." It was unclear if this kind of training helped make Fisk safer, but it made the PTO and other parents less uneasy when news broke of yet another school shooting.

The disposition of the teachers was generally positive, but they were clearly overworked. They were consumed with writing lesson plans, attempting to decipher new state and federal standards, and understand the new teacher evaluation system. The school also was stressed because they were beginning to receive new challenges, like an (albeit slight) increase in students whose first language was not English. This too added to teachers' work. Every now and again, teachers would become too concerned and overwhelmed with the mechanics and business of schooling and take it out on their kids by being sharp in tone, pressing them too hard to complete certain lessons when they were not academically ready, or by simply making the school day also mechanical and uninteresting. For the kids at Fisk, this meant that school became a drag.

The faculty was comprised of mostly middle-aged White middle-class women. There were three men on the faculty (Appendix A). They taught P.E., 4th grade, and 5th grade. The principal, assistant principal and custodial staff were also men.

Allen Reif, the 5th grade teacher lamented, "I really wish we had more male teachers in this building. It would be good for these kids. They really need to have male role models. Some of these kids come from divorced families.[2] It breaks my heart. It gets way feminized around here."

"What do you mean?" I asked.

You know, these women, I mean, don't get me wrong, they're great. They're not like crazy feminist or anything. Actually, they are some of the best teachers I know. But, they're just too touchy-feely and it doesn't relate with a lot of the boys. Boys don't need babied…and, actually, if you asked a lot of women here, they'd agree.[3]

Allen had only been teaching for three years, but by this time he was deeply commodified by the faculty as a positive male role model. This made Allen feel extraordinarily special. The on-going fable that men are needed in boys' lives is a tale that has been consistently debunked, but thrives in primary school settings. "Engaging more male teachers as role models may sound laudatory, but there is no evidence that sex of teacher has an independent effect on boys' achievement."[4] Boys do not need *male* role models; they need and want *good* role models—people who listen to their concerns, take them seriously, and offer them safety and guidance.[5] Having a penis or vagina, or identifying masculine or feminine, has little to do with anything. However, when male teachers are told they are of great value to boys, they take their role so seriously that they often act in a hypermasculine manner (putting an overemphasis on sports, joking around, and heteronormative behaviors—doing stereotypical "dude" stuff) that ultimately does not provide boys with what they really desire or benefit them in any social or academic manner.[6]

Unfortunately, boys who were taught by one of the two male classroom teachers were often reminded about how lucky they were.

"It's cool that I'm in Mr. Holland's [the 4th grade teacher] class," Gabriel told me.

"Why's that?" I asked.

"Because he understands me. Girls, I mean like grown up girls…"

"You mean, women?"

"Yeah, women teachers don't understand boys. We're different. But Mr. Holland treats me and the other boys better."

"Can you tell me how? Give an example."

"I don't know. He's just like cool. I mess around a lot in class, but he gets it."

"So, you don't get in trouble?"

"No, I still get in trouble…it just feels different."

Gabriel's conviction that Mr. Holland must simply be good for him is a typical and complicated narrative. Common sense suggests that when someone is told—particularly a child who has not yet developed a lens to which they can critically dissect and challenge complicated issues of race, gender, (dis)ability, and difference in general—that another person who has similar attributes is "good for them," they naïvely believe it. This is problematic for many reasons, but three which concern me most are: 1) it could create a segregationist attitude—which never works out well for anyone—in students that could have a long-lasting effect impacting their relationships and accomplishments as adults; 2) if students believe they cannot be successful for other teachers and adults, they might miss out on important mentoring and resulting, in some, a lack of effort and uptick in misbehavior; 3) when sameness is sought out by a quick scan of physical appearance rather than seeking diversity and working to understand shared dispositions and learning opportunities from those who are perceived different, we remain distanced from one another as people.

Gender segregation at Fisk, as in most schools, was commonplace. Of course, bathrooms were segregated, but so were groups in classes, extracurricular activities and special organized groups like Girls on the Run and "Grrl Power." It is important to note that none of the segregation that occurred was imposed by students. They were segregated based on adults' decisions and desires.

Teachers often organized students by gender, for no apparent instructionally sound reason. Teachers asked students to make small groups, boys with boys, girls with girls, to problem solve or work on projects with one another. Other times, teachers would make teams. The girls and boys competed against one another in games organized usually to test content they were supposed to have memorized. For example, Lilly Koch, a fifth grade teacher deeply enjoyed having the girls compete with the boys during a devised game that quizzed students ability to spell words that would be on their weekly vocabulary test. Tests happened every Friday, so review games took place every Thursday afternoon.

In early March, Lilly announced with great enthusiasm:

Boys and girls, you know what time it is…it's time for 'Vocab Battle.' Boys, last time you suffered a deep blow. Do you remember which word stumped you? It was 'errand.' E-r-r-a-n-d. Not, e-r-r-i-n-d. The girls knew it, but, well, after all, they are smart cookies, and you lost! Ouch. In the beginning of the year you boys were keeping up with the girls. But now, the girls have been crushing you. I wonder what's going on? Don't worry, though, today you can win one back. But if I were you, I'd be a little worried…the girls are on a roll.

While Lilly tried to "hype up" her students, some slouched in their seats, hiding their faces, wishing they could disappear. Aidan, a quiet and generally anxious kid, became teary eyed. He looked nervously at the other students, hoping they did not detect his concern. Another boy, Stephen, who had a reputation for being one of the nicest kids in the school, uncharacteristically blurted out, "But it's no fair, you like the girls more! You give them easier words!" The boys agreed, the girls protested.

"That's not true! You're just jealous," Lauren said.

Anna chimed in, "Jealous and stupid."

Several of the girls laughed hysterically, while others kept quiet because they felt awkward by this interaction.

Lilly gave Stephen a confused look. His comment either struck her as true, and it gave her pause, or she was simply caught off-guard that he would challenge her. Flustered, she said, "What do you mean?" Without giving him time to respond, she continued, "You know that's not true. Now, let's play."

The once intended jovial competition suddenly turned volatile.

Lilly ordered students to play. She drew a sharp vertical line on the front classroom white board and titled the two columns, "Boys" and "Girls." Then, she spat out words, rapid fire, drilling both teams.

The girls won again, and the boys felt utterly defeated. Lilly lightly teased the boys, sensing their loss was taken quite heavily, but keeping with her previous script. "Well," she said, "that's another one in the books for the girls. Boys, I suggest you do some serious studying for next week."

Aidan, Stephen, and the other boys, with discomfort written all over their faces, stared at her blankly. They had given up, and for the rest of the year they would hold a grudge.

Not only did games like this discourage the boys to learn vocabulary words—this was an unfortunate academic consequence—but it also made the girls "enemies." The boys, with their bruised egos, overcompensated by competing on the playground (they organized boy vs. girl kickball games and were relentless in their effort to win), heckled girls—telling them they "cheated"—on other academic achievements, and were generally unwilling to work with the girls— they wallowed in their disenfranchisement and stuck to their own "kind."

The boys' behaviors added a layer of unnecessary stress to the girls' lives in school. Several of the girls were competitive, and maintained an oppositional stance with the boys, but they were clearly in the minority. For the boys, however, any girl was a fair target. Millie, a kind, thoughtful, and academically gifted girl, was continually harassed for her achievement.

Millie whispered to me, "I feel bad because I do better than everyone else on our tests, especially the boys."

"Why would you feel bad?" I asked.

"The boys are jealous. Jealousy is a bad feeling. I've been jealous over things, and it feels terrible."

"Jealousy is a terrible feeling, you're right."

She continued, "My mom said I shouldn't feel bad, but I can't help it. I feel like I want to do bad so everyone feels better. Besides, they would like me more, especially the boys."

Millie's concern about doing well is primarily based on her understanding that "jealousy is a bad feeling," and she alludes to a dangerous desire to make other kids—particularly boys—"like her" by dumbing down her performances.[7] Other girls, particularly in fifth grade, reported that they at times underperformed, or downplayed their performances, so that boys might take interest in them as "girlfriends." Girls "hide, downplay, or deny rather than celebrate and improve upon their successes and feel the pressure to conform to normative cultural representations of (hetero)femininity"[8] that assist boys to feel smarter, successful, and more important.

Games like this also instruct kids that boys and girls should be against each other, for some reason. Not only does this help to create a long lasting belief that men and women are different (think: "men are from Mars, women are from Venus"), but that the winners are inherently better than the losers, reifying certain sextypes—e.g., girls are better at language while boys are better at sports.

By the end of the year, though Lilly recognized that the round of "Vocab Battle" in early March created some immediate tension, she did not perceive that it aided in building a consistent progression of competitiveness during the rest of the year. This is not to say that Vocab Battle was the "breaking point" per se. It is likely that Vocab Battle was just one classroom factor that helped the boys and girls think of themselves as different and create divisions. But when I asked Lilly of the potential impact the game had on her students, she contended, "Oh boys are just hotheads and the girls are too smart for their own good…that's why I had so much rivalry between these two groups. It's unavoidable." She sextyped her children, believing that they just "are" these things; Vocab Battle, in Lilly's mind, had very little to do with influencing the state of gender relations in her class. I, however, disagree. Our observations revealed that activities that enforced any gender segregation had a negative impact on students. It is important to analyze that a *well-intended* teacher made activities like this with potential miseducative[9] and harmful social and academic consequences. Vocab Battle could be, seriously, dangerous for some children.

Unique segregated programs that also provide example of how these spaces are harmful to students existed within "girl empowerment" groups. Two popular groups at Fisk were Girls on the Run (GOTR) and "Grrl Power." Both groups were exclusive to girls, and in both situations, kids had to be invited or accepted to participate.

Girls on the Run, an international non-profit organization, has approximately 200 councils across the United States and Canada. These councils encourage schools, organizations, churches, and the like to create teams of girls and their coaches to engage in a ten to twelve week packaged program. The program encourages, "positive emotional, social, mental and physical development," by providing lessons that seek to empower students to make healthy decisions, gain an awareness of their individual values, how to connect with others, among other things.[10] Teams also go for practice runs, sometimes in conjunction with lessons, and other times independently. All teams, at the end of their program, participate in a 5K race that each local council organizes. Often, the race receives sponsorship from corporations that hope to hook girls on their products; Secret tries to sell deodorant while Legos work to peddle their girl friendly (read: pink) construction blocks. Each girl runs with sponsors of their own. These sponsors can be men and are often uncles, fathers, or older brothers. Their purpose is to run alongside the girls, and encourage them during the race.

Anne Sprenkle, a kindergarten teacher, was Fisk's coach. Anne got a lot of attention, though there was no way in knowing if it was her intention.

"How would you describe Anne?" I once asked her colleague, Joanne, the other kindergarten teacher.

"Oh. Ms. Sprenkle? She's a ray of fucking sunshine with a cherry on top."

Anne exuded, and even took pride in claiming herself, "girlie-girl." She wore dangly, noisy, jingly jewelry that competed with the click-clacking of her high heels as she walked the halls of the school. Her smile was contagious and laugh charming, until her colleagues, particularly her female heterosexual colleagues, found it "overdone" and "annoying." Anne described her style as "fun and flirty." All of her personal items were pink, which from afar made her room look almost like a Victoria's Secret. Pink curtains, pink pens, pink teacher-made posters, pink picture frames, pink folders, pink lesson plan book, pink, well, everything. She displayed pictures of her husband, and often talked about him to the kids, as if they should care. "Mr. Sprenkle was so silly this weekend. He took our sweet puppy, Princess, on a walk and forgot to wipe her paws off when he came into our house. I had to remind him…" Anne was an ex-cheerleader and proud of it. She often reminisced of high school football games (she, of course, dated the quarterback) and collegiate cheer competitions. Every year, Fisk faculty challenged the graduating fifth grade class to a basketball game. Anne's contribution was that she organized a cheer squad that was comprised mostly of the perceived popular and pretty fifth grade girls to root for the boys who played. She did not intentionally discriminate by holding auditions or imposing certain criteria to be part of the squad. However, she embodied a certain type of personality and dispositions that effectively told girls who might fit. The same was true for participation in Girls on the Run.

GOTR is, I think, intended for all girls.[11] However, many of the girls who decided they wanted to participate in Fisk's program identified with representations of femininity that Anne presented. Girls had to sign-up and pay a registration fee of ninety dollars, which most of the suburban families were able to easily afford, however, a handful of girls' families could not. There were "scholarship" funds made available, but they went largely untapped because in a small suburban town like Bonstead, Rick—a parent of a fifth grader—told me, "Everyone knows your business. And if you ask for help, you'll get it, but with a side of pity. So, many of us, we just don't ask." The GOTR Fisk Falcon team was made of white middle and upper class popular girls who were all friends.

Anne took the program seriously. She dutifully helped the girls recruit sponsors and held afterschool lessons and training sessions where they would jog the neighborhood. Lessons were held in her pink kindergarten classroom typically on the carpet space, where kids would kick off their shoes and sprawl out, in the back of her room. She worked her way through each GOTR lesson, but did a fair amount of adlibbing, adding statements like:

"Remember, girls, you can do anything a boy does."

"Girls are just as good as boys."

"Girls have secret powers. We are strong and fierce…and we look good doing it!"

Part of the official program was to encourage girls to choose nicknames, ones that employed alliteration—e.g., "Beautiful Bella," "Jogging Julia," "Lovely Lilly," "Bubbly Brynn," "Delightful Danni."

The 5K was held on the campus of a local college. Teams from all over the county met at the university's track and prepared for the race by "glamming it up." They spray painted their hair pink, purple and blue. They applied make-up and face-paint. They slipped on tutus and tiaras. "Glamming it up" for the race is not part of the official GOTR curriculum, but for this council and group of coaches, this has become an annual tradition—part of the local GOTR culture. Men who were girls' running sponsors also dressed in tutus and tiaras. Some wore long wigs with pigtails. These men drew a lot of attention away from the girls because of their "unusual" (mocking) representation of "girlie."

Anne provided all the digs for her team. She personally pinned every tiara on every head. Before the race began, Anne announced, "I'm so proud of all of my girlies! You are all wonderful and beautiful! Good luck!"

I believe Anne and everyone involved in GOTR, had good intentions. Anne and others cared for these girls. And they convinced themselves, without really knowing, that this program was good for students. Programs, like GOTR, that rely on traditional pedagogies and curriculum come from a space that care "is a pedagogical virtue demonstrated by forcing students to achieve the skills and acquire the knowledge that has been prescribed for them" and that "carers, in what they see as the best interests of those for whom they care, may decide what those best interests are without listening to the expressed needs of the cared-for."[12] Certainly, despite adult imposition, one could argue that there may have been a few positive outcomes—e.g. a better understanding of exercise, acquisition of language regarding self-esteem, and so on. However, I perceive many more potentially negative consequences of participation in GOTR—particularly those that create a greater sense of difference resulting in division. Programs like GOTR transmit powerful messages about "girlhood" and how to "fit" into girl culture. Anne, coordinators of the program, parents, and other adults offered little resistance or critique. Concerns I had included:

- GOTR has become a "celebration of girl culture." What is "girl culture?" Can/should society agree on a stagnant definition of "girl culture." Is this celebration helpful in advancing the rights of girls and women? And what if some girls do not identify with the particular kind of "girl culture" that the curriculum promotes? Are they destined to be marginalized?
- What happens when girls who identify with masculinity (and/or desire to be a boy) are confronted with the possibility of participation in GOTR?
- What happens when boys who identify with femininity (and/or desire to be a girl) are disallowed participation? How do programs like GOTR define "girl?" If biologically, are schools willing to "check" the sex of their students?

- What happens when girls do not identify with femininity or masculinity?
- What are the unintended consequences and hidden curriculum of GOTR?
- GOTR was born out of white middle/upper class "feminine" culture. Is this culture/their values the values we desire to impose on other communities?
- When men dress "hyper-feminine" for the race, is it in jest or mockery of girlhood? If not, would men who dressed feminine because this is how they identify, be accepted and supported at the race?
- Has GOTR become about/for/more important to adults?
- Are nicknames infantilizing girls? Are nicknames that emphasize beauty continuing to sexualize girls and place importance on their appearance? Should the program not ban this?
- Does the international GOTR organization mind when coaches encourage "glamming it up?" Should the GOTR curriculum/ organization disallow coaches to encourage girls to "glam it up" because they receive these messages from everywhere else in society (this should be the one space that doesn't emphasize appearance)?
- Could the bombardment of "positive" messages (e.g., "girls are just as good as boys") tell girls that there is something inherently wrong with them?
- What messages are transmitted to girls when they are afforded an isolated and segregated space to explore their importance? Does it mean they are not worth our time and effort every day?
- Would it be more powerful if programs that teach empowerment and relationships are done in co-educational settings that represent the real world? Would not boys have something to gain (e.g., gender equity, sense of fairness and respect, and so on) by participating with girls? Would not girls have something to gain (e.g., positive relationships with boys, and the right to be important and valued in front of and with/by boys) by participating with boys?
- What messages are transmitted to boys when girls are perceived as "in need" of special programming like GOTR?
- Does GOTR reify stereotypes of femininity?

- Why does GOTR partner with capitalistic opportunists that peddle sexualized "tween" and "pre-teen" products/messages tethering girls' worth to beauty products.
- Could we (adults) serve all kinds of girls—including the kind who are not into living and breathing pink and lace—better with more holistic programming that believes in respecting and celebrating all children who identify along the spectrum of gender representation?
- What if the program is just downright miseducative?

Confused, Dylan, a fifth grade boy complained to two female teachers after school, "Why do the girls get to do special things like Girls on the Run, and we don't?"

They responded, with a smile and instructional tone, "Because boys always play outside and are athletic, girls don't have much interest in that…so, we help them."

Ugh.

Programs like GOTR, or Grrl Power reify stereotypes and create a public narrative that boys and girls must live separate lives with specific cultural configurations.

Grrl Power was the project of Becky Lanzalotto, Lynn McCabe, the P.T.O. president, and Suzanne Chase, a first grade teacher. Grrl Power is in its second year, and was designed to "empower" young girls. "Empowerment," however, was not really conceptualized and so for all intents and purposes Grrl Power became a mini social club. Socialization, particularly when it builds community, can be empowering, however the socialization that occurred at Grrl Power was more or less a space at school to talk about fashion, friends, and even boys.

I sat in on Grrl Power one day.

"Oh, Dr. Richardson, you are being a secret spy," Suzanne said in front of the girls.

"What do you mean?"

"This is a girl space, you are from the other team."

"Maybe I'm on your team," I provoked.

The girls and Suzanne laughed. I quieted down so that I could observe Grrl Power at work.

"Girls, how was your day?" Lynn asked.

73

Eight girls from grades first through fifth sat at the kidney bean shaped table and stared into the distance. Allison, an extraverted third grader, piped up, "I saw Tori's boyfriend today at lunch."

"Shut up!" Tori protested, "Ian is not my boyfriend!"

Another girl, Rose, teased, "Uh-huh…you and Ian always talk at lunch."

The three adults smiled. Lynn said, "Well, it's OK if Tori likes Ian. Remember, girls have special feelings and we can like who we want. It's OK."

Tori retorted, "But…I don't like Ian!" By this time, it was clear that she was feeling picked-on.

Lynn, a bit startled at how strong Tori responded—and perhaps a bit disappointed there was no romantic energy between the two elementary schoolers—said quietly, "It's OK, alright…let's move on. Anyone have any plans for the weekend?"

The girls talked about movies they were going to see, friends they would visit, and shopping trips they planned with older sisters. The adults listened and interjected with lines like, "Oooh!" "That'll be nice," and, "Your sister is such a pretty girl." After forty-five minutes of this Lynn announced, "Well girls, it's time to go! Back to class. See you next Friday."

Grrl Power was held every Friday from 1:00 – 1:50 p.m. "Like happy hour!" Becky informed.

After all of the girls left the room, I asked, "So, how did Grrl Power come about?"

Suzanne responded, "Well it really came from the P.T.O. They were the push we needed.

"Right," Lynn responded with a proud smile. "The P.T.O. is made of, basically, a bunch of moms. We just thought our girls needed a special space. So we asked Ms. Lanzalotto if we could create a group of some kind. She did some research and…"

"We did it!" Becky continued. "I asked a couple of my counselor friends and they had Grrl Power groups."

"Who gets to be in the group?" I asked.

Becky responded, "Well, usually we try to find girls who are having a rough time. So, typically girls who get referred to my office for something. Girls who need some more support because home isn't so great. Or girls who are having problems in class."

"And so it's about, empowerment, huh?"

"Yes," Suzanne said. "It's about making them feel good. Like they have a safe space."

Grrl Power raised similar kinds of questions and concerns I had about Girls on the Run. I attended several Grrl Power sessions and not once did I, or my research team, observe any purposeful effort to "empower" girls through critical conversation or activity.

SECOND GRADE WITH MARY FOX

Mary Fox was the teacher of Marisa, Dana and twenty-six other students. She was the most veteran of teachers on the faculty and admittedly close to retirement, but was enthusiastic as ever about teaching. In the mornings, each student received a hug at the door and a greeting, "Good morning, I'm so happy you're here today," "How was the soccer game last night?" or "I found a super special book just for you. You are going to love it!" Parents practically bribed the principal to get their kids into Mary's class.

Mary was one of the first teachers that volunteered to participate in my research and quickly became a primary informant—someone I could go to with questions about the school and district. She had a lot of institutional history because twenty-four of her thirty-five total years teaching had been spent at Fisk.

Mary was proud to have received her master's degree, over two decades ago, from Teachers College, Columbia University. "I made friends for life. We had a great cohort of students. When I have a problem, I just call one of them for advice. Graduate school was really one of the best decisions I ever made." Receiving this kind of external support was unusual among the faculty. Fisk teachers typically looked to one another for help. Mary leaned on her colleagues a bit, but usually over trivial things like about when the copier might be fixed or if bus #34 will be late to school again. Mary did not intend to discount her colleagues' skills. She did not have a mean bone in her body—she was, in fact, one of the sweetest people I ever met. However, it was clear to me that she knew so very much. She did not really "need" her colleagues. She was in a different stage of her career. Mary saw just about every educational fad, program, and style of administration. She knew who she was as a teacher, worked hard to understand her students, and was dedicated to bigger causes like equity and social skill development (not just reading and math).

"So, what's been going on between Marisa and Dana?" I asked.

You, know…it's a bit of a mystery to me. I am finding it more and more, with each year, difficult to know how to deal with girls. I know there have been many changes for girls, but I don't know if it's because of the media—what they are watching and listening to—their home life, or something else. Maybe it's just early on-set puberty. Kids are developing at faster rates now than ever. But in second grade?! I don't know. But what I do know is that by the time they finish first grade—probably earlier than that really—they already know how to antagonize one another.

When Mary told me this it was October. I was a bit skeptical that early second grade girls had learned the "mean girl" ways that were exhibited in middle schools and high schools. But as the year went on and I hung out in Mary's classroom, it became more evident that meanness was a true weapon that many of the girls were equipped with and ready to use at any moment.

"What kills me," Mary shared, "is that a lot of what happens is so subtle. But these teeny-tiny microaggressions make the girls hurt so deeply."

"Can you give me an example of a microaggressions?" I asked.

Oh, things like simple little eye-rolls, a crinkling of a nose, the way one sits slightly turned away from another, choice words, and even simple refusal to acknowledge each other in particular ways. They are such small events they seem insignificant to us, and we can't even detect them most times…but they devastate the girls.

This made my head and heart hurt. I wondered how a second grade teacher might proactively teach about microaggressive behaviors? How could she provide consequences for things like how a kid sits? Worst of all, I thought, these behaviors are probably so engrained in girls' understanding of "girlhood culture" that they are being performed so fluidly and effectively. So, if teachers attempt to address what girls understand as "natural" what kind of conflicts in identity and culture might they experience?

"Well, the worst of it is when they come in from recess."

"Yeah? How so?"

When I pick them up from recess, they are all hot and sweaty. And who knows what happened out there on the playground. Our playground assistants, for the most part, are great. But, when my students line up you can tell on their faces—with little scowls and smirks—that "stuff" went on. When we come into the school, I immediately take them to the bathroom and allow them to get a drink. This cools some of them down, and for the most part the boys are ready to learn. The girls, however, not so much. I try to refocus the class by reading a story to them. I keep the lights off, and if it's a mild day, I open the windows so a breeze can come in. I tell them to just rest and listen. I don't care if their heads are on their desk. I actually don't care if they are under their desk relaxing. As long as they are cooling down and getting refocused. The girls, though, use this time to continue their arguments. Of course, I'm reading so they don't have the opportunity to use any sort of verbal communication. But their bodies say it all. In-between words, I glance up from the book at the class and I see the tail-end of girls just doing little things to each other. Most of the time, I can see that they are "upset," but at the same time they try to remain composed. They only "tell" on each other for two reasons. First, if they think they have a solid case of getting the other in trouble. That in itself, is problematic. I mean, if they aren't sharing what is making them upset, then teachers are left in the dark. It doesn't allow us to help them think through their problems. And two, if it all just boils over.

"Boils over?" I asked.

"Yeah. Boils over. If they just can't take it anymore. If they are just so hurt, or crazed by the situation."

"How do you usually handle this situation?"

Well…a couple different ways. I try to make sure that I emphasize care and compassion in everything I do. So I try to meet with the girls and facilitate a conversation. But the interesting thing is that the girls have learned how to say 'sorry' and use all the right words of reconciliation without really meaning it. So, in neutral times, I try to offer opportunities where kids—not just the girls, but boys too—can talk about any problems they are having. For example, I make sure that we open and close every day with a "care circle."

"A care circle?"

"We sit together on the carpet and we share how we are feeling, any anxieties about the day, and anything they want to talk about including stuff that happened the night before."

"Interesting."

"But, even during our care circle there are some microaggressions. Girls often slight one another by choosing different partners. For instance, Jess and Amelia are usually great friends. They always sit with one another. However, if Jess gets pissed off, she'll choose someone else—sometimes even a sworn enemy of Amelia's—to sit next to."

"So what happens?" I asked.

"Amelia's just hurt. Deeply hurt. She won't know what to do with this feeling except just know she's deeply hurt. And the fucked up thing, excuse my French, about it is that Jess completely knows it too. Lovely one minute, nasty the next."

"Second grade, huh?"

"Yup. Getting back to your question about handling this…I've found it extremely interesting that when I try to engage parents in conversations about their daughters and microaggressions, they either don't get it, or they don't care. I don't mean they don't understand the behaviors the kids are demonstrating, they just chalk it up as 'normal girl stuff.'"

"Example?"

Last year I had a group of girls that were just overly concerned and involved in each other's stuff. I use the term 'stuff' loosely because they were into everything. They were interested in what each other wore, how they made friends and with whom, how they held their pencils, who went to the bathroom first. Literally everything. During parent-teacher conferences, I spoke with their parents. One after another, regardless of whether it was concerning to them or not, they made comments like, 'Oh, but, you know girls,' 'girls are the worst,' 'well, this is what girls do, right?'

"So...you don't agree with them?"

No! Of course not. I think it's demeaning to the girls...that this is just 'the way they are.' But, what my point was is that addressing behaviors, that in the long run aren't very healthy or empowering, is difficult without community support. Breaking patterns in culture, I think, and especially mainstream culture, takes a group of dedicated people.

Mary's ideas, as I would find out, were much different than those of her colleagues.

Mary's classroom was designed so that kids sat in collaborative groups. Desks of three or four together made "islands." Mary told me that students were randomly assigned seats in the beginning of the year without consideration of their academic level. She did not intentionally assign seats according to gender—which was the case in many other classrooms. Mary's colleagues decided to either arrange kids in same sex groupings or in mixed sex groupings, depending on their philosophy. They would say things like, "The boys are too rowdy and don't stay on task so I have to break them up and sit girls between them," "Girls aren't confident enough to sit with the boys," and "the boys and girls just need space from each other."

Mary used the classroom as her "lab." She ran pedagogical experiments and organized the environment so that kids could access and explore manipulatives for problem solving tasks. Admittedly, however, her teaching had become "more narrow and standardized," which limited the kind of experimentation she valued. Mary told me:

There used to be a time that I could make practically all instructional decisions on my own. Those days are gone. I am ordered to use certain math, language arts, social studies, and science programs and to 'deliver' content in specific ways. 'Delivering content' is exactly what I don't want to do. I want kids to discover. So, I try to give students certain moments to engage in ideas in a way that's more authentic…but, those times are more and more rare.

The programs Mary referenced were "boxed curricula"—teacher manuals, student workbooks, and some supplemental materials that were designed by large curriculum companies and sold in mass to school districts across the nation. The programs were touted as "evidence based" (I am deeply suspicious of this term) and "aligned to federal and state standards." These programs are known as "teacher-proof" (read: "dummy-proof") by giving teachers scripts to follow, and activities to employ, as they so-called "taught." With these programs, if the teacher were to follow directions, it is perceived that there is "no way to mess up." The school district mandated the use of these specific programs and administrators expected that teachers stuck with the script.

These programs are historically notorious for being patriarchal and "unabashedly Anglocentric"—a product of American settler colonialism.[13] Upon examination, it was clear that the language arts, math, and social studies programs given to Mary favored white boys and men—she did not have a program for science. While it was true that diversity, particularly racial diversity was more present in these programs than those from the past, they did not represent the spectrum of racial or ethnic diversity (e.g., Middle Eastern cultures went mostly unrepresented). It was also clear that assessments were attempting to capture whether they have "absorbed this white-stream curriculum."[14] And nowhere were there transgender, gender fluid, or multiple representations of masculinity and femininity. Men and boys were portrayed as athletic, smart, adventurous risk-takers and women and girls were portrayed as social and caring. Mary attempted to modify some of the lessons, clarify misconceptions and respond to sexist and racist messages. Mary admitted that she would like to embed homosexual relationships in her curriculum, but was nervous about administrative backlash. "Look," Mary told me,

I've carved out a nice space where I can ignore a lot of what the administration wants me to do. I close my door and teach.

But that's only because I am successful—my kids learn—and parents like me. As soon as I raise any 'controversy' then I'm in jeopardy of getting micromanaged. I just want to fly under the radar. Though I desperately want to expose children to a diversity of relationships and families, if I do, I'm practically inviting administration to snoop around in my daily practice. I don't know if it's worth it.

Mary was a talented teacher. She differentiated instruction, paid fair amounts of attention to all students in her classroom, and patiently listened to students' voices. She encouraged them to be self-advocating six and seven year olds. "This is difficult for the girls," Mary told me.

"Why so?" I asked.

"Because they are supposed to be more compliant than the boys. So, even at this young age, they don't feel like they can interject or have a protesting voice. They need to be encouraged to be bold."

"Who says they are supposed to be more compliant?"

"Society—everybody. Families, media, everyone has a hand in creating pretty nice girls."

FOURTH GRADE WITH JESSIE MALLOY

She's "nice enough." That's how Ian, a middle-aged father of three, described Jessie Malloy. Jessie was one of the fourth grade teachers at Fisk, and she was nice.

"That's not really a compliment, is it?" I asked.

"Nope. I mean she's just that, though. 'She's nice enough.' Besides being nice…I dunno…she's clueless…mindless."

Outside her classroom door, Jessie would stand watch and greet kids as they scurried down the hallway. She loved this ritual of hers that happened at the beginning of each day. Jessie especially liked greeting her ex-students who were now in fifth grade.

"Hey girlfriend!" she called out to Brianne. Brianne was a shy lanky student who Jessie and a few of the Fisk teachers liked to talk about. "She's a beautiful kid…the boys don't notice her now, but just wait a few years," and "She's going to grow into her body…just wait…she'll be a knock out!" they would say in the faculty room during lunch.

"How's it going beautiful?" was always reserved for Katie, a bright-eyed and always smiling kid. Katie did not feel that she was beautiful, one could tell. So, that is why Jessie liked calling her that. "It's just a shame. She's a gorgeous kid with no self-esteem. It's important to tell her she's beautiful."

"Hey bud!" and "How's it going, buddy?" were directed at boys. The boys politely entertained Jessie's greeting ritual with a tired, "Hi Mrs. Malloy," while the girls embraced it out of enjoyment or obligation. Jessie would every once-in-a-while give a boy a pat on the back or a hi-five, but insisted on hugging and squeezing the girls—as if they were girlfriends meeting up for drinks. Some of the girls were awkward about the hugs and being called "beautiful," "girlfriend," "cutie," and "gorgeous." But they played along.

Jessie claimed to know she wanted to be a teacher since the age of six. Though she was nice enough, she was, as other dad's enamored, "perfect." Jessie was an ex-cheerleader and even participated in a few beauty pageants when in high school. She had perfectly painted nails, a perfectly glowing white smile, perfectly silky deep hazel hair that lightly curled at its ends, and was perfectly dressed as if she fell straight out of a Banana Republic advertisement.

Life was easy for Jessie. Throughout her twenty-seven years she never faced any extraordinary adversity and was never confronted by serious conflict. She floated through life and received almost everything she desired because she was nice, pretty, white, and middle-upper class. She had a peachy-keen sense of the world.

"One of the kids," laughed Jessie, "called me 'Ms. Malloy.' I had to correct him. I told him I wasn't some old bat." And whenever kids called her "Miss." she was even quicker to correct. To say Jessie loved being a newlywed is the understatement of a century. After dating a few men—several of them minor league baseball players for some reason—she settled down with Tim. Tim was also "athletic" among hundreds of things she would drone on about. Tim was liable to be the topic of conversation at any moment; it was the "Tim Show" 24/7. Few people at Fisk were honestly interested in Jessie's ramblings about Tim.

Her wedding was also something she planned since she was six.

Jessie's room was "cute." It was not drastically pink, like her colleague and good friend Anne Sprenkle's, but it definitely exhibited two themes: girl and boy. Prior to the beginning of the year, Jessie made construction paper cut-outs of footballs, basketballs, soccer balls, and baseballs. She neatly wrote her students' names on these shapes—one name per shape—and hung them using a paperclip, yarn, and a push-pin pressed into the drop ceiling above each of their desks. The boys names were sporadically assigned to the footballs, basketballs, and baseballs. The girls names were written only on soccer balls.

The day before the first day of school, Jessie received word that she would have a new student, Nafy. Nafy was not on her class roster. She had no information on Nafy since this student was a refugee who just arrived from Sudan. Jessie could not make sense of Nafy's name, and became stressed wondering if this new student was a boy or girl. She went up and down the halls, asking colleagues, "Do you think Nafy is a boy name or a girl name?" and following it up with, "It would be so embarrassing if I got it wrong."

Jessie settled on making Nafy a basketball and hung it over the student's desk. The first day of school came and Nafy and two-dozen other students filtered into her classroom. Most of the students knew Jessie and immediately they shared their summertime happenings. Nafy, however, spoke no English and sat quietly. To Jessie's (short-lived) relief, she believed Nafy to be a boy thus feeling successful for choosing a "boy" sports shaped nametag. To Jessie's horror, however, she believed Nafy did not have any "American" clothes and so was sent to school forced to wear a dress. A brand new beautiful yellow and blue dress. Nafy was, in fact, a biological female but had short cropped hair, which confused Jessie. Jessie took into no consideration of Nafy's culture. By 10:30 a.m., Jessie arranged another teacher to cover her class as she escorted Nafy to the nurse's office asking for a set of "boy clothes" for Nafy to change into. The nurse had extra clothes on hand for "accidents" that children might have. Nafy was confused, but compliant. She was switched into a pair of jeans and a blue t-shirt with green letters with white trim that spelled, "IN CHARGE." How ironic.

Nafy wore her new clothes without protest. Her mother, and an accompanying social worker, at dismissal were shocked to see Nafy not wearing the new dress they had bought for her first day at school in the U.S.

"What happened?" asked the social worker.

With a smile, Jessie proudly reported that she was able to get Nafy some boy clothes that he could keep. She handed the mother a bag with the dress in it.

The social worker pulled Jessie to the side and informed her that Nafy was, indeed, a girl. The social worker emphasized how embarrassing this might be for the family. Jessie felt attacked and instead of owning her mistake, complained to other teachers that there should have been "some way to tell," and "if you send your student to an American school and it's not clear then maybe you need to tell the teacher."

Nafy had short hair and wore a dress. Jessie could not "get over it."

The social worker never meant to upset Jessie. However, Jessie for weeks talked about how she was "so rude." She was in disbelief that an act of kindness (trying to give Nafy properly gendered clothing) warranted a correction. However, what was lost on her was that she offered a "correction" of her own when she took Nafy to the nurse to change. This, however, was only the beginning of a rough year for Jessie.

Parents Mark and Melanie became very dissatisfied with Jessie's management of her classroom. Mark and Melanie were both educators and complained that their daughter, Zoey, felt like she was "under continual and unnecessary stress for stupid stuff."

"Like what?" I asked them.

Melanie shared, "Zoey is a laid back kid. She's a good kid. And [Jessie] Malloy she just micromanages every bit of the day. For kids who like time to think, reflect, be in the moment, it doesn't work."

"So, it seems like their personalities don't line up."

Mark chimed in, "Well, maybe, but, if you are the adult in the room, you should know what kinds of kids you have sitting in front of you. We're continually trying to tell Malloy that some of the stuff she does is too stressful."

Mark and Melanie started to take issue with Jessie's instruction and management of the classroom by mid-September. Zoey started crying at the bus stop, worrying in bed about the next day, and developed some general anxiety. Zoey pleaded with her parents to be homeschooled, while Mark and Melanie pleaded with Jessie, and eventually with the principal, for her to become more inquiry based, less punitive, and to be generally more excited about learning rather than approaching learning as "work." Jessie, and many other teachers at Fisk viewed learning as a banking of information[15] (that could later be tested) that required memorization, and practice (with lots of worksheets and program based workbooks).

Jessie's primary problem was that she was a "follower." Meaning, she strictly implemented canned curriculum given to her, instituted any silly and punitive rule suggested by the administration, and was relentless about "collecting data"—giving lots of assessments that measured students' so-called "achievement" so that she could report it to her supervisors (which is what they wanted). Teachers like Mary Fox knew better and refused to mindlessly employ anything, especially if it was a "new trend." And to Jessie, Mary Fox was "irresponsible."

Jessie told me, "Mary's just crazy. She's so old school." But Mary's students were happy and learning.

Eventually, Mark and Melanie had enough. By December, they directly told the principal to provide instructional support and supervision to ensure that Jessie did not continue to "kill learning" for their daughter and the other students. Melanie and Mark rallied a handful of other disgruntled parents and together began making their dissatisfaction heard. Jessie, never having faced any significant adversity, did not know what to do. Her gut response was to be dually defensive and, well, herself. "When you put a person in a difficult position," Melanie pointed out, "they start to show their true colors."

Jessie's "true colors" bled sparkly rainbow. Her instruction did not improve, but her involvement increased in organizing faculty potlucks, baby showers for any staff and faculty who were expecting, and a student program called "Monroe Valley Cheer!" Events like this not only made Jessie feel like she was doing something important, but she felt "connected" to it. Her personality and "girlie side," as she described, was able to "come out."

Monroe Valley Cheer! was Anne Sprenkle's idea, but the two of them worked together to make it happen. Anne and Jessie recruited girls from across the school district—elementary through middle school—to attend "cheer camp" on Thursdays after school. High school cheerleaders were empowered to help the other girls learn techniques and routines. During these sessions, Anne and Jessie beamed with excitement. They would become playful with the other girls, often talking about "liking boys." They would also talk about how to modify their cheerleading uniforms and hair to look cute, (un)intentionally impressing that cheerleading had a lot do to with appearance. They claimed to talk about health too. "Health is a big part of the program… we stress that it's important to make sure you are eating healthy foods and that your portions aren't too big," Jessie told me. Certainly this was a fine line since several of the girls on the high school squad had at some point received help for eating disorders. The younger girls idolized the older ones and listened intently to messages emphasizing "portion control."

The Monroe Valley Cheer! girls were mobilized to march in parades and perform during home football and basketball games. Parents wore "My girl is a MV Cheer! girl" t-shirts and sat throughout entire games to catch 3 minute routines at half-time. Boys of all ages sat among parents in the crowd and pointed at the "hot" girls and made lewd comments. Monroe Valley Cheer! became a multi-aged public display of "girlie" femininity and sexuality. They performed to songs by Beyoncé, Rihanna, and others that featured some explicit and implicit sexual themes. Their routines involved moves that elicited sexual excitement. Jessie and Anne were not naïve and actively claimed cheerleading to be "sexy." "Of course the boys are going to go crazy… put a bunch of pretty girls in tight clothes with hot songs…it happens," Jessie reported. I found this perspective interesting, particularly because the girls who participated in their program were as young as six years of age. Also, I wondered then, about how Jessie and Anne made the decision to perform with the kids. Privately, over beers after a performance, they told me, "I love dressing up…it's hot…it takes me back to cheering in college…those were the days of lots of attention…," and "fuck yeah…we're sexy bitches…it's fun getting out there…I like to see the look on some of the dad's faces…" They loved thinking about their formal teaching positions at Fisk elementary and how their cheerleading personas "clash." They deeply enjoyed being a "tease" to dads in the district. It was clear that just like many of the other programs at Fisk, Monroe Valley Cheer! existed primarily because Jessie and Anne loved it, not because it was good for kids.

Some teachers understand sexuality as a normal part of daily life, and that neither they nor their students can fully shed their desires, orientations, and interests at the school's front door. And so, some cheerleading coaches might believe that cheering could lead to positive sexual empowerment and ownership. This was not Jessie and Anne's intent. Accompanying the love of designing routines and developing athleticism, they enjoyed the salacious feeling that cheering has a flirtatious and naughty side. This was troublesome because the performances become about performing for others (a consumption of their sexuality) rather than performing for self (an owning of their sexuality).

Jessie's classroom became wholly involved with MV Cheer! She used a portion of every week to have her class do things like make banners and signs that read things like, "MV Cheer Squad Rocks!" and "Smart and Sassy – MV Cheer!" Some weeks they would take a break and go outside or to the gymnasium so that the girls in Jessie's class can "show off" some of their new routines to the rest of her students.

"I don't give a shit about cheerleading, and I'd prefer that you not involve your class," Lynn and Gail parents of Danielle, told Jessie at parent-teacher conferences in early April. This became another moment of contention in which Jessie would feel personally attacked.

"Look," Gail said, "If we could do what Mark and Melanie did, we would…but we can't afford it. So, you have to make this [class/school] work for Danielle."

This stung. Mark and Melanie felt as if they were getting nowhere with Jessie, or the principal, so they eventually pulled Zoey from Fisk and sent her to a private Montessori school. Jessie was embarrassed to know that a public perception existed that she could not satisfy the educational needs of a student.

"I don't understand," Jessie responded with a quivering voice, "Danielle isn't even on the squad."

Lynn responded, nearly yelling:

Exactly! So, if we don't want her involved, we don't want her involved, period. Your class uses time during the day to make banners and who the hell knows what else…meanwhile Danielle is complaining about being bored all day long. She's hating math, reading, everything in your room. Maybe putting some of your energy into what you're supposed to be teaching instead of cheerleading would make sense. And besides, your cheerleading program is exposing Danielle to a culture in which we don't identify.

"It's 'cause they are lesbians," Anne later half-joked, half-consoled Jessie.

"They're assholes," Jessie cried.

Lynn and Gail were not "assholes" by any stretch of the imagination. However, in this situation, they were deeply frustrated.

"We don't want Danielle to get too steeped in this petty girl drama that Jessie seems to fuel with cheerleading and her general approach to teaching girls and boys differently," Lynn confided.

"I have a working theory," Gail added, "that cheerleading and this ultra-femme persona she's continually working to maintain provides her a distraction from doing the hard work of teaching."

"I completely agree. I'm cool with people being femme…obviously," Lynn smiles and nods toward Gail, "but when it's this over fucking exaggerated and mindless that it impacts the way our kid thinks about gender and interferes with good teaching…then, something needs to happen."

Gail and Lynn described Jessie as "mindless" just as Mark and Melanie had. Gail and Lynn, however, understood her particular performance of femininity as an inhibiting condition to doing a good job as an instructor. The other parents, including the disgruntled ones—probably because they had been socialized to accept, even appreciate Jessie's version of femininity—did not connect these dots the same way Gail and Lynn had. In my observation, however, they were correct.

The physical environment of Jessie's classroom was unremarkable except for the gendered name tags hanging over students' desks, pictures of high heels lining the outside and inside doorframe, and a picture of Ryan Gosling tacked to the front board. Jessie loved shoes and incessantly talked about them. Often she made it a point to talk about the shoes she was wearing or planning on buying. Sometimes she would make an announcement, "Aren't these the cutest?!" other times she held individual conversations, "These hurt my feet, but it's worth it…"

"What's with Ryan Gosling?" I asked.

"Well…come on! He's so cute," Jessie responded.

"I know, but why do you have him hanging there?"

"Isn't it hysterical?!" she laughed. "Personally, it just helps me get through the day looking at him."

"So, it's just for your viewing pleasure?"

"Well, no…sometimes if kids tattle-tale, I tell them I don't want to hear it, but they should talk to Ryan. And sometimes I'll pretend like I'm talking to him. I'll say stuff like, 'What's that sweetheart? It's time for lunch?'"

"Sweetheart, eh?"

"Oh, yeah. I call him my sweetheart or boyfriend, but I tell my students not to worry that Mr. Malloy doesn't mind."

Again, this display of sexuality could possibly be argued positive. That is, that women have a sexuality—a fact often ignored by society—and that she is allowed to "own" it. However, Jessie's intent, I think, was to be "silly." Coupled with how often she talked about her husband to the class, it made her seem "boy crazy." In fact, she teased many of the boys to talk to Ryan who responded, "Eww…that's gross," or "I'm not going to talk to Ryan, that's your thing." She continued, "Oh, you're just jealous," and "Just wait, some day you'll have girls hunting you down." This fawning over Ryan and Tim modeled to her class how boys should be commodified and girls enamored.

In early May, at a follow-up meeting, Lynn and Gail still deeply dissatisfied, asked her, "Why is it that Danielle can't tell us any of the academic material she's supposed to be learning, but can report all the happenings of your honeymoon, what Tim's favorite ice cream is, and every other unimportant thing about your husband? We get it, teachers are people and it's great for kids to know that, but why must your husband be involved in every conversation you have with a bunch of nine and ten year olds?"

Tim was a centerpiece in Jessie's psyche and classroom. She "rewarded" the class—if they scored certain grades on tests, or dutifully completed the piles of homework she assigned every night for a month—by having Tim visit the class. These visits usually involved Tim reading a book or two.

Jessie read to her class for about twenty minutes a day. She read more "boy books" about sports, adventure, mystery, and action so that she "wouldn't bore the boys." "The girls," she said, "will put up with boy books, but the boys really complain about girl books." But every once-in-awhile, Jessie told the boys they had to "deal with it" and suffer through a girl book. On one occasion, I observed Tim's visit to the classroom. Upon entering through the high heeled decorated door, Jessie squealed, clapped her hands and announced, "Mr. Malloy is here!" For the most part, Jessie ignored me while I sat at the back of her room, but this time she called me up to meet her husband. Upon introduction he shook my hand and said, "Hey man, nice to meet you," in front of the class. The "hey man" and the obligatory need for the men in the room to meet, gave example to students of engineered male homosociality.

Minutes later, Jessie sat Tim at the front of the room and hid a book behind her back. She teased, "Tim, we just finished a book and we're moving on to a new one. So, I picked one out just for you. One that I knew you'd really like. Want to see it?"

"Yes, if you want me to read it."

"Here it is," Jessie smiled, and showed the class a copy of *Princess Academy: Palace of Stone*.[16]

"Oh, no! I don't think so! I'll leave that one to you!" Tim exclaimed.

"What? Is it too girlie for you? Well, I thought big strong guys could handle anything."

"I can handle it…it's just not my thing."

"What do you think class? Should we let him off the hook and let him read something else, or should we have him read *Princess Academy*?"

Several of the girls chanted, "Read it! Read it!"

Some of the boys who took a particular liking to Tim protested, "No! That's not OK. He shouldn't have to read a girl book if he doesn't want to!"

Some of the other kids, like Danielle, sat quietly soaking in the gendered expectations and interactions being performed.

Tim, like Jessie, was nice enough, but also mindless. If Tim came during recess time, he played basketball with the boys and chatted with the girls who watched on the sidelines. He loved encouraging a competitive spirit among the boys. Jessie would remind him how great it was that he spent time with the boys. "They really need you," she told him.

At the end of every visit Tim pretended to be serious and turned to Ryan Gosling's picture. He pointed and said, "Gosling, I'm watching you." Jessie would hold her hand over her heart and swoon, "Oh, Ryan" or "Ok, that's enough Mr. Malloy, I need my time with Ryan," and shooed him out of her room. It was a skit they would perform over and over again throughout the year.

Jessie's math, language arts, and social studies programs—like all the other grade level programs provided at Fisk—were rife with heteronormative and traditional binary representations of gender. Jessie, however, spent no energy in correcting or challenging these representations. Instead, she reinforced them. She also filled her classroom library with books like, *The Big Book of Girl Stuff, Girls Rule,* and *A Smart Girl's Guide to Boys* for the girls, and *Ninja Farts: Silent but Deadly, The Boy's Book of Survival, A Long Walk to Water,* and *Captain Underpants* for the boys. Other books in her library did not have gendered titles, but most still entailed gendered themes. A favorite of Jessie's—which she was gifted by her husband—but was too "young" for her fourth graders was *Dog-Gone School.*[17] She prominently displayed this gift on the top shelf of a bookcase. The book featured dogs in school, doing typical school stuff. It also captured stereotypical gender roles: Lucy the cocker spaniel is the teacher's pet (she is always on time to school, behaves, and performs well academically); Simon the pitbull does math; Ralphie, a terrier, drinks too much water and ponders going to the boys' bathroom; Maddie the lab works on spelling; Ellie the beagle is enthusiastic about reading; Stan, a mutt, is punished and stays after school to write "I will not eat my homework" on the chalkboard. Girl dogs behave well and are interested in language arts. Boy dogs were mischievous, but good in math.

Often, girls would reach for a "boy" book only to be discouraged and redirected to something more "girl." The "girl books" were so explicitly "for girls" that the boys avoided choosing those titles in fear of being teased. Therefore, Jessie did not police the boys' reading choices as carefully. Jessie thought it was important to have gendered literature, especially for the boys. She sextyped the boys as "non-readers and non-writers." Many of the boys, however, deeply enjoyed language arts. Midway through the school year she bought each of the boys in her class *Guy-Write: What Every Guy Writer Needs to Know*.[18] Lucy asked if she could have a copy of the book to which Jessie responded, "Oh sweetie those are for boys…they talk about boy stuff to help get them interested in writing. You don't need that." Sadly for Lucy, the book gave lots of good writing advice, especially for crafting stories that are humorous and adventure based.

Students in Jessie's room were experiencing pre-puberty. Which meant they were a little more moody and a little smellier than years before. It also meant that adults, in and out of school, began to talk—not in a serious and helpful manner, but in a teasing way—about "liking" those of the opposite sex. A few of them, both boys and girls, claimed to "like" each other and even admitted to having a "boyfriend" or "girlfriend." All "liking" and relationships were heterosexual in nature. All of the encouragement from adults also reinforced heterosexuality. This pre-pubescent phase made them especially susceptible to Jessie's influence. Jessie, unfortunately, became a model for "what's normal." So the girls often flirted with Ryan Gosling. The boys, just to be safe, often did opposite of whatever it was the girls were doing.

Beyond some biological changes and an increasing sense that they should be interested in romantic relationships, their gendered behaviors became more pronounced. On the playground, boys interacted almost exclusively with other boys. They played catch with footballs and organized pick-up basketball games. I was startled to see that many of the girls simply sat and watched. Others sat in a row against the school's wall and quietly read books. One group of girls consistently met and shared their *American Girl* and *Monster High* catalogues. They discussed which sexy monster character had a boyfriend, and which ones were "cute." Infrequently, girls would try to join some of the games boys were playing. They were consistently denied participation, unless they were deemed an exceptional athlete.

Jessie's students, like Mary Fox's, would return from recess having endured some social drama on the playground. Jessie's solution was to immediately engage her students in a "brain break." She cued up music video clips and had students dance behind their seats. Her favorite was "I Like to Move It"[19] from the movie Madagascar. She and students danced as characters from the movie also danced and sang, "I love how all the girls a move their body…Nice and sweet and sexy alright!"[20]

FIFTH GRADE WITH ALLEN REIF

"Hey, Reif, what's the white stuff you find in cheerleaders' panties?"

"What the hell?" Allen responded looking up from his computer screen to find Jessie walking through the door.

Jessie loved flirting with Allen. They were both close in age and she enjoyed the idea that she might get him excited. It was an after school ritual for Jessie to visit Allen for a few minutes.

"Well, what's the white stuff you find in cheerleaders' panties?" Jessie asked again.

"Um…" Allen paused, and glanced my direction as I buried my face into my laptop.

"Richardson doesn't care," Jessie said with a wink. "He knows you can't help yourself…you love me! Answer the question!"

"In that case, then I guess I have to say I don't know but would like to find out. What are you doing tonight?"

Jessie laughed heartily. "Nice try…it's clitty litter!"

Allen shook his head from side to side and smiled.

Jessie, Anne, and a couple other women at Fisk were overly interested in everything Allen—but in all the wrong ways. They wanted to know about his social life—who he was dating and if it was getting serious—and his professional (administrative) goals. They looked for opportunities to pry about his sex life, give advice about dating, and help him organize his instruction and classroom. Allen did not ask for any of this, however, it became convenient and so he accepted their assistance. Besides, Allen felt special because of this attention he received. He was, like many other male elementary school teachers, commodified. Jessie, Anne, and others on some level felt special too. They enjoyed the "safe" flirting space in which they learned about how Allen (and they generalized this to other men) thought about relationships. They enjoyed trying to explain how they (and other women) thought about relationships. To some extent, they felt like they were doing the women Allen dated a favor by grooming him to "treat them right."

Over the school year, I watched this grooming process happen before and after school, in the hallways, during lunch in the faculty room, at "bus duty," and during school-wide happy hours. Throughout the school year, I also watched Allen go through a process where he became more oblivious about how to teach his class because the women helped him plan so much of his instruction. In some cases, they would simply craft plans—especially in science since there was no official program—and gift it to him. Allen had three students who were identified with learning disabilities. Jessie and other women provided him with differentiated activities or arranged their schedules so that they could invite these students into their classroom for instruction. He essentially never learned how to appropriately work with these students. Because, however, he is tethered to performing masculinity, he was not able to ask for help. Admitting that he did not understand or know something and that he needed real help to become a better teacher would not be perceived masculine. So, Allen was stuck.[21]

Allen did not understand the complexity of teaching, but he knew how to get good test scores. Besides whatever plans the women gave him, he knew how to teach out of the book and assign oodles of test preparation. This was important to Allen because good test scores would build him the reputation of a competent teacher among some of his colleagues. Though others, like Mary Fox, knew better.

Good test scores also meant he received the praise of his principal, which he figured would help his case to become an administrator.

Allen, like many of the male elementary teachers I have met, had dreams of becoming an administrator. This influenced the way he taught his class. He was, for the most part, no nonsense. He expected students to follow his rules and procedures. Allen was concerned with managing his students—he believed this was the work of a teacher, just as many children believe. Procedures, protocol, and order trumped inquiry, curiosity, care, and fun. His plan was to teach a maximum of three years—the state minimum to be eligible for an administrative certificate—and move into an athletic directorship or assistant principalship.

There was nothing dynamic about Allen's teaching. Our observations in his classroom rendered us bored to tears. Whenever my research assistants and I were scheduled to observe Allen's class, we were sure to bring along a thermos of coffee. He was a robot, reading directly off of the plans provided to him by his colleagues, or directly out of his teacher manuals. Sometimes we would observe him sight reading lessons attempting what he was supposed to do in the very moment.

I have fond memories watching my little sister, when she was seven or eight years old, line up her stuffed animals in rows and pretend as though she was their teacher. She would "play school." She reprimanded students for talking, asked questions that required recalling memorized facts, and called on students if they raised their hand—and if they did not raise their hand, she had prepared a brief lecture on the importance of doing so. She entertained requests for the bathroom, modeled math problems, passed out worksheets for students to complete, and assigned homework. I imagine many young children play like this. This is how Allen taught. He too, "played school."

Boys enjoyed being in Allen's class because he would talk sports and use "guy" language that signified that he was, on some level, like them. It was obvious that Allen cared for his students, but that he understood the boys and their culture better than the girls. Of course, he sextyped what boy culture and girl culture was and aligned himself with the boys, developing an affinity for them. Boys also heard their parents sextype by talking openly about how lucky they were to have him as a teacher. Comments like, "Mr. Reif is great…the boys respond better having a masculine vibe in an elementary classroom," and "It's so important to have male teachers for boys…boys learn better from men," were commonly overheard. Again, the role modeling literature does not support that male elementary school teachers inherently benefit young boys (or girls, for that matter). However, when boys are actively told that male teachers are better for them—or they hear the rhetoric swapped between adults—then they believe it. It was unfortunate because many of the fifth grade boys who were in other classrooms "acted up" for their female teachers because they believed the reverse; that is, women were not suited for them. The female teachers, by and large, were better teachers and could have acted as significant role models, however, boys closed off the idea.

An overwhelming majority of parents told me that their boys had better academic performances since they had been in Allen's classroom. This might have been true, but only for a few. In actuality, upon an examination of students reported grades, test scores, and so on, it was obvious that boys stayed on a relatively consistent academic course between their previous female teachers and their year with Allen. For a few who did perform better, there could have been any number of explanations. One reason could have been because masculinity acted as an effective placebo, stereotype boost,[22] and/or self-fulfilling prophecy. If boys thought Allen was "good for them," then they may have been (sub)consciously more confident and tried harder, resulting in better performances.

Something quite unexpected came from our observations of Allen and his students. We predicted accurately that Allen's performances of (hyper)masculinity—exuding control, authority and toughness in the classroom, displaying typical male dress and dominant-based interactions with female colleagues, talking about "guy stuff" (sports in particular) with the boys, his particular use of pop culture as a connector (e.g., "No…I wouldn't listen to Taylor Swift if you paid me…" and "You shouldn't play *Call of Duty* (video game), but let me tell you…it's pretty awesome."), among other things—would result in homosocial bonding with boys, creating some hegemonic and complicit performances of masculinity[23] in his classroom. However, we did not expect that these performances would create such exaggerated forms of deep male solidarity at the expense of girls in the class. Certainly we understood that among adults, "male solidarity…plays a role in the maintenance of men's power,"[24] but did not know that girls would feel so "marginalized," or "on the outside" of the primary social scene.

"It's okay," Lizzie told me, "Mr. Reif always picks the boys to do special things, but I don't care."

"What do you mean?" I asked.

"Like, I never get to pick teams for games we play. Mr. Reif always picks Ben, Aidan, Connor, and like, other boys to be captains."

"And you want to be a captain?"

"Yeah…me and Gabby we always want to be captains, but we never get a chance."

"Are there other things you'd like to do?"

"Uh-huh. Lots of things. Like I never get to deliver things from the office."

The week of this conversation, the P.E. teacher, Michael, received a shipment of materials for a fundraiser. He asked Allen, in front of the entire class, if he could have a couple "strong boys" to help carry the boxes to the gym.

"I don't know, he [Allen] just likes the boys better because he's a boy," Lizzie concludes.

Many girls felt this way. They often complained, but privately among themselves (and to me when I asked), that they were not treated the same or as special. They did not actively complain to Allen or the other boys because they sensed they had little agency to do so. Ironically, the boys complained if they perceived that the girls received privileges or attention that they desired. Boys became comfortable within their patriarchal environment, policing the girls. For instance, when Allen asked questions during whole class instruction that many students knew the answer to, and he called on girls for answers, the boys complained and sighed heavily. Allen made sure that the girls were aware that the boys also knew the answer. It was a demonstration of maintaining expertise and power. Another example was when girls received turns at completing certain classroom chores. "It's no fair," "I can do it better," and "Why do they always get to…" were common comments. Allen would respond, "Well, we should give them a chance too." Note the team-like mentality with the use of "we."

In Allen's class, girls had a diminished value, but maintained agency in two particular ways: performing well and flirting. Girls' performances on standardized tests and other metrics that "evidenced learning" were a valued commodity. Girls' academic achievement helped ensure Allen's tenure and promotion; he was perceived as an effective, even highly successful, teacher. He counted on girls to do well academically, and in this domain he provided them with a substantial amount of positive reinforcement. The girls' performances were not due to the impact he had as a teacher—rather, they came to fifth grade, in comparison to boys, with strong academic skills. Allen found himself simply encouraging girls to "keep up the good work."

Girls in upper elementary school—like those in Allen's class—began to understand that "the route to 'success' is less a path than a tight-rope. Girls realize that in order to be seen as successful women in contemporary society they must be attractive, as well as high educational achievers."[25] They also began to understand that "this combination [successful yet attractive] is particularly difficult to negotiate, as there are powerful associations between cleverness and a-sexuality/unfemininity."[26] Though difficult, girls in Allen's class attempted to be both. Outside of performing well, the next most popular way they received positive attention was through flirting with Allen. Certainly, the girls may not perceive their actions as flirtatious. However, the tone of their teasing (e.g., "Mr. Reif, does your girlfriend know you're not cool?" and "I don't care if you fail me…then, you get to have me in class again next year") and acting "ultra-femme" that drew attention to their looks (by engaging him in things "girlie" like asking if he "liked" their outfits, nail polish, and so on) was certainly flirtatious in nature. They also began to carry their physicality in a way that if they were adults, it would have been interpreted flirtatious. They sat extra close to him to get attention, playfully pouted, and at times would even lightly touch his arm when speaking (particularly when trying to get or convince him of something).

"Please, please, please, Mr. Reif…don't give us homework tonight," Jessica pouted, sticking out her bottom lip and widening her eyes.

"Mr. Reif, so you know how I didn't get to sit with Ally yesterday… well, can I sit with her today?" Lynn begged, touching his arm with one hand and reaching for his hand with the other.

"I'm not going to ask you again, Mr. Reif," Bianca said smiling slyly and sashaying away from his desk, tossing her long brown hair to one side. "But if you don't want to get in trouble, I hope you start listening to me," she said and sat down at her desk crossing her legs and glancing up at him hoping she would catch his gaze.

In almost all cases where girls were flirting, or "practice flirting," he found their playfulness endearing. It was no coincidence that the most popular and "prettiest" girls were best at this practice, and received responses from Allen that encouraged their ongoing engagement.

In May, I interviewed Allen and told him that I was studying gender. This was a great surprise to him. He did not know what I could be observing that would be of any value. "You mean, this whole time you weren't worried about student achievement? I was hoping you could have put in a good word for me. And what's there to know, anyway?"

"Well, to answer your first question," I said, "I'm interested in student achievement as it is related to gender. But, mostly, I am wondering about how students learn gender."

We had a discussion about what this meant. Then, I read him some of our field notes that detailed interactions that we perceived flirtatious and asked for his interpretation. While I was reading, he smiled, seemingly like he enjoyed remembering these events.

"So, what do you make of these?" I asked.

"Hmmm…I guess you could say that I have a good relationship with the girls. Is this what you thought?"

"I don't know how to think about it, that's why I'm asking you," I deflected.

"Okay. Yeah…I think it's just that I treat girls like I treat the boys… we all get along."

This statement contrasted with our observations of how boys were deeply favored and that girls were marginalized to be "achievers" and "cute" or "flirtatious." It also exposed that he did not interpret his or the girls' actions as flirtatious.

"Interesting," I said. "I actually thought they were doing a little flirting with you at times."

Allen laughed heartily, but then quickly looked concerned. "I don't think so. I mean, sometimes they'll say stuff or I hear them talking about me being cute. This one time, at parent-teacher conferences a mom told me that her daughter had a crush on me and that she, the mom, could see why. I was like, 'Whoa! Slow down!'"

"So, then, it's possible."

"I guess so," Allen agreed.

"Then, could we call your banter, or responsiveness to their flirting, flirting?"

"Dude, that's sick!"

"What?" I asked, acting confused.

"That's sick! There's no way I'm interested in them…are you fucking serious?!" Allen raised his voice.

"I'm not insinuating that you were interested in them by any means, I'm just wondering if they are flirting, or sharpening their flirting skills on you, if you are helping them by being responsive in some way."

Allen turned red, got up from his chair pushing it hard enough that it fell over and walked out on the interview.

Later, when I apologized to Allen, he simply responded, "I have things to do," and walked away from me.

The last time I saw him was near the very last day of the school year. He had three boys in the hallway, doing push-ups because they forgot their homework. He, and the rest of the class hung out the classroom doorway, laughing and teasing, "Come on! You're strong aren't you?" "Don't be a wimp!" and "I'm going to assign so much homework so that you can't possibly finish it…you'll have to do this again tomorrow."

"ME! ME! PICK ME!"

Because my dutiful research team collected droves of data (from over one hundred observations) in such a variety of ways, I found myself wondering how else I could "see" the operations of the classroom. This weighed heavily on my mind for quite some time. Then, as I was sitting in Joyce Arango's third grade I had a hunch—I thought she might be favoring boys. [27] In particular, I thought she gave more attention to the boys in the room. I immediately began recording the frequency of interactions she had with boys and girls during that lesson. This initial experiment did not tell me much. Therefore, I developed a method of collecting data that I called a "time study," (see Appendix B) helping me to identify:

- the frequency of interactions with boys and girls (and whether repetitive interactions existed and if so, why?);
- the quality of each interaction (e.g., Did it help students think deeper? Did it reinforce a positive or negative behavior? Was it a reprimand? Was it "empty," "meaningless," or "shallow" for the student?);
- when the interaction occurred (e.g., During whole group instruction? Small group work? Independent work?);
- explanations for why and how interactions happened.

I employed time studies over six months, accruing fifty observations at Fisk.[28] Data were analyzed, primarily looking for trends, outliers, and averages (Appendix C). I was mostly interested in descriptive statistics.[29]

Typical lessons began with whole group instruction—e.g., modeling something on the board, introducing a new topic—and concluded with students working independently or in small groups at their seats—e.g., completing worksheets, reading, and so on.

During whole group instruction, boys (overall, but not in all classrooms) received slightly fewer interactions with teachers than what girls received. However, interactions with the boys during small group and individualized instruction were considerably longer. Teachers were more patient, helpful, and provided more in-depth explanations to boys' questions. At times, teachers would stop their whole group lecture/demonstration and ask the class, while looking directly at the boys, "Do you understand? Everyone OK?" The boys did not do anything in particular to garner such special attention. But perhaps teachers subconsciously found themselves zeroing in on the boys because girls demonstrated particular social cues. In comparison to the boys, girls sat relatively still in their seats, made eye contact with the teacher, and shook their head in agreement as their teachers spoke. This may have given teachers the impression that the girls were paying attention and understood the lesson. But how did they know for sure? Regardless, I theorize that these social cues helped "fuel" the teacher as they were in front of the classroom. Teachers fed off the energy of the girls, and talked actively at them, helping to "equal" the amount of attention given.

During small and individualized group instruction—and especially in younger grades—girls were, in relation to the boys, practically ignored. Immediately after teachers were finished with whole group instruction, they usually rushed to attend to, and "helicopter over," the boys in their class. The large majority of these boys had no identifiable disabilities, language needs, or other demands that warranted intensive support. Teachers for some reason just dedicated themselves to ensuring that the boys were "on track" and that they "understood" the directions and concepts presented in their lessons. Many of these interactions turned into moments where the teacher walked through the assigned small group work, what I call "helicopter teaching," until the boys "got it right." Again, boys did not ask for this kind of intensive assistance, but they did not resist the teachers' help. Meanwhile, girls were left alone to problem-solve. Girls worked alone and productively in their groups, in particular, with other girls. A fascinating phenomenon occurred frequently; girls would attempt to interrupt conversations being held between their teachers and boy students. This usually involved girls leaving their seats, walking up to their teacher and tugging at their arm saying something like, "Excuse me, I need help." Almost every time, the teacher responded by half-turning (just for a second), raising a finger and saying, "Hold on, I'll be right with you." The teacher then commenced talking to the boys. The girls, again almost every time, waited but then grew impatient and returned to their seats. These girls, still confused, then asked a neighbor or tried new strategies to figure out their problems. Girls, overall, fared better in school—they received better grades/scores on assessments, and retained content to a greater degree—in part, because they were mistakenly empowered to problem solve when their teachers ignored them. Meanwhile, I believe the intensive "support" teachers provided boys may have disallowed them the space to apply critical thinking skills and the opportunity to learn responsibility to the task at hand, hence "disabling" them over time from reaching their full academic potential.

It was quite remarkable that the ratio of who received teacher attention, and the quality of this attention, held steady across grade levels K-5. There may be many possible explanations for this. We observed very few differences in student behavior during instructional times. Certainly, behaviors among children aged five through eleven vary greatly other times of the day—during recess, assemblies, field trips, walking in the hallways, and so on—however, during instructional time the most formidable difference we observed was that kids were able to devote more attention to lessons without fidgeting and getting tired as they grew older. So, while there was a slightly higher frequency of interactions between younger children and teachers because students required "redirection" to "get back on track," overall, who received the majority of attention remained the same—boys.

Though I conducted time studies while a variety of content areas were being taught (including social studies and science) I did not have a large enough sample size to feel comfortable presenting these data sets and drawing conclusions. This is important work, however, for a future time. I accrued many time studies in language arts and mathematics simply because this was what was being taught for the majority of each day. These two content areas are state tested subject areas, therefore were standardized with scripted curricula and programs. This resulted in pedagogical practice among teachers that looked extremely similar across grade levels—remember, these programs are "teacher-proof." Also, teachers were trained to see children as "data points." Standardization may help to explain why the kind and frequency of attention given to boys and girls is relatively consistent across teachers and grades. It is problematic that pedagogical practice does not vary greatly from teacher to teacher despite their individual dispositions, capabilities, and desires to teach in varied ways. There are two particular reasons to be concerned: 1) if students only experience so-called "learning" in one way they may feel consistently (un)successful (from grade to grade) and experience deep (dis)satisfaction, and 2) specific interactions, expectations, and accomplishments between

103

genders become understood as "commonplace." And so students may grow up to believe that boys and girls are "better" or "worse" at specific things. This is dangerous and it works to limit the potential of all children.

THOUGHTS

Fisk's school-wide climate was "cheery," but it was evident that teachers were under stress. They were overwhelmed with appeasing their administration's expectations to integrate standards, teach to the test, and simply manage their day. They were busy. Which, I theorize—except for being socialized themselves—was one of the primary reasons gender was institutionalized at Fisk and the other schools we observed. When I interviewed Emma Rhodes, a first grade teacher, and revealed I was studying gender she worried, wrung her hands and turned red:

> Oh no! You don't think I'm sexist, do you? Oh no, oh no. I'm a feminist and defender of gender equality, but I think I favor the boys more. What do you think? I mean, I knew it. It's true right? But when I'm teaching I'm trying to keep straight so many things that gender just gets pushed aside. I'm happy you are studying this, but I'm so scared to learn how awful I am. But now, maybe I'll do better. But I don't know. I'm so overwhelmed.

Though most teachers did not respond as strongly as Emma, they were equally concerned that they might be "doing something wrong." Several teachers reported feeling embarrassed because they "know better" and should be more conscientious about their interactions. Interestingly, during the interview, I did not share any evaluative material—I simply revealed I was interested investigating how boys learned masculinity and girls learned femininity—and asked them their perceptions on how the school, in general, might be institutionalizing gender. Still, they were defensive and concerned about how I might be "judging them." When I asked them why they worried about what I thought about them, they told me that much of what they do in school is not representative of who they really are. In two ways, I believed them:

1. The great majority of Fisk teachers had the best of intentions. They reported that they decided to become teachers because they liked kids, and desired to be a positive influence for *all* of them. And so, even though I was not suggesting anything about gender equity, they quickly became concerned. The thought that they were inequitable was deeply wounding.
2. As previously noted, teachers were extremely overworked and overwhelmed with matters that distracted them from the work of thinking about gender.

However, to say that their actions at Fisk were completely separate, or non-representational, of who they are, is difficult to justify. All teachers, according to their understandings of gender and personal performances of gender, actively contributed to sextyping their students in explicit, complicit, and implicit ways.

Fisk, and other elementary schools we observed, provided students with a firm anchoring in how they were expected to perform gender. Certainly, most students came to school with an already deeply established sense of gender identity—both of who they were as boys or girls and who the "others" are. They policed each others' behaviors and corrected, "That's for boys," and "That's for girls."

I loved to sit in the hallway at Fisk. I would do this some days for a few hours at a time. I organized my notes, read, wrote, and silently observed the foot traffic passing by. One of the things I enjoyed was taking note of what students wore. Of course, how kids dressed depended upon their parents—I knew of no emancipated children living on their own and shopping at the local Hot Topic or Old Navy. Kids from a very young age are thrown into fiercely gendered gear. Think of the bald baby girl with a headband and big bow and pierced ears, and the boy wearing khakis and designer-looking polo shirt just like dad. So, even if parents claim, "Well, that's what my six year old likes to wear," of course it is; they have learned their entire life to "like it." Teachers often commented on students' dress. "Oh, that's an awesome Spiderman shirt, Max!" "Wow, Jenna, look how pretty that dress is!" In most cases, the younger the student, the more exaggerated their clothing screamed, "girl" and "boy." If an adult woman would wear the first grader's puffy denim skirt with bedazzled rainbow hearts and pink leopard print t-shirt with lacey bottom fringe, she might be given the title of a "crazy hooker." Though boys' clothing was not as exaggerated, if an adult man were to wear a first grader's neon green gym shorts and orange dinosaur t-shirt, he would be perceived "special."

Student dress is only one piece of evidence that demonstrates that kids come to school already deeply engrained in gender. The elementary school just continues to carry on the tradition and anchors them firmly into place: boy versus girl.

NOTES

[1] Bing Crosby, *You Must Have Been a Beautiful Baby*, by Harry Warren and Johnny Mercer, 1938, record.

[2] For an interesting review on how sexual orientation and the married/single/partnered status of parents has little impact on children see: Timothy J. Biblarz and Judith Stacey, "(How) Does the Sexual Orientation of Parents Matter?" *American Sociological Review*, 66, no. 2 (Apr., 2001): 159–183.

[3] There were many moments in history that demonstrated concern that women were "jeopardizing" boys' and their future as men. Pinar provides this example: During the post-Sputnik era and during the administration of President John F. Kennedy, "men's long-standing suspicions of women's influence on children, specifically on boys, were stimulated as the nation—in many men's minds gendered masculine—was imperiled. Never mind that it was men in the Eisenhower administration and in the military establishment who were responsible for this heightened sense of peril, having lost to the Soviets the race to launch the first satellite in space. Other men—in this case, the Kennedys—sensed the political dividends to be paid should they convince an uneasy American public that women—public education, gendered female—were to blame." See: William Pinar, *What Is Curriculum Theory? 2nd Ed.,* 108. See also: Michael Kimmel, *The Politics of Manhood* (Philadelphia, PA: Temple University Press, 1995); Michael Kimmel, *Manhood in America: A Cultural History* (Washington, DC: 1996); Michael Kimmel, *Angry White Men: American Masculinity at the End of an Era* (New York, NY: Nation Books); Michael Kimmel, *Misframing Men: The Politics of Contemporary Masculinities* (New Brunswick, NJ: Rutgers University Press, 2010); David Tyack and Elizabeth Hansot, *Learning Together*.

[4] Michael Kimmel, "Solving the 'Boy Crisis' in Schools"; Patricia Bricheno and Mary Thorton, "Role Model, Hero, or Champion?: Children's Views Concerning Role Models," *Educational Research,* 49 , no. 4 (2007): 383-396; Bruce Carrington, Peter Tymms and Christine Merrell, "Role Models, School Improvement and the

'Gender Gap'—Do Men Bring Out the Best in Boys and Women the Best in Girls?" *British Educational Research Journal*, 34, no. 3 (2008): 315–327; Geert Driessen, "The Feminization of Primary Education: Effects of Teachers' Sex on Pupil Achievement, Attitudes and Behavior," *Review of Education*, 53 (2007): 183-203; Andrew J. Martin and Herb W. Marsh, "Motivating Boys and Motivating Girls: Does Teacher Gender Really Matter?" *Australian Journal of Education*, 49, no. 3 (2005): 320–334; Laura Sokal and Herb Katz, "Effects of Technology and Male Teachers on Boys' Reading," *Australian Journal of Education*, 52, no. 1 (2008): 81–94.

5   Martin Ashley and John Lee, *Women Teaching Boys: Caring and Working in the Primary School* (Saffordshire: Trentham Books, 2003); Elina Lahelma, "Lack of Male Teachers: A Problem for Students or Teachers?" *Pedagogy, Culture & Society*, 8, no. 2 (Dec. 2006): 173–185.

6   Richardson, eleMENtary School.

7   Phenomena like this—girls participating in an intentional "dumbing down" so that boys will "like them"—may help to convince girls over time that they are actually not as talented as they once believed. See: Anna Stetsenko, Todd D. Little, Tamara Gordeeva, Matthias Grasshof, and Gabriele Oettingen, "Gender Effects in Children's Beliefs about School Performance: A Cross-Cultural Study," *Child Development* 71, no. 2. (March/April, 2000): 517–527.

8   Emma Renold and Alexandra Allan, "Bright and Beautiful: High Achieving Girls, Ambivalent Femininities, and the Feminization of Success in the Primary School," *Discourse: Studies in the Cultural Politics of Education* 27, no. 4. (December, 2006): See also: Suki Ali, "To be a 'Girl': Culture and Class in Schools," *Gender and Education* 15, no. 3 (September, 2003): 165–182; Emma Renold, "'Square-girls', Femininity and the Negotiation of Academic Success in the Primary School," *British Education Research Journal* 27, no. 5 (2001): 577–588.

9   John Dewey defines miseducative as "any experience…that has the effect of arresting or distorting the growth of further experience. An experience may be such as to engender callousness; it may produce lack of sensitivity, and of responsiveness. Then the possibilities of having richer experience in the future are restricted." See: John Dewey, *Experience and Education* (New York, NY: Touchstone, 1938), 25–26.

10 "Girls on the Run," Girls on the Run, accessed October 4, 2014, www.GirlsOnTheRun.com.

11 Though GOTR espouses that they are open to "all girls," their events do not actively encourage girls of all types to participate. GOTR coaches tend to "glam up" events, but I have never observed any real effort to "butch up" or "androgynously be" who they desire to be. See also: Scott Richardson, "Girls on the Run: When Efforts to 'Empower' Girls Go Wrong," *Sociological Images: Inspiring Sociological Imaginations Everywhere,* accessed November 20, 2014, http://thesocietypages.org/socimages/2014/07/30/girls-deserve-better-than-girls-on-the-run/.

[12] Nel Noddings, *The Challenge to Care in Schools: An Alternative Approach to Education* (New York, NY: Teachers College Press, 2005), xiv–xv.

[13] See: Anne R. Hickling-Hudson and Roberta Ahlquist, "Contesting the Curriculum in the Schooling of Indigenous Children in Australia and the United States: From Eurocentrism to Culturally Powerful Pedagogies," *Comparative Education Review* 47, no. 1 (2003): 64–89.

[14] Ibid.

[15] Paulo Freire, *Pedagogy of the Oppressed* (New York, NY: Continuum, 1986).

[16] Shannon Hale, *Princess Academy: Palace of Stone* (New York, NY: Bloomsbury, 2012).

[17] Amy Schmidt, *Dog-Gone School* (New York, NY: Random House, 2013).

[18] Ralph Fletcher, *Guy-Write: What Every Guy Writer Needs to Know* (New York, NY: Square Fish, 2014).

[19] William Adams and Sasha Baron Cohen, *I Like to Move It*, by Erick Morillo and Mark Quashie for "Madagascar," Dreamworks, 2005.

[20] Ibid.

[21] See: Scott Richardson, *eleMENtary School*

[22] People experience a stereotype boost when they encounter positive stereotypes and it results in performing better. There are "many potential mechanisms that may underlie stereotype performance boosts, including reducing anxiety, increasing efficiency in neural processing, and activating ideomotor processes." See: Margaret J. Shih, Todd L. Pittinsky, Geoffrey C. Ho, "Stereotype Boost: Positive Outcomes from the Activation of Positive Stereotypes" in eds. Michael Inzlicht and Toni Schmader (New York, NY: Oxford University Press, 2011), 141–158.

[23] Connell, *Masculinities*

[24] Scott Fabius Kiesling, "Homosocial Desire in Men's Talk: Balancing and Re-creating Cultural Discourses of Masculinity," *Language in Society* 34, no. 5. (November, 2005): 695–726.

[25] Becky Francis and Christine Skelton, *Reassessing Gender and Achievement: Questioning Contemporary Key Debates* (New York, NY: Routledge, 2005): 108. See also: Valerie Hey, *The Company She Keeps: An Ethnography of Girls' Friendships* (Buckingham, UK: Open University Press, 2003); Valerie Walkerdine, Helen Lucey, and June Melody, *Growing Up Girl: Psycho-Social Explorations of Gender and Class* (London, UK: Macmillian, 2001).

[26] Becky Francis and Christine Skelton, *Reassessing Gender and Achievement*. See also: Diane Reay, "The Paradox of Contemporary Femininities in Education: Combining Fluidity with Fixity" in *Investigating Gender,* ed. Becky Francis and Christine Skelton (Buckingham, UK: Open University Press, 2001).

[27] In 1995, Myra and David Sadker brought national attention to the problem that girls received significantly less attention from their teachers, in every capacity. To this day, this narrative persists. However, interestingly, while teachers believe that boys are still given the majority of attention, they personally do not think that

their practice reflects this inequity. See: Myra Sadker and David Sadker, *Failing at Fairness: How Our Schools Cheat Girls* (New York, NY: Touchstone).

[28] I conducted nine time studies per each grade level (K – 5th grade) during language arts and math—the two most concentrated subjects. Each observation lasted between twenty-five minutes to a little over one hour.

[29] There are limitations to any data set. We should be reminded that it is only representational of the site/population/time in which the study was conducted, in this case at Fisk Elementary. However, I believe that there was such a remarkable trend and consistency to how girls and boys were given attention across classrooms at Fisk that future research should investigate other sites.

J. R. RANDOLPH MIDDLE SCHOOL

The Proving Ground

A woman is a woman and a man ain't nothin' but a male

—Louis Prima[1]

Kyle and Addie quietly passed each other in the west hall on the second floor of Randolph Middle School, every day between 1:47 – 1:50 p.m. Kyle walked to math, her favorite subject, while Addie walked to P.E. dreading it. Kyle and Addie did not know one another. If they did, they might have been friends, and would stop to chat for a few seconds. But they were two years apart, Kyle was an eighth grader and Addie a sixth grader which meant their schedules largely dictated with whom they would come in contact. Though Kyle enjoyed math, she did not enjoy her math teacher. Sadly, Diane Ramsey, the mid-career "advanced math" teacher, was starting to slowly kill Kyle's love for the subject. Additionally, Kyle would sit in anticipation of whispers or sneers by her classmates that she was "gay" and "wishes he had a pussy," without any hope that her teacher might intervene.

Addie's walk in the hallway consisted of a slow shuffling, clutching a three-ring binder against her stomach, looking distressed. She bit the inside of her right cheek in moments of anxiety and felt as though she might burst into tears at any moment. Addie, though young, understood P.E., particularly the locker room, to be a difficult place for a person "like her," thanks to her mother's explanation: "Girls who don't fit with other girls get hassled. That's the way it's been for a very long time. Gyms, bathrooms, locker rooms, are all tough for girls like you." Addie knew her mother loved her unconditionally and appreciated her empathy, but wished, however, that she had better ways at saying things. "Girls who don't fit" and "girls like you,"[2] made her feel like a freak.

I got to know Kyle and Addie early in the school year, during lunchtime. Occasionally I sat with a group of teachers who situated themselves in the back corner of the cafeteria, away from most of the commotion. Teachers who ate in the cafeteria were a faction who despised the absurd rumor-mill of the teachers' lounge. I sat with them, this sensible crowd, so I could ask questions and learn more about the school. Unpopular and fearful students clustered in this same area hoping that being in close proximity to teachers would save them from unnecessary harassment by their peers. Sixth and eighth grades had different lunch periods, but both Addie and Kyle sat in this section seeking refuge. I liked kids like Kyle and Addie. I enjoyed talking to students who experienced and understood life differently than their conformist, cookie-cutter peers. So, I would often try to steal a few minutes with them, talking over peanut butter and jelly sandwiches and bad cafeteria pizza.

Kyle came from a wealthy family. Her parents were both medical doctors, and her grandparents owned several large farms and other land that over the past few decades was sold for development. Her parents, since early elementary school, Kyle told me, "just loved" her. So, being "gender non-conformist" was not a big deal. She was always allowed to dress "feminine" and do as she pleased.

On a day in December, she and I talked at length.

"When I went to school on the first day, I mean in kindergarten, I wore a dress. I wore dresses a lot before I went to school. So that was pretty normal for me."

"But not anymore, huh?"

Kyle hesitated, unsure if she wanted to answer this question.

"I don't know when I stopped."

"Well, is it OK if I ask why you stopped wearing dresses?"

"It's OK, but I don't know why I stopped. Well, I kind of sometimes still do [wear dresses], but not in like school."

Addie, on the other hand, dressed as her sixth grade homeroom teacher described it, "butch." I would not have characterized her in this manner—she just was not super "femme." Addie came to school, most times, in jeans, a t-shirt, and a sweatshirt—usually alternating between a lime green hoodie with a white zipper, and a completely black one.

Addie told me that she loved being a girl, but she did not have close girl friends at Randolph.

"I had a good friend, Remi, in elementary school. But she isn't in any of my classes this year."

"So you never get to see her?" I asked.

"Only sometimes, like at assemblies or something."

Addie had been placed in a higher academic track than Remi.

"How about other friends…any guy friends?"

"A few of the guys are nice to me, but I wouldn't call them my friend."

Addie, though an athletic kid, tall and strong, never really liked sports. And she definitely did not enjoy P.E.

One day I caught up with her in the library. She was perusing the science fiction section.

"What happens in P.E. that you dislike?"

Addie stood in silence for ten seconds or so, and shifted her eyes and weight uneasily.

"I'm sorry, I just wondered. You told me before that you hated it. It's cool. Forget I even said anything."

"I just fucking hate it," she responded with tears in her eyes.

I was caught off-guard. Addie was, by all measures, a polite kid, a good kid, and swearing I imagine was not something she often did because she would deem it "inappropriate." Besides that, it took a lot of bravery for a sixth grader to talk this way to a grown-up she did not *really* know, and one who could "report her" to teachers. Perhaps she trusted me. Or perhaps she was fed up.

Everybody stares at me in the locker room. Everybody is thinking stuff about me. Everybody hates me. I don't want them looking at me anymore. Sometimes Nikki, or Cora, Kendra, or other people say stuff to each other about me. I hate them. They are all friends. I'm nobody's friend. There's no one on my side.

"What do they say about you?"

Another couple of seconds went by. She sat down, exhausted, in the aisle of books. I sat with her.

"I don't know."

"How do they look at you?"

113

"Like I'm ugly."

As the school year passed by, I watched Addie experience some very low moments. She was often depressed and always suspicious that kids were talking about her. At times, her classmates did say hurtful things, but it was a lot less frequent than Addie suspected. It was clear that she was not comfortable in school, and felt on the margins. Addie suffered, as I viewed it, from a form of post-traumatic stress disorder. The few times she actually heard students say things about and to her (e.g., "There's a boy in the locker room," "Addie's gay," and "Why do you want to be a boy?") was enough to traumatize her—making her think that she was always the topic of every conversation.

Addie, like Kyle, never experienced having teachers confront the students who harassed her, and so she remained consistently unprotected and vulnerable.

"When I was in elementary school, it was easier," Addie said one day. "It's like you always have to prove yourself in middle school."

For this reason and others, Addie was correct; Randolph Middle School was a proving ground.

SCHOOL CLIMATE

Randolph sat among farmland. It was a short distance from suburban developments, but far enough that students were brought to school via bus or car. The primary road that wound its way to Randolph was spotted with roadside vegetable stands, and near the school, was Living Waters Evangelical Christian church. This church offered tutoring to Randolph students, donated school materials to families, and often held special events that coincided with school happenings—like dances and social activities, called, "The 5th Quarter," after football games. Many Randolph students were members, along with their families. The other students had some sort of contact with the church as it was a staple in the community and partner with the school. Throughout the year, the pastor rearranged letters on the prominent medium sized billboard on the church's front lawn, offering messages to all who passed by, and specifically attempting to appeal to middle school students:

"Have a blessed school year"
"One can do all things through Christ"

"A baby's life is God's choice"
"iPod? iPad? Try iPray…God is listening!"
"All atheists will believe 1 day!"
"Good luck Panthers football!"
"A, B, C – Always Believe in Christ"
"Body piercings saved my life"
"Come huddle with us before the big game"
"God answers knee-mail"
"Evolution is just a theory. Find truth inside!"
"God sent the very first text message – The Bible!"
"Randolph M.S. Christians rock!"

Some parents turned to religious outlets, like that of Living Waters, during middle school years because they feared the prospect of their children becoming sexually active and making other "bad" decisions.

Rick, a father of two daughters at Randolph told me, "Yeah, we weren't really religious…but Riley and Samantha knew some of the kids, nice kids, at Living Waters and we thought it couldn't hurt…so we started going. I'm still not really into it all that much, but there are things I appreciate like the devotion ceremony we just had before the start of school year."

"What's that?" I asked.

It's like a formal dance. And there's a presentation that all the girls and fathers, or a man in their life attend. They talk about purity, virginity and devotion to God and elders. So Riley and Samantha both devoted themselves—said they would hold off on sex. I gave them purity rings that they'll wear until they get married…at least, that's the plan.

Joslin and her son have been long-term members and they loved the church. She sat on the prestigious Curriculum Committee that planned programming for Sunday School and special events. Often the talk of the committee was how to "counteract the damage done by some of the liberal teachers at Randolph."

"Some of the teachers," Joslin sighed, "well…they are just not Christian friendly. I'd go as far to say that they don't support our work."

"In what way?"

"I think they really want to confuse our kids. Schools aren't friendly places for Christians. We're always under attack. So, we make it our business to be around."

Jon Davenport, the principal at Randolph spoke measuredly to me about Living Waters:

Christopher, my son, went to a couple events there years ago when he was a student at Randolph. They're all salt of the earth kind of people. They grew up in such tradition that it's hard for them to reason that some of the stuff we do at the school just... how can I put it? Well, it's tricky. We are just implementing the curriculum, and often, it is heavily impacted by state standards and initiatives. Living Water's folks will see that it is in conflict with their beliefs. Or that we had a choice in the matter. I think for evangelists, they expect to champion Christianity at all costs. And they want us to champion Christianity, to be brave about it, when it's not really our business to do so. This irks them because they essentially think we are part of the family. It's complicated. I keep them involved, allow them to be involved in lots of ways, because if I don't, I think we'll have hell to pay. But, please don't say anything, OK?

"Lips are sealed," I assured him.

"I just wish they'd go away. It'd be much easier if Living Waters would evaporate. But, if the district put some distance between us and them...Living Waters would make it a holy war...they'd start tearing up this community...trying to rally their troops...everything would become more difficult."

Michelle, the mother of a son at Randolph told me:

They are maniacs. There are other churches too, in this community...don't get fooled...there are mainstream regular old Protestant and Catholic churches that want to hook into the Randolph community. I understand evangelism—to go and 'spread the word'—but to me, churches around here seem to unnecessarily police everything that goes on in school and our communities. As evidence, you should read our local newspaper. I just think it is overreaching. And it impacts our kids in some serious ways.

I carefully asked parents and teachers in the Randolph community if they felt Living Waters, and other churches—which were predominantly conservative Protestant churches in this geographic location—had an impact on middle school children.[3] In this process, I was careful not because I personally believed such matters should be sensitive, but because as the researcher I wanted to glean honest answers. Regardless of whom I asked (members and non-members of any of these churches) they claimed that these religious institutions had a significant impact on how children develop within gendered roles—particularly as it related to sexuality and traditional/"appropriate" roles.

Members of churches, for the most part, thought they had an incredibly important and positive role by teaching abstinence, how homosexuality and other non-marital based sexuality (including masturbation and fantasizing) are sins, and that boys should aspire to be proper gentlemen and girls to be caring women. It was believed that boys' "desire is a demanding physical urge, instinct, or drive, embedded so deeply in the body that it gains a life of its own once ignited...impossible to control, absolutely necessary to satisfy...it is the unstoppable artifact of testosterone overload...It is all about individual needs and has nothing to do with relationships...It is male, and it is masculine."[4] In contrast, girls should not experience sexual desire, but rather, a "yearning for love, relationships and romance. Acknowledgement of their sexual longings as an anticipated part of their adolescence is virtually nonexistent...effectively desexualized girls' sexuality, substituting the desire for relationship and emotional connection for sexual feelings in their bodies."[5] Often, the rhetoric employed asked boys to "respect girls" and to "control oneself" while girls were to remain "pure" and "loyal." They believed and implicitly taught that because abstinence is more difficult for boys "to tolerate," girls need to "fight off" boys' advances, but in a way that doesn't "demasculinize" them.[6] And confusingly, at times, the message was "don't be a prude, but don't be a slut."[7]

Non-members believed that such rhetoric, sextyping, and expectations created students who were either repressed or wild. Ron Crosby, Randolph's school psychologist, reported:

> The super Christian kids are some of the most promiscuous. Sex is so mystified and patrolled that all they want to do is get at it…and, that's dangerous, because these kids learned the least about STDs, pregnancy, and other consequences—social, psychological, and otherwise. The other kids, the repressed ones have a difficult time making and maintaining healthy friendships especially with those from the opposite sex because they are overly concerned that they could become sexual…boys socialize almost strictly with boys, girls with girls.

This was problematic because these "repressed" students had a much more difficult time understanding how to 1) be empathetic, 2) sharpen their social skills, and 3) build positive relationships with any individual different than themselves.

For many students, "girl" and "boy" cultures were established in churches, and played out in Randolph. Church members continually sextyped, having been influenced by biological essentialism—that men and women were/are created differently and "for" one another— and adhering to religious traditions informing them about what roles girls and boys should play.[8] However, beyond role expectations, the primary driving force for creating such strong divisions—making gendered factions between middle school students—was the fear that their kids might become sexually active. This is not to say that students who did not attend local churches, or have parents who had any religious affiliation, did not experience at-home/community sextyping and policing of their sexuality. They absolutely did, just in different ways. Only a handful of Randolph students had families that refrained from socializing their kids to "fit in" and maintain a narrowly defined traditional gendered identity. Even more rare were families that were sex positive and openly communicated about the realities of sexual activity without engaging in pedagogies of paranoia or sensationalism.

Carrie and Damon, two eighth graders, reported liking each other "just as friends" since fifth grade, but over the past year, they became "more serious." Both came from middle class families with all of the traditional suburban fixings: houses in nice developments, family vacations to the beach once a year, pizza and movies on Friday nights, and so on. Meaning, these kids and their families were not radical, off-the grid, hippie, or unconventional types. But they were viewed as such because they knew a lot about sex and were comfortable with who they were. Carrie and Damon openly talked about their feelings for one another. They held hands in public and at school events, like many of the other students—but their physicality did not seem childish or sneaky. They were not trying to hide under the bleachers, or cut class to make out in the auditorium. They were not like their classmates whose behaviors were erratic, unpredictable, and often stumbled into sexual experiences without thinking about their actions ahead of time. They exuded a confidence (individually and as a couple) in part because they were, for their age, sexually self-actualized and self-determined.

But Carrie and Damon unnerved parents, teachers, and other students.

"It's like they are married or something...it's so gross," Josh, a friend of Damon's reported.

"I just wouldn't want my daughter to get in so deep with a guy like that...he seems to be way more advanced than I'd want for my girls... who knows what he's teaching her," reported Amy, a mother of two daughters at Randolph.

"It's admittedly creepy. They are both nice kids. Responsible, and good students...they just seem so grown-up...I'd be happy if they weren't into PDA [public displays of affection]...I think it has some impact on the other kids, you know, telling them it's OK," Edward, the assistant principal told me.

Carrie and Damon, despite what others believed, were not having sex.

"We really like kissing, but we're not ready for anything else," Damon reported.

Carrie told me separately that they were both virgins and that their friends' behaviors discourage them from going any further. "Since we've been in eighth grade, our friends have been hooking up. And it's a lot of drama. They worry all the time about stuff...like they don't know what they want and they are kinda trying to do what the other person wants…it's confusing!"

It was ironic that Carrie and Damon had so many critics. One possible explanation was that people expected middle school students to simply behave differently. That Carrie and Damon did not "fit" their understandings, they were perceived weird, gross, and "too mature." Meanwhile:

- Josh was investigated for sexual harassment and assault. He touched two girls—who were friends—in a proclaimed "playful" way that he eventually interpreted as "bad…I guess." Allie and Monica were in many of Josh's classes and had band practice together after school. Randolph, like many middle schools, had informal and unstructured times that provided opportunities for interactions between students that were not highly supervised. In the beginning of the year he engaged Allie and Monica by telling mild sexual jokes, offered unsolicited commentary about media (particularly movies) that had sexual themes, and would generally make it a point to "be around" in their personal space. Later, he tickled, poked, pushed, and touched them in ways that he claimed demonstrated "liking," and was successful in building somewhat of a relationship. However, his touching became more aggressive and he increasingly talked about sex more pointedly. Allie and Monica felt uncomfortable but did not vocalize it directly to Josh. They reported later that they "didn't want to hurt his feelings." They pulled away by avoiding and ignoring him when he was around. After receiving less attention, his behaviors escalated and he touched their backsides and taunted them. After he touched Monica's breast, they reported him to a teacher.
- Amy's daughters—who Amy constantly dramatized whenever they showed any interest in boys—were rumored to be "hooking up"[9] with several different boys. It was "confirmed," Rachel, a friend of theirs, told me that "they give hand jobs and other 'stuff'…some boys joke that they hooked up with both of them, but separately… and they'll compare them." The kids told Amy that they were not sexually active.
- Edward was a younger (mid-30s) administrator. Handsome, athletic, and personable. In his position, he garnered lots of attention from

some of the younger and middle-aged female teachers and moms with kids at Randolph. When I asked him about whether he was flirtatious with some of the women, he said, "Yeah, I guess you could say that," with a big smile. "I have to be careful, though… there are always kids around. So, we have to do it in a way that they don't understand." But kids did understand. They whispered to one another, "Dude, I think Mr. Hunter wants to bang your mom," "Miss Connor and Mr. Hunter are going to have babies…," and "Mr. Hunter is a player!" It is possible that students making these observations perceived these kinds of flirtatious and sex-based conversations appropriate for the school setting. It was problematic that Edward actively discouraged and at times punished students (typically under the guise of "disrupting the learning environment") for flirting and engaging in sex-based conversations.

A troubling phenomenon, echoing the groundbreaking work of Deborah Tolman's *Dilemmas of Desire,* was that many students, particularly girls, reported that their first (and on-going) sexual experiences "just happened."[10]

> …that sex "just happened," is an explanation girls frequently offer for how they come to have sex. Having sex "just happen" is one of the few acceptable ways available to adolescent girls for making sense of and describing their sexual experiences; and, given the power of such stories to shape our experiences of our bodies, it may tell us what their sexual experiences actually are like. In a world where "good," nice, and normal girls do not have sexual experiences of their own, it is one of the few decent stories that a girl can tell…It is also a story that covers over active choice, agency, and responsibility, which serves to "disappear" desire, in the telling and in the living.[11]

Several of the sixth grade boys, by October, were well known for antagonizing others who have not yet been sexually active. Steven, Michael, Aidan, JP, and Brady all claimed to have "gotten far" with girls, but incessantly bullied boys who have not at "least gotten to second base." Many competed with one another, bragging, and giving every detail of their encounters. I overheard statements like, "It made my fingers stink for like a week," "I told her that she had nice boobs, but her sister's were nicer while I was feeling her up," and, "She was all crazy for me." Girls who were involved were talked about as being "easy" and "sluts." Daniel, a kind and studious sixth grader, eventually sought counseling because he was consistently physically assaulted before and after school, as well as in the hallway between classes, and called, "fag" and "gay" because he showed no interest in trying to coerce one of his female classmates into a sexual encounter. "Many of the girls," reported the guidance counselor, "show interest in boys, and so they 'became prey' [consumed] by the sixth grade boys." After sexual encounters, girls were often confused when they were treated poorly or ignored because boys demonstrated such dire interest. Sometimes boys would tell other girls about their sexual conquests, particularly if they 1) desired to embarrass the girl with whom they "hooked up" or 2) were trying to instill jealousy, getting the other girls interested in engaging in sex.

Seventh graders at Randolph were more serious about becoming "boyfriend and girlfriend." Around this age, parents approved of their children to date, and to have a "boyfriend" or "girlfriend." In eighth grade, relationships became more complex. Often, students were jealous of one another—claiming their boyfriend or girlfriend is interested in someone else or was "cheating" on them. So, many of the eighth graders looked to "fool around" but not be committed to someone in particular. This resulted in a lot of casual and informal sexual interactions.

Carrie and Damon's friends engaged in what they justified to be "playful" and "flirtatious" behaviors. However, because they "just happened"—they were not planned and consensual—they could be instances of sexual harassment and assault. Randolph middle school students were, on average, between the ages of eleven through fourteen. Not all students were sexually active, but upper grade students were increasingly and more explicitly interested and engaged in sexual banter. Students commonly joked and talked about "liking" others. Girls teased other girls about boys. Boys teased other boys about girls. Teasing became more serious, and often taken offensively, if it occurred across gender. When boys teased girls or girls teased boys, it seemed that those getting teased felt that they were placed in some kind of "social jeopardy." That is, same gender teasing was often perceived "safe" and had a bonding effect—it helped build a defined and narrowed identity of masculinity and femininity among same sexed friends—and was perceived "fun," and even "helpful"— whereas cross sex teasing was to raise serious provocation that the claim that someone liked someone else "could be true." Teasing in general is "often subsumed under, and at times conflated with, humor, play, irony, sarcasm, and bullying," but always embodies aggression (to a lesser or greater extent depending on the context and individuals involved) because the phenomenon occurs within a power dynamic.[12] Therefore, because teasing is "an ambiguous and complex behavior and is often difficult to distinguish from other types of student interaction, most notably bullying,"[13] Randolph students who were teased by someone of the opposite gender often played defense and damage control.

A sexual undercurrent ran throughout the culture of Randolph. Hormones in students raged, interests developed, and the school became a "proving ground"—a place where these new desires were expected to be carried out. It was shocking to observe students at this age to be so overtly attempting to situate themselves as heterosexual and interested in/interesting to the opposite gendered groups. Even more shocking, and quite ironic, was that teachers, parents, staff, and other adults encouraged these middle school students to be interested in each other, and to a certain extent expected kids to become flirtatious and "boyfriend and girlfriend" but became alarmed when things turned sexual between students. What were these adults expecting? To encourage loving, liking, dating, flirting, *and* complete physical distance?

The tension, fights, and drama related to sex created among teachers, parents, staff, and other adults, in this perspective were completely manufactured and engineered by adults. Throughout elementary school, students were separated and groomed to perform certain kinds of gender that would, in middle school, with adult encouragement, become the gaze of the opposite gender. Adults primed students to be these kinds of middle school students.

A small sample:

"Oh, Jess, I saw you staring at Jack at lunchtime. Uh-huh…I know what's going on," teased Myra Fleming, a 6th grade mathematics teacher.

"You know I'm cute," announced Christy Shelton, a 7th grade communication arts teacher to her class, "…but I just want to let you know, I'm taken. I'm going to the dance with Mr. Shelton. So, you'll have to choose someone else. Got it, Dallas? Hey, maybe you should ask Vanessa. You two would make a cute couple."

"Erica, you were stuck down in rehearsal with only boys today, weren't you? Well, you won't complain soon enough," smiled John Weber, a 7th grade science teacher.

"These boys are looking cute today…we should have picture day every day, what do you think ladies?" asked Caroline Stokes, an 8th grade math teacher.

"Girls, today is cheerleader tryouts immediately after school," Shawna Henry, a speech teacher and cheerleader coach, told the school over the morning news, "but boys, you aren't invited…no peeking in the gym."

"Hey handsome!" and "Hey beautiful" were frequent greetings called out to boys and girls by Essie Hudson, a 7th grade math teacher.

"Today is Friday, today is Friday," sung Annie Weber, a 6th grade communication arts teacher, to her homeroom. Then, smiling, she asked Fred, a student, "I'm going on a date with my husband…you got a date tonight?" and assured him, "Oh, I'm just teasing you."

"Get moving. Get working," yelled Jim Ritter, the P.E. teacher, to a group of boys. "How are you ever going to get girls to like you without any muscles?"

"I need some big strong boys to help me carry these things to my car. Any volunteers?" asked Martha Westbrook, a 6th grade science teacher.

"Oh, now I know you ladies will love my selection, and I think the boys can be romanced too…because who doesn't like a boy interested in *Romeo and Juliet*?" asked John Riley, an eighth grade language arts teacher.

Teachers flirted with one another, at times in front of their students. There were several teachers rumored, and others confirmed, to have had romantic affairs with one another—often outside of their committed relationships. The school oozed a certain kind of eros. Perhaps the mixture of teachers' expectations for students to be "interested" in one another, combined with students being bathed in preteen/teen hormones, resulted in a cocktail of sorts—an environment that "encouraged" teachers to engage in playful, risky, and borderline criminal behaviors.

Extracurricular Activities

Sixth graders experienced several major shifts when they became Randolph students. The student population tripled—fed by three elementary schools (Fisk, Waters, and Fieldcrest)—expanding students' social scene. Students also had to adjust to having several teachers for different content areas. Switching between classes provided an opportunity to learn "self-control" and "responsibility" while socializing—or for kids like Kyle and Addie, surviving—unstructured school spaces. Perhaps the biggest change from elementary school was the opportunity to participate in extracurricular activities. The school had organized athletics, arts, service oriented clubs, and other seasonal activities.

The "Randolph Leaders" club volunteered in the community. Service clubs such as this were non-gender specific, however, on average more girls than boys actively participated. Service clubs typically coupled volunteer activities with social events. Randolph Leaders went out for pizza, bowling, or the movies after visiting nursing homes, cleaning up local parks, and doing other good deeds. This gave students an opportunity to contribute to something important while socializing with one another. There was nothing particularly unique about how teachers and parents sponsored and organized service clubs at Randolph. This also means that they did not orchestrate extracurricular activities that would challenge or address gender based discrimination and (in)equity.

Arts based clubs focused on enrichment activities for students who were interested in performance and visual arts. Hank McCain, one of three art teachers at Randolph, organized the Visual Arts Club. Hank was a well liked and helpful teacher. Therefore, student membership swelled at any given moment to forty or more students. Hank engaged students in the creation of work, after school, every other Tuesday. Each fall and spring, he would take them to museums, like the American Visionary Art Museum in Baltimore, the Museum of Modern Art in New York, and the Andy Warhol Museum in Pittsburgh. Students loved these trips. Parents thought the world of Hank. Interestingly, Hank adopted a stereotypical liberal interpretation of how art—all art—should be accessed without any censorship and little intervention. He wanted students to "be exposed" so they could "develop their own ideas...push their thinking." This meant that much of the male produced, deeply misogynist work that unnecessarily commodified women's bodies in simplistic and hyper-sexualized manners went without critique. Museum trips resulted in students being exposed to an overwhelming number of nude female bodies in various sexualized forms, while male bodies were mostly clothed. This possibly conveyed that female sexuality (just like the sixth grade boys figured) was something to be "consumed." Randolph students walked museums, giggling, and making lewd comments (e.g., "She has pancake boobs!" and "I wish she were real."). Hank, if he overheard them, would respond, "Guys, don't be immature...I want you to take this seriously...think about what you are seeing," but never truly intervened or provoked them to think about what they were saying.

Athletics shaped Randolph's school culture, and deeply influenced the manner in which students performed and understood gender. Students literally had to try out to be certain kinds of boys and girls. Only a specific kind of masculinity was rewarded a spot on the football team; only a specific kind of femininity was rewarded by the cheerleading squad. "As an institution that makes visible people's bodily abilities and limitations, sport has historically created and conveyed cultural assumptions and values about essential differences between women and men" and boys and girls.[14] A residue of pre-Title IX ideology influenced the kinds of sports available and encouraged for girls. Cheerleading was, by far, the most popular and visible sport. Boys were encouraged to engage in contact based sports, which evoked praise and fame from the faculty, parents, and students. Boys' sports were consistently featured in local newspapers. Athletics were an area that adults and children implicitly and explicitly claimed that boys and girls "naturally" differ.[15] Often, adults would report sports as important for boys because it allowed them to "get their naturally aggressive energy out"—they assumed that boys were mostly "driven by 'testosterone,' and by their natural predispositions to be active, aggressive, and competitive."[16] Adults would only occasionally praise girls playing sports like basketball and softball because it offered an opportunity for them "to learn more conventionally masculine traits that would benefit them in public life." Boys who were interested in tennis, swimming, and other non-contact sports were devalued in comparison.[17] This is another example of how girls doing "masculinity" manifests as appropriate because it pays homage to patriarchy, while boys doing "femininity" violates patriarchy.

Practices were vastly different for boys and girls. Boys were coached with sternness, harsh words, and an expectation to be yelled at while on the field or court. Often coaches swore and used phrases like, "don't be a baby," "come on girls, you can do better," "toughen up," and "be men," to rally and inspire the team. Girls' coaches who were men, however, treated them softly, reporting that they were emotional and did not want to upset them. Women who coached girls were also not as abrasive—for example, they did not yell much when their girls made errors—but took pride in having multiple ways to coach. "Coaches' different treatment of boys and girls serves as an add-on to differences that have been socially constructed through a myriad of gendering processes that shape boys and girls at deeply emotional levels."[18]

Athletics, thus masculinity and femininity, invaded every space—even purely academic ones—at Randolph. Every morning, announcements featured athletic match-ups and reported scores from previous games. Football was the most prized sport—making cheerleading an important commodity too in that it supported the fight of the boys—and so, every Friday during the season players wore their jerseys, and cheerleaders their uniforms, to school. Teachers and other adults pumped up the boys by saying things like, "Good luck tonight, you're gonna crush them!" and commented on how cute the cheerleaders looked. With this positive reinforcement, football players and cheerleaders carried themselves like their existence was the most important thing to ever happen at Randolph Middle School.

Academics

Although dozens of teachers claimed to be interested in gender equity, while in school they flirted with one another, teased students, embedded "liking," "loving," and "crushing," into many of their normal interactions, and embraced extracurricular activities that aggressively taught the stereotypical gender binary. Additionally, they made no attempt to advocate for, or address, equity. They did not even provide students with balanced well-rounded representations of women and men. While it was true that administrators made most choices about programs to be used—helping to minimize teachers' ideas and obligating students to trudge through content in irrelevant ways—and faculty felt like they could not actively object, I was not convinced they would opt for curricula that would work to deinstitutionalize gender. Teachers, administrators, and parents were comfortable living within and emphasizing boy and girl culture and so they made no true attempt at trying to modify some of the cultural messages transmitted; just like in elementary school, curricular programs relentlessly emphasized heteronormative lifestyles and Eurocentric thought.

Also, despite teachers' concerns that students were too sexually active, they did not advocate for a robust sex education program. Health classes were taught by P.E. teachers, who perceived this as a chore and political hazard. Nancy Roland, a mid-career P.E. teacher, lamented, "I don't think there's anything worse than teaching health to middle school students. Sex education is the worst. A bunch of giggles or stares, depending on the section. But that's not the main problem; parents are always concerned…"

"So, how do you teach Sex Ed.? Is there a program?" I asked.

Well, that's the one area that isn't provided a program. So, not really, though we have some loosely based standards. But honestly,

I just go brief and shallow. I rather do that than get parents coming at me from every direction. And by the way, the administration… yeah…they aren't going to really back us up. It's all on us.

"What do you mean?"

"I'm told to teach Sex Ed., but if we taught anything minimally important, and parents freaked…well, they just direct the parent to address us. It's not worth it. It's really not worth it."

"What are the complaints?"

Varied. They are all over the map. Mostly, though, a call for abstinence. And to ensure that we aren't teaching 'gay values' whatever the fuck those might be. Whatever. I don't care. I'm just not getting too deep. I've seen the writing on the wall for a long time. I will do the bare minimum and try to fly under the radar.

Obviously, Nancy *did* care. However, the culture of the school and community informed her that she was not going to be able to teach a comprehensive sex education program. "My hands are tied," she reported.

"Academically," reported Jane Fenwick, a social studies teacher, "girls do better. There are more of them in Honor Society, they achieve better in all subject areas…they are just better all around."

"Even in STEM [science, technology, engineering, mathematics]?" I asked.

Yes. Often girls are better on average. This doesn't mean we don't have high achieving boys, but generally speaking, and I think the faculty would agree that the average girl knows more, does better, than the average boy. Again, we have some talented boys. And often, these boys get much more attention and praise for their accomplishments…the same kind of accomplishments of girls, but yes, girls do well.

It was difficult to assess "achievement" given the multiple definitions and measures that could have been employed. However, Jane's perception that girls in general outperformed boys resonated with her colleagues. Many male faculty members, however, disagreed and argued that boys' and girls' achievements were not equally celebrated. Rick Warner, a technology teacher, argued:

> Look, boys are being left behind. Schools are bending over backwards for girls. What's left for boys? Society doesn't value masculinity either. What good jobs are left for men? Everything is feminized. I mean it's just so apparent. Girls are doing better than boys…we have a real boy crisis and no one is willing to admit it.

Rick was not shy about sharing these sentiments with colleagues. He tried to excite and rally male teachers to "take action," but was never clear about what was to be done. He attempted to antagonize Randolph women and diminished girls' accomplishments. I found no examples of female faculty who worked to diminish boys' accomplishments.

Jane and the majority of her colleagues also pointed out that girls were more well-rounded than boys. She astutely observed,

> I have lots of teacher friends at elementary schools. In fact, I started my teaching career in an elementary school…and let me tell you, boys are not expected to be multi-dimensional. The only, or at least primary, expectation boys have is to be a 'boy'—also known as, sorry to say, 'a little asshole'…And so, they are! The teachers will reprimand the boys for their behaviors, but they won't actively teach boys social skills…they don't teach boys how to be successful. I know people like Rick would push back and say that boys act out because school is a feminized institution…and so boys would 'naturally' create disruptions because they can't handle whatever elements make it feminized—I suppose things like order, sitting in seats, reading—but that's complete bullshit. Boys are trained by society, media, family, and schools to think they need to be rough, tumbly troublemakers. But boys are not trained by society, media, family, and schools how to actively listen to others. Saying, 'you need to pay attention,' or 'focus,' isn't enough. We need to teach boys how to connect with their feelings, develop effective communication skills, learn how to be patient, and how to recognize when they are monopolizing all of the attention in the room or group. Boys are *totally* capable. We just don't teach boys how to be successful. So, they get to

middle school, and well, guess what? They have fewer skills, are less well-rounded. This definitely harms them academically. But socially too. It's crazy, sometimes painful, to see when girls get involved with boys who have the language skills of a Neanderthal and has no idea how to recognize the way they feel or think about certain social situations, well…it's a disaster. Of course, girls are immature too in their own ways, but in my observation, they have some skills and are more dedicated to trying them out. I am really confused. Why don't we just teach boys the skills they need?!

In my observation, middle school boys fell into three primary categories: 1) checked-out 2) class clowns, and 3) engaged. Checked out students actively disengaged with instruction. Class clowns acted silly, joked, and drew attention away from the instructional tasks at hand. The engaged boys were mostly students who did not exploit and rely on teachers to do over everything for them in elementary school. Of course, all students are different, and there were some who did not fit one of these categories, and others who slipped in and out and fit multiple categories. Regardless, these three categories were omnipresent at Randolph.

I believe there were two factions, motivated by different perspectives on achievement, among boys who performed "checked-out" and "class clown." For some boys, it was to avoid being figured a failure. (Hyper)masculinity demands boys and men to be knowledgeable. I theorize, that boys have suffered greatly from not being taught how to be successful, as Jane suggested, and by receiving so much intensive and unnecessary teacher assistance. Many boys were not prepared to enter middle school. They lacked the academic and social skills necessary to participate actively in an educational setting that was significantly different. Therefore, for some, these performances were manifestations of a defense mechanism aimed at not looking stupid. Another faction of middle school boys who were "checked out" or "class clowns" began to believe that what it means to be a guy is "at odds with succeeding in school. Stated most simply, many boys regard academic disengagement as a sign of their masculinity…How little they care about school, about studying, about succeeding." [19] Masculinity, by some middle school boys, was being perceived as "anti-work." [20]

While teachers in elementary school taught students content, teachers in middle school taught content to students. These are two very different pedagogical orientations. Randolph teachers did not scaffold or differentiate instruction as much as their elementary counterparts. Instead, they expected students to memorize content. Randolph faculty consistently reported that they became teachers because they loved their subject area so much that they felt it important to pass on content[21] and the passion they have for their fields of study[22] to their students.

Certainly, some students who experienced helicopter teachers in elementary school learned to adapt to the content driven pedagogies employed at Randolph. I was curious how some of these students made this switch—perhaps it was simply due to personal maturation, maybe the new content excited them, or maybe this "hands-off" approach empowered students to think. "If we can hook them in sixth grade… get them to be engaged…they'll often remain engaged throughout their middle school years," Jane reported. "Of course, there are distractions along the way, and some kids lose focus, but for the most part, I think it is true…Actually, I think most sixth grade teachers could, with reasonable reliability, predict how successful students will be in high school." To me this was a scary notion.

I did not conduct time studies in the middle school, but in my observation, teachers gave comparable attention to boys and girls. Again, that teachers were interested in content might have resulted in a pedagogical approach that made learning "business-like." Teachers taught "stuff" and students either "got it" or did not—the onus was on the students.

SEVENTH GRADE MATHEMATICS WITH JOSH HAYES

During one of the very last days of August, and first days of the school year, I stood in front of the entire Randolph faculty and described my study, asking if they would agree to participate—to have me and my research assistants in their classrooms throughout the year. Most were responsive and asked good questions about the design and reasons behind my research. Of course, I was faking it. I made up phony answers on the spot and dared not allude to gender. By the end of the meeting several teachers and staff committed their time.

Josh Hayes, a seventh grade math teacher, and twenty-one year veteran, was most enthusiastic about working with me. I quickly learned that he was lonely and perceived "odd" by the rest of the faculty. "I think he's on the spectrum," the assistant principal told me in confidence. Josh was easily excited and often interrupted conversations or spoke out of turn during meetings by interjecting strong messages of dissent. He was pessimistic about the motives of the school district and the direction of public education. He framed his arguments in an abrasive manner that made others feel he was overreacting or imagining conspiracies. This was unfortunate because Josh's thoughts were often steeped in facts and they paralleled his colleagues' ideas.

Josh was also noticeably extremely intelligent—he was a walking encyclopedia. This, coupled with his tall, six-foot-four-inch lanky stature, intimidated newer faculty. When Josh spoke to his colleagues he invaded their personal space by standing too close which made them stare directly up his hairy nostrils. Josh had no sense of style, nor did he consume himself with worrying about his fashion choices. Often, he wore a simple white dress shirt—short sleeve in the fall and spring, long sleeve in the summer—and black pants. He loosely knotted a dated tie around his neck.

Though excitable, he was consistently tired. Anytime he walked the hallways he did so slowly. In meetings, he slouched over in his seat perpetually rubbing his eyes while he flipped through piles of papers. I wondered if he had a secretly wild alternative life at night, but as I got to know Josh, it became clear that he was tired because he did not know how to relax his mind.

Working with teachers who are on the "margins" is always a risk because it becomes more difficult to convince others to work with you. It is like sitting with the unpopular kid at lunch. So, selfishly, our first meeting was not at the school. I met Josh on a Saturday over coffee near his house.

"It's the administration, it's parents, it's everything," Josh told me.

"That things are the way they are...like at Randolph?" I asked.

"Yeah. No one is satisfied, and it's all a big game. We're just pawns," he said while he haphazardly dipped his scone in his coffee and quickly raised it to his mouth, slurping, and getting drops on his beige v-neck t-shirt. Crumbs tumbled to the floor and the papers that lay between us on the table.

"So this year, I'm teaching out of this program," Josh continued. He reached into his bag and held up a student workbook that was named after their state's standardized assessment. "We just practice, all year long, to take the test. But next year, I think we'll have something aligned with Common Core and whatever our fearless leader and Emperor Bill Gates wants. I dunno...students hate it...and I didn't become a math teacher to do this. But, whatever."

"Whatever?" I asked.

This provoked Josh to go into a forty-five minute rant. He was incredibly animated and visibly upset.

"I used to be a good math teacher," he asserted.

"Not anymore?"

"Not for a few years now. Not since this bullshit," he held the workbook up hastily and threw it back in the bag as though he could not stomach the sight of it any longer.

This first meeting concluded by talking about the multiple educational initiatives he "survived"—his term—but that by now he was feeling emotionally and intellectually frayed. He admitted that he elected to participate in my research because it gave him "a person to talk to about things." He said, "I need something to help me get through this year."

Because we observed dozens of classrooms in the beginning of the school year, I did not get to Josh's class until late-September. I sat in his fourth period that was described as a "level 3/4." This meant that students in this class performed proficient (3) and advanced (4) on their state assessments. I situated myself in the back of the room at an empty student desk and five minutes in, I wanted out. I scanned the room for possible exit plans and I pondered if I would survive jumping from his second story window. "Bend your knees and roll," I told myself. Class was dreadfully boring. Students entered the room, found their workbooks, sat at their desks, and worked through pages of problems. Josh sporadically interrupted students reminding them to remain quiet, and on rare occasions would go to the board to explain a concept. As students completed sections in their workbooks, they shared with Josh. He circled problems with incorrect answers, and then students returned to their seats and attempted to correct them. This procedure was repeated class after class, day after day.

Josh's classroom was one of the most sterile learning and social environments at Randolph. He had no connection with his students; Josh had difficulty reporting how well his students *actually* understood certain mathematical concepts, or who they were as people. And his students hardly interacted with one another while in Josh's room. If they did, Josh quickly broke it up, and asked them to get back to work. Though with each passing minute I wished I were doing something else, my intuition was telling me to stick it out, and continued to come back for more observations. I wondered how gender might present itself in such a seemingly sterile setting.

Students were explicitly groomed to perform stereotypical heteronormative versions of masculinity and femininity during all parts of their day at Randolph. For example, in Alice Mory's third period language arts class, she subtly reinforced, and at times actively enforced, the gender binary by saying things like, "Boys, you know better than that...ladies first." While discussing a short story she advised, "Girls, when you find a cute boy, you can't seem too eager. Like our character, Bella, here...Donovan knows she's into him, so he acts disinterested..." And at times, she would address her class as "princesses and princes" or "lords and ladies." In fifth period, students attended lunch where most of the boys would socialize with other boys and talk about sports, class, and girls. Girls would sit with other girls and talk about class, fashion, and boys. Each of these groups would also demonize the kids that "didn't fit" their particular social clique. Wedged between Alice's adult imposed heterosexism, and lunch's free for all, was Josh's class.

Students were well trained. Daily, upon entering Josh's class, they immediately found their workbooks and got to work. Students who were most likely to "act up" were those who had disabilities, spoke a primary language other than English, could not handle the boredom, or struggled constantly. These students would attempt to socialize with their neighbors. Josh would warn them, and if their behaviors persisted, he would eventually write them up and send to the office for disciplinary action. All other social interactions were subtle and were difficult to detect. Students who were considered the best mathematicians navigated the strict prison-like environment. Josh did not closely monitor them as he did the others. Over time I observed Abbie and Wendy, two high performing and popular students, who liked to silently try to catch each others' gaze by sneakily making sexual gestures—e.g., sticking their wiggly tongue between a "v" they formed with their fingers. Gil, an equally high performing student, would wait until his classmates and Josh were not looking his direction. Then, he would quickly lean forward and softly slide his hand between Francesca's ribcage and inner arm to briefly touch the side of her breast. Francesca would wiggle and smile. After completing a section of her workbook, she stood up, turned around, arched her back—sticking out her chest—and slyly smiled at Gil as she walked back to Josh's desk. Jackie, a daughter of two engineers who had a mathematical mind of her own, flirted with several of the athletic boys. She had a reputation for grabbing boys' genitalia. She successfully did this in Josh's classroom too. Her favorite target was Ross, a football player who was not mathematically gifted and sat next to her. While Jackie could "fool around" and quickly complete her work, Ross could not. He was often reprimanded for not making any progress.

I got the sense that since Josh's classroom was so dull and businesslike that flirting and sexual interactions were excitedly taboo among his students.

The sterility of his classroom also represented a missed opportunity to build a learning community. A dynamic learning environment, where all (non)gendered members of the community are valued, could have provided Josh with opportunities to replace flirtatious and sexual behaviors with interesting academic tasks. If a learning environment was appropriately facilitated, Josh's students might not have been focused on garnering attention and agency via gendered/sexual performances, but rather through participation in mathematical ideas. Additionally, a learning community might have created social opportunities for Josh to weave important narratives that would address gender and sex based issues. Being an involved teacher would have provided him credibility among students, which he could have used to disrupt some of the sexist and sexualized notions that exist in middle school.

Josh, however, had given up. Despite his fiery attitude toward his colleagues and administrators, he felt deeply helpless, and embarrassed, as a teacher.

As a researcher, I had an obligation to report the sexual behaviors I witnessed in Josh's classes to Jon, the principal. Jon scheduled a meeting with Josh. I thought this might make Josh upset, but instead he invited me to the meeting, and used it as an opportunity to address his supervisor.

Josh and I simultaneously walked into Jon's office, and she immediately objected to my being there, "This meeting is closed. Scott you'll have to leave."

"No problem," I said and turned to walk out.

"Wait," Josh said, grabbing my arm. Mid-stride, I awkwardly hesitated while Josh said, angrily, "Scott can stay. I want him to know what Randolph is truly like."

"This isn't a meeting for Scott."

Still holding onto my arm, he complained,

I'm not stupid. I know students are bored out of their freaking skulls in my class. That's not my doing. That's your doing. I didn't assign the curriculum. You did! And if you believe my classroom is the only place that students are doing these kinds of things… well…then we have some bigger issues. Sex at Randolph is an epidemic. What do you want me to do, teach out of a workbook and stroll the aisles like a policeman? How about I put them all in cubicles? Or better yet, why don't we just let them stay home? Honestly, what do you expect if the school takes no responsibility? Sex education isn't allowed…oh, wait, I know what you are going to say, 'We have sex education.' But, c'mon! Virtually no sex ed., no social skills training…and then we are going to take these hormone driven preteens and force them to sit at their seats for seven hours a day? They all know their education is irrelevant.

So, Randolph, in my view is a pressure cooker…eventually, they can't take it…so, yeah, they're going to fuck around. Empower us teachers…let us teach, and things might get better. Otherwise, I don't want to hear it.

Josh let go of my arm, and stormed out of Jon's office.

Jon was a reasonable administrator who understood the frustration of his faculty. On several occasions, he privately complained about the perils of standardization. This interaction with Josh had become commonplace.

"Well," I said, finally breaking the silence, "uh…ok…see you later."

The next day, I ran into Josh in the hallway.

"Hey!" he said cheerily, "Are you coming to my room today?"

"Sure," I said.

It was back to boredom and groping.

EIGHTH GRADE LANGUAGE ARTS WITH TAYLOR AMES

Taylor Ames, a second year teacher, was a self-proclaimed feminist. Like many of the younger women faculty—like those who led girl power groups in schools—she believed that "girls need positive role models…more now than any other time."[23]

"What do these role models look like? Who are they?"

"Well, I think the biggest feminist of our time is Beyoncé. I love her. She's smart, pretty, and amazingly talented."

"What if you don't perceive yourself, or no one else perceives you as, 'smart,' 'pretty,' or 'talented'?" I asked.

"But that's the point. She's telling all young girls out there that it's possible. And you don't have to be slutty."

"So feminism values those who are smart, pretty and talented?"

"Well, sure…but that's not what feminism is about…it's that it's possible."

"Oh," I said. "What's slutty?"

"You know, some of the other female pop-stars…they are barely clothed, really provocative…and Beyoncé's all about her man…not like having sex with multiple or random men. You know, she's 'Mrs. Carter,'" she said laughing, throwing her hands in the air.

"What about Katy Perry?" I asked, wondering if she earned a "feminist" seal of approval.

She's not a feminist. She's way too sexual. But that's a good example...my kids listen to all of this pop-music. I think it's to my benefit that I'm younger, and I can have conversations about it. I'll talk up Beyoncé, but Katy Perry, or Iggy Azalea, I kinda try to tell them how they are absurd. Have you heard Beyoncé talk about how she's a feminist?

"Yes, I have."

"So, you know! She's way different from the likes of Katy Perry."

"Well, I dunno...I have mixed feelings...I've come to wonder if it's useful to judge and ascribe labels..."

Cutting me off, she interrupted, "Trust me, Beyoncé is a feminist! Did you hear 'Flawless?'"[24]

"What about Madeline Albright?" I asked, and immediately felt guilty.

"Who?"

"Never mind." I quickly responded. I carefully worded my next question, "So Beyoncé is a good feminist role model for boys and girls?"

"Not for boys!" Taylor laughed.

"Why not? And don't boys need good feminist role models?"

"Well, of course, but boys aren't interested in Beyoncé, and I don't blame them. Well, on the other hand, maybe they are [interested], but just to look at her! They need male role models. But I don't know," Taylor paused, "...can men be feminist?"

"Well, what is a feminist?" I asked.

"It's someone who thinks girls can do and be anything boys are."

Taylor reminded me of many of my undergraduate female students— particularly the white middle-class suburbanites who have been trained to understand that if they work hard, they can be "just as good as boys." They fully embrace the popular gender binary and do not understand (perhaps they do not seek to understand?) gender beyond specific archetypical male and female representations in their culture. In fact, they are happy to take their cues from pop-stars, avoiding painful wrestling with the complexities of continually (re)defining constructs like race, equity, freedom, patriarchy, and yes—feminism. They point to performers who self-proclaim to be feminist, and do so with flare, fame, and within promising marketing opportunities. I find Taylor's generation (she is twenty-four years old) fascinating because they do not understand the roots of feminism—they believe feminism used to be simply "man hating"—and are currently informed that some of the primary functions of "new feminism" is that it is sexy and hip.[25] Also, they understand femininity and "being a girl" as something only in relation to masculinity, within a deficit model. When they define "feminism" as "a movement that tells girls they can be as good as boys," I want to reply, "Shouldn't feminism be like, 'Of course girls are as good as boys! Why are we even saying this?'"

Throughout the school year, I witnessed Taylor enact her understandings of feminism by making sure she called on girls during class ("Wait a second, boys, it's time that I call on a girl."), by asking girls to do tasks traditionally perceived masculine ("I need help carrying all of these heavy books downstairs to Mrs. Stewart's room—I'm going to pick some strong girls to do it. Boys aren't the only ones with muscles are they?!") and by trying to confront students ("It's not OK to talk that way [harshly] to girls. You need to apologize. Boys need to respect women!"). She constantly policed her classroom, and in my observation, attempted to make things "equal," which had little/no relation to equity.

Taylor volunteered to coordinate the school-wide talent show, held on a Thursday night in January. Proceeds benefitted the National Cervical Cancer Coalition. In the months leading up to the show, Taylor used class time to encourage her students to think about how they might participate. She structured lessons that prompted students to write about "the ideal talent show performance," "what makes a good judge," and "performance etiquette."

There were two tryout sessions, in which Taylor invited her colleague, Travis Flanders, "so there would be an equal representation," to judge and admit acts. The acts were predominantly of girls singing songs by women artists—that talked about liking boys—and boys rapping songs by male artists—that talked about being "boss" and having girls like them. Only a few kids did something different. One boy did a stand-up routine, and a few girls performed dance routines.

The night of the talent show, Taylor walked on stage, dressed up in a femme representation she usually does not perform, and welcomed the crowd.

"Good evening, ladies and gentlemen. I'm so happy you decided to come out and support our talented Randolph boys and girls…" As she walked off of the stage, the audience clapped as several of the male parents worked in a few whistles and yelled, "oww!" Their middle school children sat among them.

Talent shows invite critique. And with each act, parents made rumbling comments about how "handsome" the boys were, and how "developed" and "pretty" the girls have become. Students' performances were representative of mainstream pop culture. Girls moved suggestively, boys performed cockily, and the crowd (which included students, families, and teachers) loved it. Many of the girls were "glammed" up with sparkly low-cut tops, high-cut skirts/ dresses, heels, and make-up. Boys wore primarily hip-hop gear. Older boys wore tight shirts and tank tops to show off their muscles, and baseball caps unbent with stickers. As the show progressed, kids in the audience slipped away from their parents to sit with clumps of same-sexed friends. They talked, giggled, pointed, and yelled suggestively. I overheard Richie, a typically quiet and respectful kid, show-off to his male friends while a seventh grade girl danced to a Christina Aguilera song, by saying loudly, "You should dance right here," pointing to his lap. I witnessed a group of girls scream, "I love you," "Sexxxxxxy!!!!" and even, "I wanna be your baby's mama," for laughs, when Ty, a popular Black student, walked on stage to perform. Ty was a tall eighth grade boy who physically resembled a high school upper-classman. Many of the girls at Randolph boasted that they "hooked up" with him. Bragging about sexual conquests in middle school typically resulted in being called a "slut." But in this particular case, it was a rite of passage. One could become a popular, worthwhile girl by hooking up with Ty. Ty rapped—terribly—a Drake song. The audience cheered wildly.

Everyone waited for Isabella to perform. She was purposefully last in the program, Taylor made sure of it. Isabella was an incredibly gifted singer and one of the few Latinas at Randolph. Her family was very religious and traditional in their conception of gender. Isabella walked on stage, wearing a heart-shaped v-neck form fitting sparkly blue dress. Girls' choice in how to dress certainly does not warrant obnoxious and sexual comments from boys. Isabella, however, while making her way across the stage, stopped, put her one hand up to her ear, spread her legs apart and briefly tugged at the bottom of her dress provocatively. Isabella, like Ty, physically resembled a high schooler. The crowd whistled and cheered. Isabella's girl classmates yelled, "Yeah, girl! Get it!" I wondered if she had performed this sexualized act, and were lesser known, what kind of reaction she would have evoked from the audience? Taylor shook her head and smiled. She nudged Travis, who sat next to her at the judges table, as he shrugged as if to say, "What are you going to do? There's no stopping her." She sang, upon Taylor's request, a Beyoncé song, which included some trademark provocative dance moves. The audience loved every second of it.

At the closing of the show, all contestants lined up on stage and were re-introduced. Popular and cute students received loud applause, while students who were less popular received little applause, and even some heckles. Ashley, a talented but "overweight" seventh grader, who sung an absolutely beautiful rendition of a Taylor Swift song, was the target of many boos and a few stray but loud oinking noises by boys who sat in the back of the dimly lit auditorium. Her mom sat a few seats away from me while this happened. She forced a smile on her face, stared straight ahead, and clapped for her kid pretending she could not hear the insulting chaos behind her. Finally, Taylor stepped onto the stage and announced Ty and Isabella the winners.[26] Isabella jumped up and down and Ty pumped his fist against his chest and threw it into the sky raising one finger to signify he's the best. Taylor ushered the two together, joining them in the middle of the stage so that dozens of parents, teachers, and kids could take their picture. Ty and Isabella were the "right kind" of boy and girl, and they were thusly celebrated.

After the auditorium lights came on, parents and relatives gifted female talent show participants with flowers. Boys were greeted with handshakes and high-fives. Students took the opportunity to flirt with one another. They hugged, playfully touched, and joked. Families stood in the wings proudly watching, and exchanged gossip about which kids were interested in each other. I stood next to a grandma and had a lovely conversation about the architecture of the school, until she said, "My granddaughter performed tonight."

"Oh, great!" I said, "Who is she?"

"She's that one over there," she said, pointing at Bella, a seventh grader.

"She's a great kid," I responded.

Thank you. She is just lovely. Her sister is in high school. Sara is her name. Sara's cute, but Bella is gorgeous. Thing is that Sara has a boyfriend...a really good looking kid. But I don't hear Bella talking much about boys. Her mom and I, though, we notice some boys interested in her, like this kid Peter. He's over there with that group of boys. If she's not ready for a boyfriend, she better get ready, because some other girl is going to come scoop him up! He's a very popular boy!

The day after the talent show, Kyle—the student who identified secretly as a girl—slouched in her seat, during Taylor's second period class. Taylor, at the beginning of the class, talked about the talent show, which made Kyle squirm a bit. "Did you see how great everyone looked? We have some really talented students here. I'm so impressed and proud of everyone!" Kyle was disinterested in participating in the talent show. She wanted nothing to do with any event that could possibly bring her any additional attention. She, however, felt small in comparison to the students who received such over-the-top praise during the past few months by her teachers. Taylor went on to talk about the performance by Jenna, who sat a row behind Kyle: "She was so perfect! She had it all going on for her...not a nervous bone in her body...she killed it. Look," she continued as she pulled out her phone, "I have a picture of her back stage...isn't she pretty?" Kyle sighed and thumbed through a book of poems.

143

Finally, Taylor was ready to move on. She was surprised to see Kyle already reading, "Oh, look, Kyle's ready for poetry. Everyone get your books out. Kyle, I thought poetry would be your kind of genre." Kyle, confused, looked up at her smiling, well-intending teacher.

Taylor worked hard, tried to stay current with pop culture so she could connect with her students, and was friendly to everyone. Extracurricular activities helped define her in-class personality, which in the case of Kyle, was not particularly helpful. Her teaching was standards driven, like all of her other colleagues' instruction, so she perceived this as keeping her from digging deep into the literature they read. She had to keep a steady pace, conquering various genres within specified timeframes. Regardless of whether or not Taylor would help facilitate a thoughtful feminist critique in her classroom, it did not matter; she felt like she was not given enough time to do so. As the year went on, it became more apparent that Taylor was what I call "a winner at school." In fact, she was such a successful student when she attended school as a child, that she decided to do it the rest of her life. Her easy, even enjoyable time as a student, helped to make her a wildly utopic teacher. School worked for her, so she reasoned that school should work for everyone else. Stories of her former classmates who did not do well in life often followed with accounts about how they did not perform well in school. Taylor did not understand the varied lifestyles students led, and believed that students just needed to "try harder" if they wanted to be successful. But middle school for kids like Kyle was not the environment they desired; they did not want to be king or queen of a school that they disliked, that did not understand them for whom they were. Taylor's privileged school experiences kept her from understanding the realities of her students—and, at this point of her career, she did not yet recognize she did not understand them. Though a "feminist," she easily mapped on what was good for her must be good for her students, and so she easily reified stereotypes of achievement, masculinity, and femininity—all wrapped up with a bow.

SPECIAL EDUCATION WITH JEN SPIRO

"So three of my grandparents, my mom, two uncles, an aunt, my sister, my brother's wife, and, well, my daughter is a high school senior now and she wants to become a teacher…and then, there's me…so yeah, education is kinda like the family business," Jen laughed. "Honestly, I don't know what else I'd ever want to do. Helping kids…that's what we're about."

Jen Spiro taught special education for the past twenty-four years, which is more than most other teachers at Randolph. This made her the go to person when anyone had questions regarding students who were struggling or were receiving services. "It's exhausting," Jen reported, "but I love it." She was a bit of a control freak.

Jen's daily schedule consisted of equal parts push-in and pull-out instruction. In the morning, she gathered between nine and twelve students across grade levels, and gave them intensive language arts and math instruction in her classroom, 227B. In the afternoon, she found herself in other teachers' rooms, helping to modify instruction. "Actual co-teaching would be nice, but we rarely have time to plan together. So, the classroom teachers email me their plans, I try to give them a look-over prior to class, and then I make modifications for students who are on my caseload," she told me.

Observing Jen teach was interesting and exhausting. She was continually on the move. I was able to get a good sense of what instruction at Randolph was like by following her from class to class. During self-contained instruction, Jen was a stern but loving teacher. She expected students to produce when they were under her watch. She held students to high expectations, but did so in a way that transmitted care. Her greatest talent was how masterful she was at getting to know her students. She knew everything about her students' families, social lives, happenings at home, and so on. This allowed her to connect with her students. It also allowed her to impose her own cultural understandings of gender. I often overheard her conversations with students:

"Well, your mom is lucky she gets to stay at home with the baby. Not many moms get to do that anymore. She should be very thankful of your dad."

"I can't believe you're getting so tall…look at those legs, girl!"

"I think your parents must be concerned about all these boys getting interested in you? It's perfectly normal, Amber, just remember to make these boys respect you…they have a hard time controlling themselves."

"Oh yeah, I know who Luis is…he's that new cute boy in Miller's homeroom, right?"

"I like that song. It's fun. But what's she [Miley Cyrus] saying? It's sexual right? Just watch what you are listening to. You know old Mrs. Spiro…she's a bit of a stick in the mud…but not all songs are good ones."

One piece of advice was particularly unsettling. After school one day, Colleen, an eighth grader with down syndrome, visited Jen's classroom. Jen often had students visit her room because she was warm and likable.

Jen asked, "So, are you going to go to spring fling?"

Colleen replied, "Yes. Of course!"

"Do you have a date?"

Colleen blushed, "Noooo, but, I hope Daniel goes. We can go as friends my mom said."

"Friends. Yes, that is a good idea. Colleen, do you know what boys are interested in at your age? Has your mom talked about this?"

"Yeah, I know what boys are into, like sports, and cars, and video games…"

"I don't think your mom would mind me telling you this," Jen said, inviting Colleen to sit at a table with her, "She might have already told you this, but they are also into sex."

Blushing again Colleen replied, "I know."

"Do you know what sex is, Colleen?" Jen asked. The question hung in the air, heavily, for a few seconds.

"It's like for making babies, or like when someone wants to touch your body…"

Jen informed with seriousness,

Yes, it is your body. You don't let anyone touch your body. You tell them, 'no' and then tell a grown-up. You don't let boys touch your body even if they are friends and they ask you. Boys want to touch girls' breasts, and in-between their legs. Even the boys you know want to do this. This is what boys who are your age want to do, but it's not okay. Look at me, it's not okay. Some girls might let boys do this, but you don't want to let them. And if they tell you to touch their bodies or put your mouth on their bodies, you say, 'no.' Boys are a lot different than girls and it's your job to keep yourself safe…"

On one hand, I was happy to hear that a teacher was attempting to be straightforward about sex to a student—any student regardless of (dis)ability. But on the other hand, it was awkward for me to sit in the room and listen to Jen's babyish tone and overcautious advice. Jen continued to make overgeneralizations about what all boys want and try to do to girls. She villianized boys and victimized girls. Perhaps she simplified and overexaggerated because she did not believe that Colleen could be sexually self-actualized and self-determined and make good decisions based on the various possible situations that might present themselves. Meaning, Jen probably believed it was just safer that Colleen took extreme caution in all situations. However, I found it unfair that Colleen was learning that 1) all social interactions with boys—nice, kind, innocent—like with Daniel (her best friend) are dangerous ones; 2) sexual interactions were "violations" of her body and; 3) friends of the opposite sex—not of the same sex—should be held suspect.

Kids, (dis)abled of all ages, endure comments from adults that they must be "boyfriend and girlfriend" or "like each other" if they hold mixed-gender/sexed relationships. I often witnessed parents of young children, who joke about how their kids are dating or will get married to one another some day.

Paradoxically, despite Jen's advice to Colleen and her other students (particularly girls) to be wary of the opposite sex, her other casual conversations incited romantic and sexual excitement, or at the very least, normalized heterosexualism. Jen was a popular and engaging teacher, and students tuned-in to every word she muttered. She loved talking about her family life, particularly about her children. She had one son, a sophomore, and one daughter, a senior, in high school. She talked about how athletic, handsome, and smart her son was. She often joked about how "girl crazy" he had gotten since he went to high school. "What a lucky guy. He goes to a big high school, and let me tell you, there are quite a lot of pretty girls. Lots of options.

I think he feels like he died and gone to heaven," she told a small group of girls in the hallway. Jen particularly loved nosing around in every aspect of her daughter's social life—particularly her romantic relationships and would talk about (process) them with kids in her classes. Jen announced in May, "Abigail is getting ready for the prom. We've been shopping for weeks to find just the right dress. And we found it!" Jen showed a picture of her daughter wearing the dress and many of the girls huddled around to take a look. Then, she showed a picture of her date and said, "And here's the boy she's going with...I couldn't be happier. He's such a great guy. They are going to make a great couple." Students asked questions like, "How old is he?" "Does he have any brothers?" and "Are they going to go to that like after-prom party at the school?" Jen loved engaging her students in this conversation. Finally, quite satisfied, smiling, she said, "Okay, I think we need to get some work done today..."

Jen, like many other teachers at Randolph, were also guilty of talking about their spouses, and other personal business, in the hallways, over lunch, and places in which students could overhear. That these teachers were people who were significant in their lives, students paid close attention to them. Students gained insight about how their teachers thought. It became an opportunity to examine adult heterosexual norms. They over heard things between their teachers like:

"I just don't understand men. Mike just can't respect that I need my special girl time. Sometimes we just need to pamper ourselves. We deserve it. So, I don't care, this weekend, he's going to have to figure out what to do with the kids."

"She's dragging me to some chick flick tonight. I said I'd go only if I get to pick the next three movies. I'm going to be bored out of my skull."

"I know Maggie is pressuring Jim for that ring. She's ready to get married. But you know how guys are, so noncommittal. She is totally ready for wedding, honeymoon, house, kids, the whole thing. I was like that too. I don't think she'll stick with him through the summer if he doesn't propose."

I gained the sense that Jen's interactions and conversations with colleagues, in front of her students, and to her students, were quite intentional. Jen told me that it was her duty, as a special education teacher, to give her kids the "low down" on how people, schools, society works and how they should "fit." "I want them to be normalized...I don't want them to stick out," Jen reported. This meant, for her, that she should instruct students how to perform within the well-defined rules of masculinity and femininity—that she should explicitly gender her students, some of whom, like Colleen, were most comfortable being androgynous. Several of her students with autism demonstrated no preference in what they wore, but Jen (and their parents) encouraged them to wear clothes that demonstrated extreme representations of masculinity and femininity. For example, during math lessons, Jen used clothing catalogues to practice math skills. She would assign students a hypothetical amount of money they had available to spend, and asked them to peruse the catalogues and decide what they would buy. However, she insisted girls look in the "ladies section," and boys look in the "guys section." If they were to wander outside the assigned section, she would make comments like, "Now, you'd look silly wearing those pants...those are boy pants. Why don't you look at some of the pretty skirts on these pages?" and "Jon, are you shopping for your sister? Come on, get back to the guys' section." Encouraging her students to be self-determined was not on her radar. She had a problem if students were nondescript or androgynous, let alone embodied queer representations.

On a day in early June, I accompanied Jen when she visited several other elementary schools. The purpose of these visits were to meet some of the students who would be transitioning to Randolph next year. When she met these students, she shook their hands and spoke in an even-more-than-usual baby tone. She called the girls "sweetie" and the boys, "buddy." Departures ended in hugs for the girls and hi-fives for the boys. Many of the students reminded me of Colleen. They were androgynous, or disinterested in being gendered, but wore clothing, had backpacks, and owned school supplies that were clear attempts by their parents to gender them—an overcompensation of sorts, trying to give them a "normal" identity.[27] The teachers too, gendered them by organizing active experiences for boys, and socially based activities for girls. It was obvious that these teachers, just like Jen, adopted an ethic of trying to groom boys and girls so that they would "fit."

At the very end of the year, I interviewed Jen and told her that the focus of my research was gender. Excitedly, she responded, "Oh, Scott, this is such important work! I'm so happy you are doing this! Kids with disabilities don't know how to be like the other boys and girls. It's so important that they learn."

Typically, I follow a semi-structured interview protocol, and have questions I want to ask in a particular order, but in this case I quickly abandoned it and jumped in, "Is it important they learn how to be boys and girls?"

"What do you mean?" She responded.

"Well, you said kids with disabilities need to learn how to be like other boys and girls, right?"

"Right."

"Well, are you sure it's important? If so, why?" I prodded.

"It's absolutely important. It's the essence of what special education is all about. Inclusion…we want kids to be included. And they are most successful if we work with them so that they meet some 'likeness' to the other kids…it's just the way it is."

"So, what kinds of things must a boy be or do, and a girl must be or do?"

"Well, their interests, their appearance, the kinds of roles they take on."

I pushed back:

Isn't this sorta…well, in my conceptualization of the purposes of special education…I could be wrong, by the way, or my thinking could be immature…I think that the teacher's role is to help students to become self-actualized/self-determined in every facet of their life. So, if a student isn't demonstrating a desire to "fit" traditional boy or girl culture…then we should be open to what it is they want…right? Or am I off here?

"Sounds like you live in a different world or something. Men and women have different roles to play, and my job is to get kids ready to play them."

"And if you don't?"

"Then they'll be misfits, outsiders, the retarded freaks," she said angrily. "I don't want that. Do you?!"

Who could argue with that rhetoric? "Well, no, but…"

"Then we have to give our special education students the keys to being a successful man or woman. What else is there?"

PLEDGING THE PATRIARCHY

Jen's reality was the only one that mattered. She sextyped girls, boys, women, and men, was determined to anchor students to how she understood the world, and taught so that her students could prove they "fit."

I sensed when interviewing Jen that her responses were coming from a place that was attempting to defend her twenty-four years of what she believed to be good teaching. No doubt, she was an effective teacher in many ways. And I was not trying to be combative—I was just attempting to understand her thinking. The majority of special education teachers I met held similar ideas about helping their kids successfully join mainstream patriarchal culture. I did not work extensively with guidance counselors or with any English as a Second Language teachers, but wondered if they coach, socialize, teach—institutionalize—the gender binary in an exaggerated manner. Essentially, do people who provide support services institutionalize gender to a greater extent because they view their students "on the margins" or "outside" of what is "normal" or "mainstream" culture?

Regardless, the entire school structure explicitly and implicitly taught students to prize (hetero)sexual experiences, and perform masculinity and femininity in separately discrete manners that maintained the privileged space of patriarchy. It fell on the shoulders of students to prove to the adults in their lives, and their peers, that they embraced this culture. Middle school was essentially a hazing, requiring students to pledge fully to a socially constructed world (in and out of school) to which they would honor by joining when they dutifully played their parts. Kids, like Kyle and Addie, who found themselves unwilling to be hazed, and/or were actively marginalized, would become "outsiders." While it is true that schools have become more open to the needs of queer and beyond-the-binary-gender-identifying students, Randolph and the other middle schools we observed did not truly and actively try to adopt an inclusive, queer, or desinstitutionalized environment.

151

They instead defended the patriarchy—clearly defined roles that ultimately privilege boys and men in society. Though pervasive at the elementary school level, patriarchy, from top to bottom and bottom to top, was even more pervasive at the middle school. In one way or another, it suffused all aspects of school culture. Middle school offered a shift from care to content, an über competitive environment of "performance," and the adherence to rules, regulations, and procedure (not compassion, effort, ingenuity, and intuition) within predominant (white supremacist capitalistic) patriarchal ideals. Though teaching has historically been a popular occupation for women—partly because it was underappreciated (not recognized as a true profession, rather perceived as an extension of mothering) and then later because it was unionized, protecting certain rights like fair wages and maternity leave—it has been heavily governed by men. The National Governors Association, CEOs of industries, independent meddlers like Bill Gates, curriculum companies, and so on are all male-dominated. They determine how schools function in America. Since the creation of the federal Department of Education under President Jimmy Carter two women and six men have served as the Secretary of Education. President Barack Obama appointed fellow basketball buddy Arne Duncan to the top executive spot. Duncan, however, was never a teacher. If this—a man can appoint another man who never did the primary job he is tasked at overseeing (in the entire country!)—does not convince you that education is a patriarchal institution, then I figure you do not want to believe it.[28]

Male administrators and teachers at Randolph established the tone. They were boisterous and omnipresent. Bro hugs, bro banter, bro handshakes, bro culture were shared not only between faculty, but also with male students. Girls were not invited or admitted to participate in this culture, so they were sideline observers taking note of how their feminine performances should be constructed in a deficit paradigm of who they were not. Masculinity was the constant focus, even when celebrating student accomplishments. For example, Edward challenged the school to pass, on average, a series of standardized assessments. And if they did, he promised to shave his head into a mohawk and dye it orange and black, the school colors. Students were not particularly motivated by this challenge, except for a few of the most hypermasculine boys who held "bromances" with Edward, and a handful of girls who thought he was cute or funny. The school performed well on the tests, and so a special assembly was called and covered by the local newspaper and two television stations. The entire student body attended while up front, on stage, Edward briefly congratulated the students. Then, Mark, a P.E. teacher, rallied the students to shout "Shave it! Shave it!" Edward pretended to not want to go through with it, while Mark shaved large swaths of hair. "Randolph Middle School Assistant Principal Steps Up and Gets Shaved!" read the newspaper headline. Another example was when Gary, the baseball coach (and social studies teacher), challenged the field hockey team to have a winning record by the end of the season. As a reward, he pledged to wear a field hockey uniform—"skirt and all"—to school for a day. They had a successful season, and he kept his promise. Men who embody hypermasculinity are typically afforded leniency to perform femininity without a critique of being "gay" or "weak."[29] It also provides them opportunities to make a mockery of hyperfemininity. Gary, who was perceived one of the most masculine faculty members, paraded around the school—swirling in the skirt upon students' request—and acted "girly" which the majority of all children and faculty found hilarious. If Gary were to naturally represent femininity, like if he wore a skirt to school because he liked it, he would be held suspect because he was violating the terms of masculinity/patriarchy. But because he performed a mockery of femininity, it was all good. "He's such a wonderful sport...what a great guy...how awesome for our kids..." female faculty exclaimed, commodifying him. The accomplishments of the female student athletes were practically forgotten.

Not all students at Randolph were developmentally ready to be interested in romantic relationships, and others did not feel easy about being squeezed into masculine or feminine boxes. For some, they did not know who they were, and to "be" something everyone else wanted them to be felt disingenuous. For others, they knew they did not belong. Many students just wanted to come to school, have kind teachers, learn some stuff, have a good time, and make friends.

Near the end of the school year, I found Kyle in the office. She sat, waiting, with her head buried in a book. The clock above the secretary's desk read 3:19.

"What's going on?" I asked.

"I think my parents forgot about me," she joked.

"Oh. Bummer. Did you get in contact with them?"

"Well, we called, but no answer. Sometimes they do this. They have some sort of emergency. It's OK," she said, flipping a page.

"What are you reading?" I asked.

"It's really none of your business," she smiled and emphasized, "Scott!"

The secretary paused from whatever it was she was doing, and looked over her glasses and shook her head in disbelief. Calling an adult by their first name was the equivalent of committing first degree murder at Randolph.

I smiled. "C'mon…let's walk. We can reminisce about the year."

Kyle hurriedly shoved the book in her bag, and jumped out of her seat. "Is that OK, Ms. Wogelmuth? Can I take a walk with Dr. Richardson?"

"I suppose so," she grunted.

Out in the hallway, I asked, "So where should we go?"

"This way," Kyle said and led me down the east wing.

We walked the long and, by this time of the year, smudged and dull tiled floors. As we passed by classrooms, Kyle pointed out the teachers she had, followed by simple evaluations. "She was OK, but boring." "I didn't like Mr. Charters at all. He was an a-hole. He picked on students." "Mr. Wright was pretty cool. I like him, but he made us do a lot of work."

"Are you ready to no longer be a middle schooler? Are you excited to go to Central High?"

Kyle took several seconds to think about it, then finally she said, "I guess. How could things get any worse?"

"Worse than what?"

"Worse than here!"

"It's really that bad?" I asked, but already knew the answer.

"It sucks. I talked to my mom about going to a cyber school. But she doesn't want me to miss out on social stuff. But that's what I want to miss."

I didn't respond and allowed some quiet to pass. We continued to walk. Kyle grazed her hand over lockers.

"Central is going to suck too. I know it. But, Mr. Dilinger [guidance counselor] said there will be 'more kids like me.' So, maybe I'll make some new friends."

"More like you?"

"Yeah. I know they have a Gay Straight Alliance. He said I should check it out. But I don't know what I am. I'm just me."

"That's pretty wonderful…you just being you. I really like you."

More awkward silence passed.

"So, you want to know a secret?" I asked.

"Yes," Kyle immediately answered.

"You know, whenever an adult asks you to keep a secret it is usually a bad idea. So, you can tell people. But, don't say anything to your teachers yet. You can tell others though."

"Juicy," Kyle teased.

"OK, well, I've been here all year wondering about gender. Like how the school treats boys and girls. I wanted to know if boys had different expectations than girls."

Kyle's eyes became watery. "What do you mean?" she asked.

"Like, I think it's not really helpful when schools encourage boys to act one way and girls to act another way. I think people can act lots of ways—like why must we have only two ways kids can act?"

With a few big tears, Kyle said, "You think that?"

"Yup."

"So, what do you think about me?" she asked.

"The truth?"

"Yes," she nervously responded.

"You are you, and that's amazing. That's what I think. Ask me what I think about the school."

"What about the school?" she said with wet cheeks and a smile.

"Meh."

This solicited a big laugh.

155

"Randolph," I said, "is like many schools...they are just something that some kids really like and lots of others really don't. I think the trick for you, and other kids too, is to try to find ways to build resilience. Do you know what I mean? It's like how can you make the best of what you have, while knowing you are worthwhile and important. But that's hard."

"It's really hard."

In my head, I thought, "To be honest, it's not just about resilience that I want...I want you, and kids like you, to change schools. To demand it." But I knew saying this, particularly in this moment, would be too overwhelming.

"You told me near the beginning of the semester that you identify as a girl, but at school you are a boy. Do you feel like there are expectations for you to be like a boy?"

"Yes. All the time."

"Can you give an example?"

"All the time, like everything. If people think I do anything like a girl, they have a problem with it. So, it's like all the time I have to be like a boy."

Kyle's astute observation spoke to the heavy current of patriarchy. Binary boy and girl culture, defined by patriarchy, was everything and anything students experienced. It was so seamlessly woven into the culture, and overwhelming, that Kyle—even though she has been victimized by it so deeply—could not tease out examples. She just felt like she was disallowed to be her.

"Are you going to say I'll be OK in high school?" Kyle asked.

"Wow. Umm...do you want me to say that?"

"Yes."

"OK. Truly, you'll be fine in high school, but it might suck too."

NOTES

[1] Louis Prima, *Jump, Jive and Wail*, 1956, record.

[2] GLSEN Executive Summary reported "Over a third [of LGBT students] avoided gender-segregated spaces in school because they felt unsafe or uncomfortable (bathrooms: 35.4%, locker rooms: 35.3%). See: GLSEN, "The 2013 National School Climate Survey," accessed November 20, 2014, http://www.glsen.org/sites/default/files/NSCS_ExecSumm_2013_DESIGN_FINAL.pdf.

[3] Monroe Valley School District was located in a county that "leaned conservative." While there were some "mainstream" and "liberal" Protestant churches, as well as a few Synagogues and a Mosque, they were tucked away from the suburbs in urban areas. The churches, that most influenced the suburbs of Monroe Valley School District were conservative Protestant or non-denominational "mega churches."

[4] Deborah L. Tolman, *Dilemmas of Desire: Teenage Girls Talk about Sexuality* (Cambridge, MA: Harvard University Press, 2005), 13.

[5] Ibid., 5.

[6] Ludger H. Viefhues-Bailey, *Gender, Theory, and Religion.* (New York, NY: Columbia University Press, 2010).

[7] Deborah L. Tolman, *Dilemas of Desire*, 7.

[8] See: Charles W. Peek, George D. Lowe and Susan L. Williams, "Gender and God's Word: Another Look at Religious Fundamentalism and Sexism," *Social Forces* 69, no. 4 (1991): 1205-21; John R. Bartkowski, *Remaking the Godly Marriage: Gender Negotiation in Evangelical Families* (New Brunswick, NJ: Rutgers University Press, 2001); John R. Bartkowski and Xu Xiaohe, "Religion and Family Values Reconsidered: Gender Traditionalism Among Conservative Protestants," ed. Christopher G. Ellison and Robert A. Hummer, *Religion, Familes, and Health: Population-Based Research in the United States* (New Brunswick, NJ: Rutgers University Press, 2010); John P. Hoffmann and John P. Bartowski, "Sex, Religious Tradition, and Biblical Literalism," *Social Forces* 86, no. 3 (2008): 1245–1272.

[9] "Hooking up" means many things to pre-teen/teens. In some cases it meant kissing and holding hands, intercourse, oral sex, and so on. This term "hooking up" was used often, because it was intentionally nebulous enticing peers to wonder what actually happened.

[10] Deborah L. Tolman, *Dilemas of Desire.*

[11] Ibid., 2.

[12] Dacher Keltner, Lisa Capps, Ann M. Kring, Randall C. Young and Erin A. Heerey, "Just Teasing: A Conceptual Analysis and Empirical Review," *Psychological Bulletin* 127, no. 2 (2001): 229.

[13] Cristina L. Ruffner and Emily C. Graybill, "Teachers' Perceptions of Teasing in Schools," *Journal of School Violence* 9, no. 2 (2010): 2. See Also: Diane Jones, Jodi Newman, and Sheena Bautista, "A Three-Factor Model of Teasing: The Influence of Friendship, Gender, and Topic on Expected Emotional Reactions to Teasing During Early Adolescence," *Social Development* 14, no. 3 (2005): 421–439; Deborah Land, "Teasing Apart Secondary Students' Conceptualizations of Peer Teasing, Bullying and Sexual Harassment," *School Psychology International* 24, no. 2 (2003).

[14] Michael A. Messner, "Gender Ideologies, Youth Sports, and the Production of Soft Essentialism," *Sociology of Sport Journal* 28, no. 2 (June, 2011): 161.

15   Ibid. See also: Michael A. Messner, "Barbie Girls Versus Sea Monsters: Children Constructing Gender." *Gender & Society* 14, no. 6 (December, 2000): 765–784.

16   Ibid., 162.

17   Boys who were "viewed categorically as individualists, whose essential nature is played out in sports" were deemed "gay" aggressive or "confused" when they chose "feminine" sports, or if they were disinterested in athletics. See: Michael A. Messner, "Gender Ideologies, Youth Sports, and the Production of Soft Essentialism,"162.

18   Ibid.,164.

19   Michael Kimmel, "Solving the 'Boy Crisis' in Schools," *Huff Post Parents*, accessed November 20, 2014, http://www.huffingtonpost.com/michael-kimmel/solving-the-boy-crisis-in_b_3126379.html. Francis & Skelton note, "Studies have found that the highest status versions of masculinity among boys are 'ladish' [hegemonic and complicit] constructions which value rebelliousness, risk, 'having a laugh', sporting prowess and heterosexual activity above academic study and achievement…The disruptive behavior of many boys in school has been shown to have negative impacts both for their own learning and for those of their male and female classmates." Becky Francis and Christine Skelton, *Reassessing Gender and Achievement*, 9. See also: Becky Francis, *Boys, Girls and Achievement* (London: Routledge, 2000); Molly Warrington and Michael Younger, "The Other Side of the Gender Gap," *Gender and Education*, 12, no. 4 (2000): p. 493–507; Christine Skelton, *Schooling the Boys* (Buckingham: Open University Press, 2001).

20   Wayne Martino, "Cool Boys, Party Animals, Squids and Poofters: Interrogating the Dynamics and Politics of Adolescent Masculinities in School," *The British Journal of the Sociology of Education*, 20, no. 2 (1999): 239-263; Martin Mac an Ghaill, *The Making of Men* (Buckingham: Open University Press, 1994).

21   See: Molly Mee, Heather Haverback and Jeff Passe, "For the Love of the Middle: A Glimpse Into Why One Group of Preservice Teachers Chose Middle Grades Education," *Middle Grades Research Journal* 7, no. 4 (2012): 1–14; Susan H. Marston, "Why Do They Teach? A Comparison of Elementary, High School, and College Teachers," *Education* 131, no. 2 (2010): 437-454; Rich A. Radcliffe and Thomas F. Mandeville, "Teacher Preferences for Middle Grades: Insights into Attracting Teacher Candidates," *The Clearing House: A Journal of Educational Strategies, Issues and Ideas* 80, no. 6 (2007): 261–266.

22   For an interesting read about teaching as immortality see: David J. Blacker, *Dying to Teach: The Educators Search for Immortality* (New York, NY: Teachers College Press, 1997).

23   The evidence that proves that male role models do not provide boys with academic or social benefit, also proves that girls do not benefit from female role models. However, more pressing is for teachers to understand girls' experience with stereotype threat. Catherine Good and colleagues took more than 100 university students enrolled in the same calculus class and gave them a test of questions from

the Graduate Record Examination (GRE) Math portion. The students were split into two different groups so that their GPAs/course grades were similar to that of the other group. The first group was told that this test was designed so that the researchers could gain a better understanding about what makes some better than others in mathematics. The second group was told that this test was used many times before and that male and female students scored equally as well. All students in both groups scored about 19 percent correct on this test. However, women in the second group, the one that they believed there was no gender difference, scored an average of 30 percent correct. See: Catherine Good, Joshua Aronson and Jayne Ann Harder, "Problems in the Pipeline: Stereotype Threat and Women's Achievement in High-Level Math Courses," *Journal of Developmental Psychology* 24, no. 6 (2008): 17–28. Women's understandings, provoked by common lore in media, society, word of mouth, is that they are inferior in mathematics than men. So when they "record their sex at the beginning of a quantitative test (which is standard practice for many tests); are in the minority as they take the test, have just watched women acting in air-headed ways in commercials, or have instructors or peers who hold—consciously or otherwise—sexist attitudes" they do worse, when the reality is they are just as likely to be equal performers in mathematics. See: Cordelia Fine, *Delusions of Gender: How Our Minds, Society, and Neurosexism Create Difference* (New York, NY: W. W. Norton & Company, 2010), 31–32. See also: Glenn Adams, Donna M. Garcia, Valeria Purdie-Vaughns and Claude M. Steele "The Detrimental Effects of a Suggestion of Sexism in an Instruction Situation," *Journal of Experimental Social Psychology*, 42, no. 5 (2006): 602–615; Kelly Danaher and Christen S. Crandall, "Stereotype Threat in Applied Settings Re-examined," *Journal of Applied Social Psychology*, 38, no. 6 (2008): 1639–1655; Paul G. Davies, Steven J. Spencer, Diane M. Quinn and Rebecca Gerhardstein, "Consuming Images: Howe Television Commercials that Elicit Stereotype Threat Can Restrain Women Academically and Professionally," *Personality and Social Psychgology Bulletin*, 28, no. 12 (2002): 1615–1628; Michael Inzlicht and Talia Ben-Zeev, "A Threatening Intellectual Environment: Why Females are Susceptible to Experiencing Problem-Solving Deficits in the Presence of Males," *Psychological Science*, 11, no. 5 (2000): 365–371); Christine Logel, Gregory M. Walton, Steven J. Spencer, Emma C. Isserman, William W. von Hippel, and Amy Bell, "Interacting with Sexist Men Triggers Social Identity Threat Among Female Engineers," *Journal of Personality and Social Psychology*, 96, no. 6 (2009): 1089–1103.

[24] Beyoncé's song "Flawless," [See: Beyoncé Knowles-Carter, *Flawless,* with Terius Nash, Chauncey Hollis and Rey Reel, March, 2013 by Columbia, digital release.] sampled Chimamanda Ngozi Adichie's TEDxEuston speech [See: Chimamanda Ngozi Adichie, "We Should All be Feminists," (presented at TEDxEuston, December, 2012)]. This song was quickly marketed and hailed as a feminist anthem, particularly by the mainstream media—who, in my opinion, are consistently sexist and misconstrue gender. On the fringes, fair critiques emerged.

For example, Catherine Traywick claimed, "Beyoncé bookends Adichie's words with distinctly less thoughtful lyrics of her own: She shallowly trumpets material wealth and physical beauty and, working in a few lines from her spring single, advises others to 'Bow down, bitches,'" and "Beyoncé gives us a heavily-edited, watered-down version of Adichie's speech that aligns with the singer's banal brand of beginner feminism: She reduces Adichie's powerful message to an overly simplistic, inoffensive pro-girl anthem that does little to challenge trenchant gender ideals." [see: Catherine Traywick, "Beyoncé's New Album Got FP Global Thinker Chimamanda Adichie All Wrong," *Foreign Policy*, accessed November 13, 2014 http://blog.foreignpolicy.com/posts/2013/12/13/Beyoncés_new_album_got_FP_global_thinker_chimamanda_adichie_all_wrong].

[25] On hipster feminism, see: Alissa Quart's, "The Age of Hipster Sexism," *The Cut*, accessed November 24, 2014, http://nymag.com/thecut/2012/10/age-of-hipster-sexism.html.

[26] The talent show was organized to have one boy and one girl winner.

[27] Research in this area is desperately needed.

[28] Arne Duncan's appointment without major outcry by the American people also demonstrated how devalued education is in our country. Could you imagine the hoopla the media would stir if a president would nominate a Surgeon General who never practiced medicine, or an Attorney General who never practiced law?

[29] Raewyn Connell, *Masculinities*.

CENTRAL HIGH SCHOOL

Playing Life

Yeah the boys 'round here
Drinking that ice cold beer
Talkin' 'bout girls, talkin' 'bout trucks…
Yeah, the girls 'round here, they all deserve a whistle
—Blake Shelton[1]

This dude named Michael used to ride motorcycles
Dick bigger than a tower, I ain't talking about Eiffel's
Real country ass nigga, let me play with his rifle
Pussy put his ass to sleep, now he calling me NyQuil
—Nicki Minaj[2]

I often write in bars. Not a good habit, I suppose, but it is usually productive. This one night, I was enjoying a rare sour and intently watching two women in their late twenties, both very attractive, having drinks. I observed the outskirts of the room and tried to predict if any men would try to chat them up. As a social scientist who is constantly watching people, I have found bar behaviors to be very predictable. A twenty-something guy, smartly dressed, approached and struck up a conversation with the blonde. She was the cuter of the two. Her brunette friend seemed to have recognized this situation, probably from it happening in the past, and so she turned her body square with the bar, and swiveled her drink with a stir. This gave her friend a little room to talk. The guy did not come on too strong, and had a great smile. She seemed to enjoy the conversation. He asked a few questions and learned that she was a high school English teacher.

"Ok, so really, can I ask you something?" he said with a grin.

"I guess so," she responded.

In a poor attempt to flatter her he said,

> So did you see this teacher who just got sentenced to four years of jail for sleeping with one of her students? She was hot. The kid was like sixteen. I remember what it was like to be sixteen, and I never had any teacher that looked like that, or like you. If I had you as a teacher...oh my...I wouldn't be able to concentrate. I would be distracted.

The woman looked puzzled and worried, unsure where this was going. He persisted,

> And, yeah, I'd totally want to sleep with you. And how could I resist if you were to come on to me? I mean, it would just be too hard. Usually the male is the sexual deviant, the aggressor...but if you are a young boy and any girl wants to have sex with you, but especially someone like mature and knows how to take care of a man...I don't see how you can resist it. And call that rape? The boy, I'm sure, loved it. He's going to go back to his buddies and brag, "I'm the man!" and you can't blame him. Right? Girls have lots of opportunities to sleep with older men, but boys don't have opportunities to sleep with older women. So...you're beautiful...

While he talked, she slowly turned her body toward the bar, and glanced at her friend, signaling for help. He desperately tried to get his point across by leaning closer, into the bar, attempting to maintain eye contact.

"It's rape," she replied with a quick and serious glance.

"No, I mean, it's just..."

"Rape."

At Randolph, and other middle schools, students practiced flirting with faculty.[3] Faculty members perceived this as innocent playfulness by kids whose hormones raged. The high school faculty, however, recognized this as actual flirting. High school resembled "real life"— kids were anchored in boy and girl cultures during elementary school, had proven themselves masculine, feminine, and sexual in middle school, and high school was where "real life" was played out. Faculty and parents expected kids to have more serious relationships that were often sexual in nature. One way this was demonstrated was by how teachers would supportively listen to students lament when their boyfriend or girlfriend "cheated" on them.

Watching students flirt with faculty was difficult. Most teachers were uninterested in having romantic relationships with students. However, a few of the women, and several of the younger male teachers, often traded comments during lunch, or before and after school, raising my suspicion.

Female teachers:

"If I were in high school, I would so be into Ryan. Such a cute boy…and I'm sorry, but he has a great body."

"Yeah, OK…yes, it's true…I think there's a little crush going on. Zach has been really flirty with me during class, almost embarrassingly. I can't say it doesn't feel a little good. But, I have to put a stop to it because the other kids are watching this all go down…he's become kind of brazen about it."

"Jack is a nice kid, but I think he's the one who has been sneaking in and writing, 'MILF' on my board during second period, while I'm not in my room. He wouldn't even know how to handle this!"

Male teachers:

"Oh, shit…it's getting hard to have Brooke in my class. She's way too mature for her age. You can tell she's having sex…good wild sex… It's in her body language. If she were to really come on to me, I don't know what would happen. She's said suggestive stuff to me before… I'm just getting to a point now that I don't know what would happen."

"So, I was working late, and I left school and walked into the parking lot. The girls soccer team had just pulled up and they were all changing in the bus. I could see right in. I literally saw a bunch of them topless, and a few of them just in their sports bras. And they're hot! Fucking fit! One or two totally saw me looking and they just smiled."

"Beth Anne every day looks at me like she wants to fuck me. She just sits there in class and gives me those eyes. Whenever she talks, her mouth turns upward in a little smile. I keep thinking I should keep her after class one day…"

The teachers felt safe to exaggerate and say ridiculous things about their students. But I could not help to wonder if shreds of truth existed within these stories. If these teachers were to be truthful and reflective, could they recognize any desire to be in sexual or romantic relationships with some of their students? Of course, this was too taboo to ask about: "So, do any of your students turn you on?" "Do you have any desire to be with your students?"

Besides flirting with students, telling stories about their students, and engaging in conversations with students about their love life, there were instances of actual physical contact that was sexual in nature. Surely, emotional relationships were also formed between students and faculty, but these were difficult to prove.

The Physics teacher, Eric Bradshaw, taught at Central for sixteen years. During his fifth year, he had an affair with a senior girl and married her a month after graduation. Two years after that, he became divorced and married another former student. Since then, it has been rumored that he has had several affairs, even currently. A few years ago, an astounding five girls in his remedial Physics class became pregnant during the school year. This created a lot of suspicion and though none of the girls claimed any intimate contact with Eric, he liked to joke about the possibility. He enjoyed being perceived desired by high school girls. Certain girls, too, played into his reputation by flirting heavily with him. For all parties involved—except for parents—it was a good time.

Central had a problem with band teachers. Three years ago, Central's band teacher was arrested and convicted for statutory rape after he was caught having sex with a color guard member in the parking lot of the high school, and again behind a Ruby Tuesday's. The community was in an uproar. They hired a new band teacher who also slept with his students. This teacher was fired just before the school year. The superintendent told me that they tried desperately to hire a woman, but that they could not find one with the right credentials. They hired another man, who over the time I was at Central would also become known for unethical behavior: like watching the color guard change on the bus before and after away performances, holding private meetings with girls, unnecessarily coming in physical contact with several girls—usually as he walked by them or talked to them, he placed his hand on their back or shoulder and sometimes rubbed their arms. The principal could not afford the public to think that yet another band teacher was sexually assaulting students, so he actively talked about how great and different the new hire was.

Until a knee injury ended her career, Melissa Williams was a semi-professional field hockey player. "I trained with Olympians, and now...I teach Spanish," she told me, laughing. "Well, and also coach. That's really how I got this job." This was Melissa's first year teaching. Melissa took her job as the varsity field hockey coach very seriously. Several of the players felt she was too hard on them and quit mid-season. Several of the older female faculty took offense to her being hired so she could coach. "I guess gone are the days that only unqualified men are hired to teach so they can coach sports," Barbara Stills, the French teacher complained. "And look at her," added Rosalind Daniels, a Social Studies teacher, "She's freaking Ms. America. Perky and pretty. You can't tell me those douchebags [the superintendent, principal, and athletic director] didn't take notice when they interviewed her." While it was true that Melissa was hired for her coaching abilities and was an extraordinarily attractive and physically fit twenty-four year old, she did not deserve the negative campaign launched against her. The female faculty spread rumors and joked that Melissa was a lesbian—a rumor many of the female coaches endured—and that she enjoyed hanging out with her players in the locker room. This rumor trickled down to students. Damian, a twelfth grader told me, "those hockey girls are fit...you can't blame her." The younger male faculty, as well as some of the high school boys who took cues from their teachers, incessantly talked about how "hot" Melissa was and that if she were a lesbian, they were going to "change that." Since the beginning of the school year, they took every opportunity available to hang out and flirt with Melissa. Being a nice person, as well as young and naïve, she was not aware that their getting close to her was a game. As the year carried on, male faculty members and students pushed physical and psychological boundaries. It was initially difficult for Melissa, however, to identify when these boundaries, her boundaries, were being crossed. Hugs became more frequent, longer, and more intense—colleagues and students pulled her body closer, and placed their hands lower on her body or wrapped around the small of her back, brushing the side of her chest. They sat too close to her during meetings and in class; often a part of their knee would brush up against hers. They also said more sexually suggestive things to her, "Why don't you have a boyfriend, Ms. Williams? You're too much for them?" and "Field hockey…it's a game with stick and balls…I get it." By May, Melissa was thoroughly confused. On one hand she felt sexually harassed and hopeless. On the other hand she was groomed to feel like this was her role at Central.

Against all good judgment she agreed to a few dates with Tony Hall, an English teacher. She had "made out" with him once, but decided she did not want a relationship with him. Tony, at first, bragged to the other male faculty about "landing" her, but then quickly turned embarrassed when they teased him about not being able to "keep her." They nicknamed him "One Trick Tony." Tony used the last month of school to build a case that Melissa was "inappropriate" with students as well as faculty. While it was unsettling to see that male students and faculty were unnecessarily physical with Melissa, it was more unsettling to know that she was indoctrinated by a culture where the female faculty wanted nothing to do with her—they did not advise, mentor, or assist her social or academic transition. Tony's accusations were taken seriously. Second to last day of the school year, Melissa and the principal held a closed-door meeting. Details of their conversation were not discussed with me or anyone else. On the last day of the school year, Melissa quietly packed up her personal belongings and left Central without saying goodbye to a single soul.[4]

As I previously said, though droves of research indicates that students do not look to their same-sex teachers as role models because of their gender, adults' actions at Central gave cultural cues as to what was "normal" and expected by men and women. Adult behavior firmly mapped out the landscape of how stereotypical masculinity and femininity should be played. And the students at Central played it well.

There were a few students who were marginalized by those who "fit" typical male/female culture. A few brave others chose their own path and presented different variations of gender despite the pressure to conform. These students faced discrimination, mostly by being looked upon as "alternative," or "different," which over time had become burdensome. The every day social consequences—being completely ignored, enduring passive aggressive snide remarks, and explicit heckling—were non-stop.[5] Some of the students who identified queer[6] were active members of the school's Gay Straight Alliance. Others who did not identify queer, but simply not identify male or female, were resistant to joining a "gay club." Regardless, Central students understood the rules of masculinity and femininity. They performed it perfectly, regardless of whether or not they understood why they did.

SCHOOL CLIMATE

Central's climate was like Randolph Middle School's climate, but on steroids. Faculty expectations for students were high, in the name of "preparing them for college." I often overheard teachers saying, "You're going to need to know this in college…" Also, "Guys, you're going to have to learn how to treat a girl right…learn some chivalry, before you go to college," and "Girls, when you go to college, it's important to not put yourself out there…be careful of everyone…it's not going to be OK to dress in tight and sexy outfits and go get wasted at a party."[7]

Academics and athletics were most prized at Central, but participation in extracurricular activities (like clubs, Honor Society, homecoming court, band and orchestra) were also highly valued. Just like at Randolph, the school wove specific gender expectations throughout all activities. The expectation to narrowly perform masculinity and femininity were higher than ever.

When I was a high school student from 1990 - 1994, students were involved in drug use, sexual escapades, fights, and criminal activity. Central High School was no different, except, it shocked me about how openly students aired their business.

On September 28th at 9:35 a.m., between periods, I walked behind two girls who were talking loud enough for the entire hallway to listen in on their conversation.

"He acts like if I don't give him head every day, that he's gonna get it somewhere else," said Jenna.

"Well, give him fucking head," her best friend, Madison giggled.

"I do!' Jenna replied.

"Well, give it better!"

"I'm getting so much protein…he says it's good for my skin."

Jenna and Maddy, laughing, walked into a classroom and greeted Saul Keiser, their social studies teacher at the door, "Hi Mr. Keiser."

Saul Keiser stared straight ahead and responded, "Good morning, ladies."

Madison continued, "He better be returning the favor…if not, I know who loves doing it," she says with a smile.

After class, I asked Saul if he knew what Madison and Jenna were talking about.

"I don't know exactly, but to be exact, I didn't want to know," he responded.

"What do you mean?"

"High school students these days, there's very little filter. So, I could constantly try to intervene, but what's that going to get me? 'Mr. Keiser tried to talk about oral sex with his students.' And if I write them up…well, nothing is going to happen there. Students know. They know they can do whatever."

"Has it always been like this at Central?"

"No," the veteran of twenty-seven years responded, "I think this has to do, somewhat, with the explosion of social media. Kids are just constantly interacting and being fed garbage. I imagine any fleeting thought that comes to their head is fair game for the world to know."

Later that day, at 1:20 p.m., less than a mere four hours later, Jenna's boyfriend, Mike turned to his friend, Ty, and said, "Where's Jenna? I haven't seen her around."

Ty closed his locker and glanced down the hall. "I haven't seen her all day."

"I know, right, that's the problem," Mike said while grabbing his crotch.

Both laughed hysterically.

"Calm down, man…" Ty offered, "school gonna be over soon."

I, an adult they did not know, stood within ten feet of this conversation. Surely they knew I could hear them.

And Now We Should be Concerned?

Faculty at Central presented a great paradox: they fully expected that students performed gender, tethered to heternonormative representations, which included demonstrating sexual interest/ participating in sexual experiences; however, they claimed deep concern that students were "too advanced for their age." A perfect example of this paradox presented itself around the prom.[8] The prom marked a pinnacle of high school. It was perceived as a rite of passage into adulthood. The school spent several months hyping the event. Dates, dress, transportation, and anything prom related dominated talk at the school and in many kids' homes. Teachers and parents nosed their way into which students were going together, the local newspaper and television station covered the event, and parents snapped hundreds of pictures, uploading them to social media sites so they could brag how handsome and beautiful their children looked. However, in the midst of the hoopla, faculty and parents shared grave concerns of students drinking, using drugs, and having sex. Of course, the school did very little to help prepare students to act responsibly.

I will say it a slightly different way: the adults at Monroe Valley School District, from kindergarten through high school, taught students to be stereotypical boys and girls who craved an identity within the traditional gender binary—which included sexual interest in the opposite sex. To be clear, students were the products of adult desires and imposed culture. Then, unfairly, when students perfectly performed their roles, as they were taught, adults became alarmed.

COFFEE (TURNED MIMOSAS) WITH SAGES

Every faculty has a group of sages, veteran teachers who have deep institutional history. Central's sages gathered in Jane Duncan's chemistry lab. Every morning, an hour before the school day began, David Parks, Shelley Ruiz, Byron Simmering, Jeff Walsh, and Sallie Armstrong[9] met for coffee. Jane fashioned a contraption, fitting long and curly glass tubes together, hovering over a Bunsen burner that brewed a strong Hawaiian blend her sister sends religiously from the island every month.

169

I was unaware of this daily tradition until mid-year when I was chatting with Byron and Shelley about something after school. Byron said, "We can talk about it more tomorrow…I have to run."

"When tomorrow?" I asked.

"How about over coffee, in the lab, before school?" he suggested.

Shelley awkwardly looked sideways at him as if he left out a secret.

"Oh," I said, sensing I might not be fully welcomed, "I don't think that will work, I won't be in during the morning…I'll just catch up with you later."

Over the next several months I found it exciting to try to spy on who might be meeting. I would quickly walk by Jane's lab in the morning, trying to match the voices I heard from the hallway. Finally, in May, I was invited in.

Shelley, as if I never heard about it, asked, "So, there's a bunch of us who get together for coffee in the morning? Interested in joining us?"

The next morning, I showed up, mug in hand, and settled in. No one I know would describe this group "cool," but it felt like I was just invited to the "cool kids table" at lunch and I did not want to spoil my invite. So, I listened. I was quiet. I was not overbearing. I tried to get invited back, and I was successful. I spent many more mornings listening to them talk about their work. Sometimes one would bring in a stack of papers and grade while they talked. Mostly, they talked about their families and the news. Once in a while, they talked about school. David explained, "This has become a tradition for us. We just like having a moment before the day begins." It was a nice way to begin the day. These teachers were thoughtful, evenhanded, and deliberate. They were excellent teachers who have learned resilience—that is, they learned how to be effective within their political machine of a school. To see them teach was inspiring.

Between them, this group had 138 years of teaching. They have enjoyed great years, and endured rough years where everything seemed to go wrong. They have seen dozens of educational fads, administrators, students, and colleagues come and go. And they have also seen dozens of researchers come and go too.

"So," Sallie said smiling, setting down her coffee cup on a book of poetry she has been carrying around, "you can be straight with us… why are you really here at Central?"

Jeff quickly pulled his coffee cup to his mouth to block his grin. David looked over the top of his glasses and sat back in his seat. Jane and Shelley cocked their heads inquisitively and waited for an answer. They all knew something was up. I was not fooling them, like I had the teachers at Fisk and Randolph. They were a wise crew.

"What do you mean?" I asked, trying to play it off.

"You know," Jane responded, "you're not the best liar."

Smiling, knowing I was clearly caught, "I don't understand the question."

This elicited great laughter. David spit his coffee back into his cup rather than spraying it over the clean epoxy resin lab table.

"Ok, well, here's the deal…" I admitted. I detailed what I had been doing in Monroe Valley and explained how the high school was important to my research. I begged them to not share this information with any of the other people at Central. "Well, then, that means you'll be bringing bagels next time," Shelley half-joked.

The school year wound down and I tried to make it to coffee every morning I had an opportunity. And, yes, sometimes I brought the bagels. The group, for the most part, continued to talk about the normal stuff, but they increasingly asked me questions, and in turn, I asked them questions. The very last day of the school year, I said my goodbyes, but they invited me to brunch on the very next day. "It's something we old folks like to do. A little celebration at the end of the year, if you will. You should come."

Abagail's on Main was a cute restaurant in the center of Pierce. We slid into a large corner table with long benches. Coffee was set aside for mimosas…a lot of them. Our session began as if we were in Jane's lab, but it quickly morphed into an intense conversation about my research. It became clear to me that they wanted to help. They were open and willing to tell me anything I wanted to know. So, I did not waste this unique moment. Over omelets and French toast they analyzed the cultural landscape at Central.

"So, shoot!" ordered David.

"Okay," I said while pulling out my notepad and tape recorder.

"Here he goes...'the professor!'" joked Jeff. They all chuckled. I had endured on-going ribbing because they thought it was funny that I was a couple decades younger than them.

"Here's something I wrote just last night," I reported:

Being at Central for the year gave me the opportunity to collect hundreds of examples about how the school institutionalized gender—how the school's culture taught masculinity and femininity. But, in my analysis, these examples were only different from middle school in one primary way: by the time students became high schoolers, they were expected to have figured out their sexual identity—which meant that teachers, students, parents, and administrators naïvely assumed that students have "settled" into a simplistic sense of gender identity. The high school was not an environment that allotted students space to find themselves. Instead, high school replicated "real life," and expected "real" (a.k.a., "traditional") gendered performances. For example, dances at Randolph middle school were designed as opportunities to "test" students, or to give them practice within the heternormative traditions of masculinity and femininity. This included students asking someone of the opposite sex to the dance, determining how to dress (not for self, but for other), setting expectations for what kinds of physical (sexual) interactions deem one masculine and feminine, and so on. Dances at Central assumed that students should be fully interested and successful in participating in these traditions and culture. Additionally, it was expected that students saw these experiences as replications of the real world.

"Super interesting!" Shelley responded.

"Yes!" agreed Byron.

"I think it's right on," replied Jeff.

"It's like the prom...it represents a wedding!" Sallie shared.

The crew agreed.

"Do you mind sharing some of the examples of how Central standardized gender?" David asked.

"Institutionalized gender," Jane corrected.

"Oh, sorry," David apologized.

"No worries, I think 'standardized' works too…maybe even better than institutionalized. Well, I'll give some obvious examples, and sort of seemingly benign ones too." I rattled off a list:

- Posters in the hall advertising picture day showed one girl, one boy—both cute. The boy, cool and sporty. The girl, sweet and adorable.
- You have male and female organized athletics. That in itself might be problematic. Separate is never equal…right? Boys' sports gets a lot of attention and press, and are practically worshipped—we should be honest, the stars of these teams are worshiped. Female teams, or specific female players, will get attention too, but they have to be really exceptional. The school maintains expectations of exceptional female stars, to continue to perform well academically, socially, etc.
- Titty Tuesdays, Slap-Ass Thursdays, and Freaky Fridays – I can't really figure out if this is organized sexual harassment…sure seems like it for girls walking down hallways who do not desire to have her breasts squeezed or ass slapped. On "Freaky Fridays," as I understand it, students challenge one another to have sex. I suppose there may be instances where students are forcing themselves on others.
- Senior Week – we all know what happens there. This is not a school sponsored event, however, teachers and others talk about it…just by asking simple questions like, "Where are you going? Do you have any plans? Are you going with friends?" This is, yet another example, of parents, teachers and other adults who fret over drugs, alcohol, and sex, but commodify rituals that embrace drugs, alcohol, and sex.
- "Think Pink Week" was an interesting week of fundraising for breast cancer…but students made a mockery of it…or turned it into an opportunity to talk about breasts. Some wore bracelets reading, "I love boobies." This was tolerated by the school during this week. Some of the boys and several girls challenged each other to flash their breast during school. "Show pink!" I heard a few student chant. One student confided and said that pink was also being applied to vaginas. That is, it was encouraged for girls to show their breasts

and vaginas—as a so-called "game"—to one another. I know the administration knew about this, some kids received consequences, but there was no real effort to address what was going on.

- The Prom and other dances. Homecoming King and Queen. Need I say more?
- Students actively use words like, "slut," "bitch," "bro," "boss," and others—they all have gendered meanings, and typically (re)entrench the binary. Teachers stand by and rarely correct or intervene. If they do intervene, it's typically a "Hey, watch your language" or, "C'mon...not in school."
- School dress code policies police female bodies more than male bodies. Just recently, your school made the decision that girls shouldn't wear yoga pants. The narrative put out by the administrators and teachers wasn't that yoga pants were some how indecent, but that they distracted boys. So, an active policing of female bodies for the sake of the patriarchy. It's also demeaning for girls because in their ruling, it objectifies/sexualizes women. Boys too are damaged by this, because it sends a message that boys can't possibly act responsibly around girls and women who wear certain things. When will the school get over that girls and women have bodies?
- Social media is not an official part of the school curriculum, however, students access it throughout the day. Narratives posted on Facebook, Twitter, Instagram, Yik Yak, Snapchat, and others include students actively talking about friends and sex. They sneak pictures of their peers, sexualizing them—sometimes publically, sometimes privately.
- Teachers' affect and word choice. Girls and boys are talked to much differently. It doesn't actually matter how word choices and affect differ, the point is that it differs. It transmits that there are two separate gendered cultures that deserve, for some reason, different treatment—even in the simplest ways.
- The expectation that boys will be angry, and that there are "justifiable" times for violence.[10] Yet when girls are violent, psychological services are immediately suggested.

"I could go on and on," I said. "Am I crazy?"

A collective smile emerged. "No," Jane said.

"But, I can only imagine that this is kind of a never ending project," Byron interrupted.

"And exhausting to even think about," said Jeff.

Totally! Well, but...I felt it was important to start with just scratching the surface—pointing out that we are teaching gender in everything we do in schools. I think some of the most dangerous stuff is embedded in our everyday interactions...the stuff we just don't even think about. Like we've all just gotten really sloppy and started using 'you guys' to describe entire groups of people. First, it's just wrong. Second, it's argued that this makes femininity invisible and devalued.[11] But, why use gender as a descriptor for any group?

Shelley, a linguistics nerd, piped up, "That's so true. 'You guys' is a relatively recent phenomenon."

And it honors patriarchy. Sometimes when I talk about this to students, they argue with me that it is 'no big deal.' Many of the women in the audience make it a point to disagree with me. Then, I typically respond, that if it's no big deal, walk into a mixed room of people and call them all girls. See what happens. My prediction that there'll be at least one guy in there make a big deal about it...grunting, groaning, pointing out he's not a girl. Again, "you guys" pays homage to patriarchy, while "you girls" used in a mixed gender group violates patriarchy.

"So what are you trying to do with this work?"

I think just bring thoughtfulness to schools. I think we can just be a whole lot more deliberate. I think schools should be a good model for society. Schools should stretch, actively change society for the better. We shouldn't have high schools like Central reify the heteronormative stereotypical gender roles that are perpetuated in our white supremacist capitalist patriarchy.

"That's a mouthful," David laughed. "But do schools even care about this stuff?"

"That's a great question. Mostly, no. I had to work hard to have schools agree to the study. They always asked me if this work would

175

help raise their test scores or worked on new state standards. When I said, 'no,' they became disinterested."

"What about the teachers? Do they care about gender and gender equity?" he followed up.

Well, every teacher I interviewed, several dozen, all claimed gender equity and child development to be on the top of their lists. Meaning, they care about it deeply. However, when I point out the ways their schools, and sometimes their instruction, sextypes and simplifies complex human beings, they are typically horrified. They respond, 'Well, it makes sense. Even though I want to think about gender, when I'm in front of my students I'm so worried about keeping a rapid pace so we can cover content, ensuring my instruction is aligned with standards, trying to get ready for tests, and so on…' So, I think teachers might care, at least they report they care, but there are more pressing issues on their minds.

"Wow," David replied, "that's kind of telling."

"What do you mean?"

"I mean, that teachers so easily sacrifice issues of social justice for standardized/test-based instruction."

Shelly asked, "But, David, what's your take? Do you think most of our colleagues are truly interested in gender equity?"

"Or a reconceptualization of gender?" I added.

David responded, "They'd say they were interested in gender equity, yes. Do I really think they are? Umm…I don't know. I guess it's in how we define it. I think none of them would claim they are for inequity. I think the majority of them, however, would think you are nuts to believe we can reconceptualize gender."

"Do you think it's a nutty idea?" I asked.

"No, but our students have learned masculine and feminine traits their entire lives. And our teachers too, for that matter. So, when we ask for a reconceptualization, people must recognize that they have actively constructed something first. They don't see gender the way we might…that it's been constructed. Gender just is." Turning to me, he asked, "Right?"

"Right."

"So, I think your work points out some problems," Jane said while signaling the waiter for another round of mimosas.

"What's that?" Jeff asked.

"Well," she paused:

I think it's problematic that by the time students get to us, they have already been hardcore socialized boy and girl. If we were to try to help them deconstruct that, they would think we are crazy. I almost feel like it is too late. Parents would complain. A big problem too is that we have no space in our day or curriculum to think of doing such work. We are to deliver content. And that's yet another problem, many high school teachers forget that children, technically, are the curriculum. Most teachers think school is about delivering content material. So, it's educating them too. Changing their minds about things.

"Agreed," Shelley chimed in. "With social media, their parents, and other outside influences, it's an uphill battle."

"Yeah, but shouldn't it be a battle we take on?" I asked.

They somberly sat with that question hanging in the air for a moment.

"Yes, but it seems hopeless," Shelley finally replied.

"Totally," Jeff agreed.

"We have our own examples, too…stuff that's just as bad or worse than what you reported to us," Byron blurted.

The group became excited.

Byron shared:

Certain stairwells are known for sex in-between periods…faculty just tend to avoid them sometimes because we don't want the hassle of being accused that we somehow were trying to watch. We are somewhat laissez faire about sex…we don't educate, we don't intervene, we just don't do much…we should do something.

Shelly reported:

I know for a fact that the school discourages girls from taking some of the top levels of our classes. I have had several conversations with our honor roll kids and they say that their

177

guidance counselors, and their parents too, will softly guide them to easier math and science classes. That infuriates me!

David added:

Homecoming is the worst. It's a popularity contest. It's like a bad fucking reality television show. They all go around worshiping the popular kids…who of course, many of times, are terrible people. But they look good. It gets so commercial…and, of course…we have some LGBT kids in our school who want to qualify for king or queen, and that always becomes an issue of contention. And to top it off, the King and Queen go down in history by being documented in the school yearbook…preserving for all time our sexist and ridiculous ways.

Jane said:

Many of those kids, the kids who are in the GSA, or are LGBT, they have very little agency around here. And then there are other kids who just present themselves differently. I feel really poorly for them. They are just trapped in-between worlds. I really wonder if it actually gets better for them in college. Because high school is brutal.

"How about how the school has different colors for boys and girls at graduation? And they aren't allowed to use their preferred names. Why is it that boys get the red gown and the girls get the white gown? Remember Amber?" Jeff asked. The group let out a collective sigh. He explained:

Amber was born Aaron. She was in the process of transition and wanted to be announced as 'Amber' at graduation. The administration refused. She was crying in my room at the end of last year. I actually approached our principal and demanded an explanation. He simply said that Amber was a boy. I asked if he was sure…if the school district was going to actually physically check, and if so I had a problem with that. Then I stormed out of his office. Talk about infuriating!

"So, yeah, we totally get it," Jane said.

We totally understand. So, it's important to note. But I think if we, I mean as a faculty, were to slow down and think about it, we could easily become so depressed out of our minds. Or we would just say, 'it's too much to handle,' and go about our jobs as they always were.

"'Oh well, too hard.' And that's it?" I asked.

"I'm turning to straight hard liquor now," Byron joked, "waiter!" Everyone laughed.

"What I think is we need a culture shift," Jane spoke calmly.

"So we wait for it?" I asked.

"No, hold on," Jane said, "maybe schools should be the place where we begin to generate a collective consciousness."

"Conscience morale," exclaimed Jeff.

"I don't know what this entails. I don't know what the process is, but education seems fundamental on all fronts, doesn't it?" I asked.

"Yes," they agreed.

NOTES

[1] Blake Shelton, Pistol Annies and Friends, *Boys 'Round Here*, by Rhett Akins, Dallas Davidson and Craig Wiseman, March 26, 2013 by Warner Bros., digital release.

[2] Nicki Minaj, *Anaconda*, 2014 by Young Money Entertainment, Cash Money Records and Republic Records, digital release.

[3] As a researcher, I had a duty to report any behaviors in which I believed to be illegal or unethical. I reported two teachers in the course of my research.

[4] A week after the school year, Melissa William's Facebook profile picture was featured on a website dedicated to "ranking the hottest female teachers who slutted it up with students." Melissa was never found guilty of inappropriate relationships.

[5] The 2013 GLSEN Executive Summary reported that out of 7,889 LGBT students between the ages of 13 and 21: "71.4% of LGBT students heard 'gay' used in a negative way (e.g., 'that's so gay') frequently or often at school, and 90.8% reported that they felt distressed because of this language;" "64.5% heard other homophobic remarks (e.g., 'dyke' or 'faggot') frequently or often;" "56.4% heard negative remarks about gender expression (not acting 'masculine enough' or 'feminine enough') frequently or often;" "A third (33.1%) heard negative remarks specifically about transgender people, like 'tranny' or 'he/she,' frequently or often;" "51.4% of students reported hearing homophobic remarks from their

teachers or other school staff, and 55.5% of students reported hearing negative remarks about gender expression from teachers or other school staff." See: GLSEN, "The 2013 National School Climate Survey," 5.

[6] Again, students preferred the term "queer" over "gay," "lesbian," "transgender," and so on. Queer students in middle and high school did not experience positive school environments, however, high school students were able to find outside support systems—in-person and through social media—that pushed them to be more brave and "out" at school. They understood that by claiming themselves queer, publically, that it was "a way to disrupt and simultaneously expose the construction of the reified binaries of heterosexual and homosexual and the static, constructed gender assignments male and female. In seeming contrast to GLBT identities, queer points to the fluidity and multiplicity of sexualities." See: Erica R. Meiners, "Remember When All the Cars Were Fords and All the Lesbians Were Women? Some Notes on Identity, Mobility, and Capital," in *Queer Theory in Education*, ed. William F. Pinar (Mahwah, NJ: Lawrence Erlbaum Associates, Inc., 1998), 145. See also: Charles Nissley, Ella West and Madison Grey, "*Queer on Campus*," *Vitae Scholasticae*, 30, no. 2 (2013): 66–89.

[7] "Slut shaming" like this was commonplace at Central.

[8] Many school organized activities created around the premise of dating, like the prom, puts students in the precarious situation of feeling like they have to engage in sexual behaviors—particularly for girls. Girls are, "perhaps more now than at any other time—to experience sexuality on boys' terms. The bacchanalian after-parties that have become as important as the proms themselves are ones in which the manufactured romance of the school-sponsored event is replaced by a frenzied attempt to embrace the most coarse and vulgar aspect of the common culture, in which girls change from prom wear into sleazy clothes and drink to the point of passing out, both of which seem to be inclinations supported wholeheartedly by the boys." See: Caitlin Flanagan, *Girl Land* (New York, NY: Back Bay Books), 134.

[9] Jane Duncan taught 11th & 12th grade chemistry, David Parks taught Psychology and Civics, Shelly Ruiz taught 9th grade English, Byron Simmering taught choir and general music, and Jeff Walsh taught French.

[10] "There is only one emotion that patriarchy values when expressed by men; that emotion is anger. Real men get mad. And their mad-ness, no matter how violent or violating, is deemed natural—a positive expression of patriarchal masculinity." See: bell hooks, *The Will to Change*, 7.

[11] Audrey Bigler, "On Language: You Guys."

DEINSTITUTIONALIZATION, NOW!

The sex/gender system that is expressed in our classrooms through contemporary forms of curriculum, classroom discourse, and theater is an atavism that expresses church/state, school/family, social class, and sexual politics more appropriate to the 1820s.

—Madeline Grumet[1]

It is no measure of health to be well adjusted to a profoundly sick society.

—Jiddu Krishnamurti[2]

I became involved with this research for selfish reasons. I wanted to understand the girl/boy culture in which my kids would be subjected to for thirteen years of their life. I also wanted to understand if it was possible to deinstitutionalize gender in their schools, and if not, how to help my kids become resilient.

I do not expect that I will fully protect Mali and Maria from becoming and feeling socialized as girls/women in our society. However, while they are children I want to provide them with an environment that honors them as individuals. On that front, things have improved for Mali. While I was in the middle of conducting this research, Mali was in third grade. Her teacher was a lot like Jessie Malloy at Fisk Elementary. Mali was clearly misunderstood. Her teacher held narrow and senseless academic and gendered expectations that became the source of much anxiety. Therefore, we withdrew Mali and enrolled her in a Waldorf school. I am happy to report that she is back to enjoying life and feeling less pressure to perform like Barbie. It feels like by taking her out of the clutches of a teacher who did not bother to *see* Mali for who she was, and by sending her to a Waldorf school in which the curriculum seems to (in a relative nature) "neutralize" and "interrupt" stereotypical gendered behaviors among children, we have given her the gift of being a child for a few more years. Mali is detoxing from her old school and is rebuilding a strong identity and sense of agency. It is helpful that she has great friends, who have various and more fluid gender identities, at her new school.

Maria, on the other hand, refuses to join her sister and has decided to stay at the same public school that had students participate in Mardi Gras parades that simulated flashing and bead throwing. We cannot convince her to leave a few good friends. We do not want to destroy her sense of agency by not giving her a voice, and so for now, we have allowed her to stay at her school even though we cringe frequently. Unfortunately, I have seen no true commitment or shift by the school to become more thoughtful and gender equitable, or even wonder what their students' gendered experiences have been like. So, we worry, greatly, about Maria.

To begin the process of deinstitutionalization I suggest that we must continue to research and narrate how schools teach students how to perform gender in the boy/girl binary. Additionally, we must recognize the multiple possible ways that the institutionalization of gender harms students. Here I offer two separate but related reasons why institutionalization and sextyping is harmful:

1. When adults teach children that they must perform in any prescribed manner, to stay within the traditions of a particular group, and in this case to develop identity tethered to only two separate options (boy/girl), when neither of these might be personally adequate, you limit them. You limit children from realizing and becoming whatever is right for them.
2. Separate is _never_ equal. Schools' efforts to establish discrete boy/girl gender categories do no good for anyone. Equality and equity will never prevail.

It is my prediction that generations from now, people will wonder why society, and schools in particular, were so hell-bent on perpetuating an overly simplistic gender binary that was deeply limiting and discriminatory to students. They will ask: Why did schools not value accuracy? Why did schools not portray gender as multiple, flexible, fluid and ever changing?

My greatest hope is that publicly funded American schools begin to understand the complexities of gender, and adopt policies and curriculum, train teachers, and interrogate their practices so that they might produce and serve a better, more well-rounded citizenry. I want schools to become interested in gender equality and equity—at least, at first—but then move toward a more radical space of supporting students' actualization of individual desires and capabilities. I have no objection to a biologically determined girl choosing to play princess or to be a passive and quiet learner who chooses reading over math. I have no objection to a biologically determined boy choosing to play army or to be a rowdy class clown who chooses math over reading. That is, as long as they made these choices while being *truly provided* and *actively encouraged* to take up any and all gendered options imaginable—including new, not yet fully realized versions.

I argue that it is our collective responsibility to think about how schools can do this work. Studies like mine narrate what the institutionalization of gender within the traditional binary looks like in schools so that we can begin to think of concrete steps to decentralize, queer, or marginalize sextyping. Deinstitutionalization is certainly a lengthy process, but with the help of teacher education programs and professional development for in-service educators, schools can begin the process sooner than later. It is my opinion that individual teachers have the most impact on how students learn gender, and so it is imperative that the educational system as a whole supports teachers' work. Our teaching force should confront patriarchy and sextyping by learning to:

- see their students, from a holistic perspective;
- understand the flexible spectrum of gender, and interpretations of performativity and socialization housed within gender theory;
- honor and embrace each student as a sophisticated individual who is capable of embodying and desiring several changing gendered identities;
- identify and interrupt heteronormative, heterosexist, Eurocentric, and patriarchal practices (including current educational policies, extra curricular activities, and informal social opportunities—like lunch, recess, and hallway socialization);
- eradicate gender based language that privileges the boy/girl binary;

- modify curricula (formal/imposed/standards based/informal/ hidden/etc.) to widely represent and encourage the study of gender and sexuality;
- learn from students who identify as transgender, genderqueer, and so on;
- be deliberate about the hundreds of seemingly small decisions made daily (like teacher affect, student grouping, the length and quality of attention devoted to students, etc.);
- be aware of their personal representations and embodiment of gender, and how it might impose expectations for student behavior and influence students' understandings.

This list is not comprehensive. And, of course, there is much work to be done by administrators, school boards, parents, staff, policy makers, communities, and students themselves.

ALTERNATIVE AND INTERNATIONAL CURRICULAR MODELS

Deinstitutionalization should also rely on pulling from funds of knowledge beyond what is readily available to us within our westernized public school system. Due to an egocentric disposition, the public school system—and the U.S. in general—cares very little about learning from alternative and international curricular models. However, I think these models may hold some key insight about practice that could help to deinstitutionalize gender in American public schools.

Democratic, Montessori, and Waldorf Schools

The vast majority of democratic, Montessori, Waldorf, and other "alternative" schools have been established with deep philosophical roots and operate with an intentionality that teachers can easily talk about. The core tenets of these models do not change, providing teachers the opportunity to concentrate on learning their students and practicing their craft. Unfortunately, public schools in the U.S. are under constant "reform" and a dizzying slew of new demands/ things to know (e.g., curricula, policy, teacher evaluation systems, standards, schedules, and so on). This leaves teachers with a confused perspective of what the philosophy/mission of public education is and distracts them from the work of knowing their students. Remember, when I interviewed teachers at Fisk Elementary though many espoused concern over gender equity, they were too overwhelmed by other external demands to develop pedagogical practice that was intentional about equity, social justice, or about realizing students' desires and capabilities. Whereas public school teachers are policed by administrators and policy makers to continually modify their practice, the primary mission of teachers at alternative schools consistently remains to support the development and emergence of individuals—which includes students' gender identities.[3]

Democratic schools perceive students:

> not as passive recipients of knowledge, but rather as active co-creators of their own learning. They are not the products of an education system, but rather valued participants in a vibrant learning community. Democratic education begins with the premise that everyone is unique, so each of us learns in a different way. By supporting the individual development of each young person within a caring community, democratic education helps young people learn about themselves, engage with the world around them, and become positive and contributing members of society.[4]

Staff members in democratic schools conceptualize learning as "meaningful, relevant, joyous, engaging and empowering," and that schools should offer an approach to "interacting with all members of your community in a way that respects, honors, and listens authentically to each voice within it."[5] Democratic schools are self-governing. All students and staff members have shared power in deciding *all* matters of the school.

> Typically, rules are made and business is handled at a weekly School Meeting, where each student, like each staff member, has one vote…In practice, democratic schools look more like a cross-section of real life, more like a vibrant town or village, than like traditional schools. There are no assigned groups or rooms, no specified activities or time periods, no preferred curriculum

or dress code, no agenda for pressuring children into endless compromise and compliance. Here children decide for themselves how to spend their time, what to do, and when and with whom to do it.[6]

Traditionally, many democratic schools do not have formal lessons, assessments, grade levels, transcripts, or diplomas—that is, unless students desire them. Democratic schools also do not quarantine students according to age, providing them the opportunity to learn who they are in relation to others. This is practice so that in the future, as adults, they can make sense of who they are in the world.[7] Students, when given a democratic environment that does not institutionalize static representations of gender, build strong and independent identities. In the handful of democratic schools in which I have observed, students often redefine and reimagine genders that are outside traditional masculine and feminine conceptions. Students freely make friends of multiple genders and are naturally empowered to be self-determined and self-actualized. To an outsider's gaze, one might classify many of these students as gender fluid and androgynous. Jim Rietmulder, co-founder and staff member of The Circle School,[8] reports, "The freedom (and responsibility) for self-authorship in democratic schools extends in many dimensions. Exploration and adoption of gender identity is about as remarkable or unremarkable as other aspects of self-definition, such as clothing, hair color, piercings, political views, personal beliefs, relation to authority, and so on."

The "hallmarks" of Montessori education include,

> multiage groupings that foster peer learning, uninterrupted blocks of work time, and guided choice of work activity…The teacher, child, and environment create a learning triangle. The classroom is prepared by the teacher to encourage independence, freedom within limits, and a sense of order. The child, through individual choice, makes use of what the environment offers to develop himself, interacting with the teacher when support and/ or guidance is needed.[9]

Montessori teachers play the role of "unobtrusive director" as children practice self-directed activity.[10] Teachers are trained to make astute observations of their students so that they can provide an atmosphere of "productive calm…alternating between long periods of intense concentration interspersed with brief moments of recovery/reorganization."[11] Montessori students "are more likely to feel safe enough to take risks, make mistakes, and share parts of themselves that would, in a more traditional setting, probably go unnoticed or be left at home."[12] Montessori education, with an emphasis on gentle teacher guidance, development of self-regulation and autonomy, and mixed-aged cooperation, provides students with space to become themselves. Mary Cae Williams, head of The New School,[13] reports:

> Maria Montessori, herself, followed a path that was atypical for women of her day. The focus of a Montessori education is on the individual nature of children. The vision includes each teacher's responsibility for tapping into that individual nature to make the learning environment fit the students rather than making the students fit a prescribed scope and sequence of tasks and content. There is no codified program to ensure that sex-stereotyping [sextyping] does not occur; there is a foundational acceptance of the "rightness" of each child's individual path or potential on which such efforts can naturally be built…Over the years, many children at The New School have expressed themselves in ways that are considered "gender atypical" in our general society. Most of the time they have been met with acceptance and supported to be "who" they were and not "what" they were supposed to be.

Waldorf schools do not have mixed aged grouping like democratic and Montessori models. However, they are similar in that they are deeply child focused. Unique to this model is that students stay with one teacher from first through eighth grade. Teachers become students of their students, watching them grow over nearly a decade, which enables them to support their children's emergent identities.

With an experiential approach, and a woven curriculum,[14] Waldorf education strives to help students "cultivate a lifelong love of learning as well as the intellectual, emotional, physical and spiritual capacities to be individuals certain of their paths and to be of service to the world."[15] Waldorf schools are concerned about, as I argue necessary for the deinstitutionalization of gender, students' capacities. Teachers' pedagogical decision-making relies on "applying intuitive thinking to the nature of the human being, child development and the evolution of consciousness"[16] and the purpose of the curriculum is "not to make a student into a professional mathematician, historian, or biologist, but to awaken and educate capacities that every human being needs."[17] This, in my observation, extends to gender identity.

When searching for a new educational environment for Mali, my partner and I observed several teachers with their students at the Susquehanna Waldorf School.[18] We were, for many reasons, moved to tears. Our first reaction was one of great loss, while we stood in the middle of a bustling kindergarten with mixed gender groups of students playing dress-up, singing, building forts, orchestrating a play, and cooking lunch. We felt that we had squandered an opportunity to have provided a nurturing environment for our children during their early years. The Waldorf kindergarten was an environment that honored children and their natural desires, unlike many public school kindergartens where academic skills that are developmentally inappropriate are pushed onto five and six year olds. In third grade, we watched (Mali's now teacher) Melissa McIntyre evenly provoke and engage students in a science lesson. Girls and boys alike were eager to contribute. She showed no favoritism or gendered expectations, but rather created an environment focused around the joy of inquiry and exploration. In eighth grade, we watched Sal Martino offer a mathematical problem to his class, and what transpired next deeply impacted the manner in which I think about Waldorf education. Students eagerly turned to one another and began proposing solutions. They sketched diagrams, bantered with one another, and (again) excitedly engaged in learning. Girls and boys together, with Sal, created a true learning community in which all members were important. Students interacted with confidence, a sense of self-worth, and purpose. Waldorf education values individual identities within communities, anchored around principles of curiosity and growth.

As we have seen, public schools create gendered communities. Waldorf schools, in my observation, create learning communities that embrace all children and expect them to engage in subject material—

like handwork (sewing and knitting), woodworking, music, art, languages, mathematics, sciences, and so on—equally. In Waldorf schools, boys do not perceive handwork as feminine, and girls do not perceive woodworking as masculine. Melissa reports, "there is a comfortableness between students...they become like siblings because they have so many shared experiences from early on through middle school with each other and the teacher. The purpose of the teacher in Waldorf education is to open up each student's path. I'm always asking, 'Am I clearing the path so they can become themselves?'"[19]

Looking Elsewhere

Why do Nordic countries (Iceland, Finland, Norway, Sweden, and Denmark) consistently outperform the majority of all other countries on academic measures (such as the Program for International Student Assessment—PISA) and are also deemed some of the most gender equitable societies?[20] Is there a correlation? What is happening in these schools?

We should be looking elsewhere too, asking lots of good questions.

It should have been of great interest to us, and the rest of the world when the French government attempted to have their teachers teach lessons about gender equality. It was a step in the right direction— and possibly one of the largest and most progressive educational attempts at a federal level to address the complexities of gender. It should have been of great importance to us to study how it also met so much resistance. I argue that we still have a lot to learn from France's attempt, and it has (in my mind) become an example of how the world is getting closer to change.

In September of 2013, the Women's and Education ministries of France helped launch a curricular program, "Les ABCD de l'égalité" (ABCD of Equality) aimed to have primary and secondary teachers trained in methods, and armed with resources, to infuse lessons about gender equality in their curriculum. This program was to be piloted and then eventually fully implemented in 2014-2015 in all schools across the nation.[21] The primary principle of the program, which teaching unions for the most part endorsed, was that schools would transmit cultures of equality and respect.[22] However, conservative reactionaries incessantly reported two narratives in an attempt to rally opposition:

> In a letter to chief education officers dated 4 January 2013, the French Minister for Education, Vincent Peillon, said that the government had decided to focus its effort to change mentalities on young people. In his view, the purpose of school is to "remove students from all forms of determinism, whether familial, ethnic, social or intellectual." (L'Experess, 2 September 2012)[23]

> In a December 2012 report, the General Inspectorate of Social Affairs recommended that schools should start the "fight against gender stereotypes at the earliest possible age," deconstruct the "ideology of complementarity" between the sexes, and replace the words "boys" and "girls" with sexually neutral terms such as "friends" or "children."[24]

Personally, I think these two statements—though they have been constructed as propaganda and are taken largely out of context—might have some important implications for deinstitutionalization.

The French government was so deeply committed to this program that it promised to train teacher candidates (approximately 25,000 students every year) and offer on-going professional development and resources for in-service teachers to teach gender equality.[25] The government, particularly the Minister for Women's Rights, Najat Vallaud-Belkacem was serious about taking on sexism and gender inequality.[26] However, the opposition was strong. "Antoine Renard, president of the French Catholic Family Associations, said that critics feared 'a confusion in children's spirit, disassociating the physical dimension with the behavioural dimension.'"[27] Other conservative critics claimed that the program would turn students gay. A text messaging campaign, targeting conservative Muslims, led people to believe that their young children would be subjected to "masturbation classes," which of course, was false.[28] Hundreds of students were withdrawn from schools in protest.

Unfortunately, the French government succumbed to political pressure and abandoned Les ABCD de l'égalité. France could have been a powerful model, leader, partner in solidarity, for the U.S. and the rest of the world. I fear that any educational program taken up by the U.S. government to teach gender equality, or to deconstruct gender, in our schools would meet just as much or more resistance than what the French had endured. This, perhaps, is the reason why we continue to resist developing national education standards that would address issues of social justice and social-emotional learning. Or again, perhaps we Americans are just addicted to our patriarchy.

Regardless, I argue for less egocentrism and more interest in studying countries who are more equitable, and who are making attempts toward deinstitutionalization.

...YES, NOW!

Deinstitutionalization, above all, demands schools to champion children—to see them equally similar (as humans) and dissimilar (as individuals).[29] Schools need to recognize each child as unique and worthwhile. I think it is important for schools, and adults in general, to situate children not as passive recipients, but to partner with them as active agents in their reimagining of gender.[30] We need to stop doing gender to kids. Let their futures be their own, not a relic of our sexist legacy.

I hope that we all recognize our individual responsibilities to children, and that even small changes might make large waves. However, perhaps our even bigger calling, as Central's sages suggested, is for us adults to: develop individual and collective consciousness that vehemently objects to the victimization of children at the hands of organized institutionalization; recognize the positive and transformative influence our schools could have; work to identify and disrupt all gender based practices; challenge our tendencies to sextype; and let kids be themselves...individuals.

Schools, I believe, need to lead the way.

NOTES

[1] Madeline Grumet, *Bitter Milk: Women and Teaching*, 47.
[2] Jiddu Krishnamurti, *3rd Public Talk*, accessed November 14, 2014, http://www.jiddu-krishnamurti.net/en/1966/1966-11-05-jiddu-krishnamurti-3nd-public-talk.

191

³ Alternative school teachers are also empowered to set policy and make decisions about pedagogy, curriculum and administration. See: Freda Easton, "Educating the Whole Child, 'Head, Heart, and Hands': Learning from the Waldorf Experience," *Theory into Practice*, 36, no. 2 (Spring, 1997): 87–94.

⁴ Dana Bennis, "What is Democratic Education?" *Institute for Democratic Education in America*, accessed January 3, 2015, http://democraticeducation.org/index.php/features/what-is-democratic-education/

⁵ Isaac Graves, "What is Democratic Education? Sure, We Teach Democracy in our Schools—But We Need to Practice it There, Too," March 9, 2011, http://www.yesmagazine.org/happiness/what-is-democratic-education

⁶ Daniel Greenberg, "R-E-S-P-E-C-T: What Children Get in Democratic Schools," *Mothering Magazine*, 103 (2000): 66.

⁷ An espoused goal of education aligned with the philosophies of progressive educators like John Dewey, John Taylor Gatto, Paulo Freire, Ira Shor, Bill Ayers, and others.

⁸ See: The Circle School: http://circleschool.org/

⁹ American Montessori Society, "Introduction to Montessori," accessed January 3, 2015, http://amshq.org/Montessori-Education/Introduction-to-Montessori.

¹⁰ Carolyn Pope Edwards, "Three Approaches from Europe: Waldorf, Montessori, and Reggio Emilia," *Early Childhood Research and Practice*, 4, no. 1 (2002).

¹¹ Ibid. See also: Todd Oppenheimer, "Schooling the Imagination," *Atlantic Monthly*, 284, no. 3 (1999): 71–83.

¹² Mark Powell, "Gender Play and Good Governance," *Montessori Life*, no. 1 (2008): 26–29.

¹³ See: The New School: http://www.newschool.net/

¹⁴ The core curriculum integrates visual, musical, and tactile arts in all subject areas from preschool through high school.

¹⁵ Association of Waldorf Schools of North America, "Waldorf Education: An Introduction," accessed January 2, 2015, http://www.whywaldorfworks.org/02_w_education/

¹⁶ Iddo Oberski, "Rudolf Steiner's Philosophy of Freedom as a Basis for Spiritual Education?" *International Journal of Children's Spirituality*, 16, no. 1 (February 2011): 14.

¹⁷ Henry Barnes, "Learning That Grows with the Learner: An Introduction to Waldorf Education," *Educational Leadership*, 49, no. 2 (October 1991): 54.

¹⁸ See: Susquehanna Waldorf School: http://www.susquehannawaldorf.org/

¹⁹ Another notable factor that could help minimize strong stereotypical performances of masculinity and femininity is that Waldorf schools do not use computers and encourage parents to monitor the quantity and quality of screen time at home. Melissa reported, "I wondered why I had less issues at the Waldorf school, with boys and girls creating separate cultures, than I did as a public school teacher. And I think it is because from early on, we help families become mindful around

media." Waldorf students are subjected to fewer representations of stereotypical masculinity, femininity and heteronormativity.

[20] See, for example: Organization for Economic Co-operation and Development, "PISA 2012 Results in Focus: What 15-year-olds Know and What They Can Do With What They Know," OECD, (2014); Nordic Council of Ministers, "Gender Equality in the Nordic Countries," accessed January 3, 2015, http://www.norden.org/en/om-samarbejdet-1/areas-of-co-operation/gender-equality/gender-equality-in-the-nordic-countries; World Economic Forum, "The Global Gender Gap Report 2014," accessed January 3, 2015, http://reports.weforum.org/global-gender-gap-report-2014/

[21] République Française, "Increasing Action for Equality Between Girls and Boys in Schools," June 30, 2013, http://www.gouvernement.fr/en/increasing-action-for-equality-between-girls-and-boys-in-schools.

[22] Irena Barker, "Society – Could Equality be as Simple as ABCD?" *tesconnect,* October, 18, 2013, https://www.tes.co.uk/article.aspx?storycode=6367563.

[23] Parliamentary Assembly, "Obligatory Deconstruction of 'Gender Stereotypes' and Violation of Parents' Rights," June 4, 2013, http://assembly.coe.int/ASP/Doc/XrefViewPDF.asp?FileID=19774&Language=EN

[24] Ibid.

[25] République Française, "Increasing Action for Equality Between Girls and Boys in Schools."

[26] Irena Barker, "Society – Could Equality be as Simple as ABCD?"

[27] Ibid.

[28] Joshua Melvin, "Government Slammed for Equality Classes U-Turn," *The Local*, July 1, 2014, http://www.thelocal.fr/20140701/french-leaders-slammed-for-u-turn-on-equality

[29] We should work to understand childhood as a culture—rather than parceling out, and unnecessarily overemphasizing, "boyhood" and "girlhood" culture. Also, I think it is important to be clear here: there has been a plethora of empirical research that has demonstrated that boy and girl brains "are more similar than different, and these differences do not result in behavioral differences or preferences." Scott Richardson, "Blurred Lines of a Different Kind," 31. "Much of what we assume to be differences in the brain—distinctions that would cause boys and girls to relate differently or learn differently—are simply reflections of how parents unconsciously socialize their children about gender at an early age." Kate Lombardi, *The Mama's Boy Myth: Why Keeping Our Sons Close Makes Them Stronger* (New York, NY: Avery, 2010), 47. See also: Cordelia Fine, *Delusions of Gender;* Lise Eliot (2009). *Pink Brain, Blue Brain: How Small Differences Grow into Troublesome Gaps—and What We Can Do About It* (New York, NY: Houghton Mifflin Harcourt Publishing, 2009).

[30] For some insight on the problems of the male/female binary and reimagining gender, see: Bronwyn Davies, *Frogs, Tails and Feminist Tales: Pre-school*

Children and Gender (Sydney: AU, Allen and Unwin, 1989); Valerie Walkerdine, "Femininity as Performance," *Oxford Review of Education* 15, no. 3. (1989): 267–279; Allen James and Alan Prout eds., *Constructing and Reconstructing Childhood: Contemporary Issues in the Sociological Study of Childhood, 2nd ed.* (London, UK: The Falmer Press, 1998); Bronwyn Davies, *Shards of Glass: Children Reading and Writing Beyond Gendered Identities, Revised edition* (New York, NY: Hampton 2003); Valerie Walkerdine, *Schoolgirl Fictions* (London, UK: Verso, 1990); Alison Jones, "Becoming a 'Girl': Poststructuralist Suggestions for Educational Research," *Gender and Education* 5, no. 2 (1993): 157–167; Becky Francis "Discussing Discrimination: Children's Construction of Sexism Between Pupils in Primary School," *British Journal of Sociology of Education* 8, no. 4 (1997): 519–32; Peggy Ornstein, *Cinderella Ate My Daughter: Dispatches From the Front Lines of the New Girlie-Girl Culture* (New York: NY: HarperCollins, 2011); Elizabeth J. Meyer, *Gender and Sexual Diversity in Schools* (New York, NY: Springer, 2011). On adults, see also: Carol Queen and Lawrence Schimel, *Pomosexuals: Challenging Assumptions About Gender and Sexuality* (San Francisco, CA: Cleis Press, 1997); J. Jack Halberstam, *Gaga Feminism: Sex, Gender, and the End of Normal.* (Boston, MA: Beacon, 2012).

APPENDIX A

Fisk Elementary: Faculty, Staff, and Administration

Principal	Sam Borders		
Assistant Principal	Rob Drake		
K Teachers	Michelle North	Lora Robinson	Anne Sprenkle
1st Grade Teachers	Suzanne Chase	Emma Jones	Emma Rhodes
2nd Grade Teachers	Mary Fox	Sandra Major	Jo Singleton
3rd Grade Teachers	Joyce Arango	Lori Greene	Norma Reeve
4th Grade Teachers	Annie Breshears	James Holland	Jessie Malloy
5th Grade Teachers	Lilly Koch	Allen Reif	Karen Wilson
P.E. Teacher	Michael Louie		
Art Teacher	Nora Cummings		
Music Teacher	Kathryn Bell		
Librarian	Maryann Rozek		
21st Century Teacher	Tracey Dye		
Special Ed. Teachers	Lena Han	Denise Hauck	
ESL Teacher (part-time)	Julissa Hill		
Reading Coach	Brianne Flanagan		
Guidance Counselor	Becky Lanzalotto		
Secretaries	Karen Arcinega	Joan Moreno	

APPENDIX B

Sample: Time Study

Time studies collected the frequency and duration of interactions/ attention given to students. Each time study was conducted in tandem with another researcher collecting data using our negotiated observation tool. This allowed us to cross-reference/analyze our data for quality and type of interaction/attention.

SAMPLE – 1ST GRADE MATH LESSON

Teacher = M2OMx		MATH – 10:30 a.m.

1st Grade: 10 boys, 9 girls

Key: B - Boy; G-Girl;

A - All; N - Nobody

Instructional Grouping	Time (sec)	B/G/ A/N	Notes
vocabulary whole group	0	A	showing video of new vocab words
	11	G	shallow - "how'd you like that music?"
	16	A	
	21	B	
	26	B	
	34	G	
	41	G	
	56	B	
	107	A	video
	217	G	girl put up hand before teacher asked ? - could predict a ?
	232	A	

307	G	reprimand
310	G	Yes/No ?
315	A	
339	B	? requiring explanation
343	B	? requiring explanation
352	B	? requiring explanation
410	B	? requiring explanation
418	B	reprimand
420	A	
439	b	
444	a	
510	g	Clarification
525	a	
553	b	
556	g	g making eye contact entire lesson
559	b	
604	a	
614	g	
620	a	
632	b	
700	g	
702	a	
705	a	brain break - "shake break" youtub another video (superhero male providing vocab words "Mr. Phone Home")
921	a	
1040	g	
1044	g	
1054	b	
1102	b	
1115	b	"Nathan, did you forget?"
1131	g	turns to g for correct response
1139	g	

	1147	g	
	1154	g	
	1202	a	video
	1311	g	
	1317	b	
	1321	a	
	1349	b	waited for his processing
	1358	a	
	1421	g	
	1511	g	descriptive/details
	1531	a	
	1539	g	did not wait for processing, opened up to whole class
	1545	a	
	1547	g	
	1548	g	
	1551	g	
	1553	b	reprimand
	1554	a	
	1632	b	reprimand
	1634	a	
new kids: ratio 8b; bg	1749	b	
independent work	1824	n	
	1906	b	
	1923	b	
	1938	g	girl was able to interrupt teacher only for 2 sec., rt to seat
	1940	b	
	1957	n	
	2009	a	
	2014	n	looking at lesson plans
	2026	g	

	2028	n	
	2036	b	repeated directions
	2044	b	
	2058	b	asked for a deeper interprtation
	2124	n	
	2209	b	
	2221	b	
	2237	a	
whole group	2304	g	t asked ?
	2313	a	
	2322	b	abt baseball
	2327	a	
	2334	b	
	2341	b	
	2344	g	
	2349	g	
	2351	b	
	2352	b&g	
	2354	b	
	2357	b	
	2410	g	
	2417	a	
small group/indep work	2517	g	split kids up randomly "eenie, meenie.."
	2741	b	what is stamina?
	2749	b	how will we have stamina (behavioral expectations)
	2812	a	
	2909	b	
	2914	b	
	2931	n	
	3023	b	girls watch boys getting attention, but don't bother interrupting

	3029	b	
	3034	b	
	3039	n	
	3045	b	
	3951	n	
	3113	b	
	3127	b	
	3140	n	
	3353	b	
	3357	n	
	3419	b	
	3426	b	
	3441	n	
	3604	b	
	3627	n	
			raised hand, teacher answered ?
	3631	g	quickly
	3636	n	
	3810	b	
	3819	n	
	3854	b	
whole group on carpet	3917	a	
	3930	n	
	4220	g	
	4232	g	G initiated
	4244	a	
small group/ independent work at desk	4256	n	
	4414	b	T initiated
	4650	b	T initiated
	4654	b	T initiated

4700	g	G initiated
4704	b	
4709	n	
4737	g	
4741	n	
4749	b	
4803	b	
4810	a	
4911	a	
4933	b	"hands…hand sanitizer, buddy" - picking his nose
4937	a	
5001	end	

APPENDIX C

Time Studies: Averages

1ˢᵗ Grade Math

Total Observations = 5
Avg. time per observation = 2723 seconds (approximately 45 minutes)
Avg. ratio = boys : girls = 1 : 1.04

Average Time Spent Giving Attention During Large Group Instruction
Boys: 45 interactions lasting 522 sec. total = 11.6 sec. average/interaction
Girls: 51 interactions lasting 553 sec. total =10.84 sec. average/interaction

Average Time Spent Giving Attention During Independent/Small Group Work
Boys: 22 interactions lasting 489 sec. total = 22.23 sec. average/interaction
Girls: 12 interactions lasting 60 sec. total = 5 sec. average/interaction

1ˢᵗ Grade Language Arts

Total Observations = 5
Avg. time per observation 3012 seconds (approximately 50 minutes)
Avg. ratio = boys : girls = 1 : 1.07

Average Time Spent Giving Attention During Large Group Instruction
Boys: 55 interactions lasting 623 sec. total = 11.32 sec. average/interaction
Girls: 57 interactions lasting 617 sec. total =10.82 sec. average/interaction

Average Time Spent Giving Attention During Independent/Small Group Work
Boys: 27 interactions lasting 530 sec. total = 22.23 sec. average/interaction
Girls: 18 interactions lasting 112 sec. total = 6.22 sec. average/interaction

2ⁿᵈ Grade Math

Total Observations = 5
Avg. time per observation 2630 seconds (approximately 44 minutes)
Avg. ratio = boys : girls = 1 : 1.12

Average Time Spent Giving Attention During Large Group Instruction
Boys: 28 interactions lasting 298 sec. total = 10.64 sec. average/interaction
Girls: 26 interactions lasting 303 sec. total =11.65 sec. average/interaction

Average Time Spent Giving Attention During Independent/Small Group Work
Boys: 20 interactions lasting 694 sec. total = 34.7 sec. average/interaction
Girls: 8 interactions lasting 144 sec. total = 18 sec. average/interaction

---

2nd Grade Language Arts

Total Observations = 5
Avg. time per observation 3290 seconds (approximately 55 minutes)
Avg. ratio = boys : girls = 1 : 1.06

Average Time Spent Giving Attention During Large Group Instruction
Boys: 35 interactions lasting 330 sec. total = 9.42 sec. average/interaction
Girls: 39 interactions lasting 341 sec. total = 8.74 sec. average/interaction

Average Time Spent Giving Attention During Independent/Small Group Work
Boys: 67 interactions lasting 1,809 sec. total = 27 sec. average/interaction
Girls: 24 interactions lasting 342 sec. total = 14.25 sec. average/interaction

---

3rd Grade Math

Total Observations = 5
Avg. time per observation 2978 seconds (approximately 50 minutes)
Avg. ratio = boys : girls = 1 : 1.05

Average Time Spent Giving Attention During Large Group Instruction
Boys: 32 interactions lasting 307 sec. total = 9.59 sec. average/interaction
Girls: 33 interactions lasting 321 sec. total = 9.73 sec. average/interaction

Average Time Spent Giving Attention During Independent/Small Group Work
Boys: 21 interactions lasting 799 sec. total = 38.05 sec. average/interaction
Girls: 15 interactions lasting 261 sec. total = 17.4 sec. average/interaction

---

3rd Grade Language Arts

Total Observations = 5
Avg. time per observation 3329 seconds (approximately 55 minutes)
Avg. ratio = boys : girls = 1 : 1.02

Average Time Spent Giving Attention During Large Group Instruction
Boys: 34 interactions lasting 286 sec. total = 8.41 sec. average/interaction
Girls: 34 interactions lasting 244 sec. total = 7.18 sec. average/interaction

Average Time Spent Giving Attention During Independent/Small Group Work
Boys: 68 interactions lasting 1,916 sec. total = 28.66 sec. average/interaction
Girls: 37 interactions lasting 560 sec. total = 15.14 sec. average/interaction

4th Grade Math

Total Observations = 5
Avg. time per observation 2102 seconds (approximately 35 minutes)
Avg. ratio = boys : girls = 1 : 1.04

Average Time Spent Giving Attention During Large Group Instruction
Boys: 19 interactions lasting 119 sec. total = 6.26 sec. average/interaction
Girls: 22 interactions lasting 134 sec. total = 6.21 sec. average/interaction

Average Time Spent Giving Attention During Independent/Small Group Work
Boys: 18 interactions lasting 591 sec. total = 32.83 sec. average/interaction
Girls: 10 interactions lasting 173 sec. total = 17.3 sec. average/interaction

4th Grade Language Arts

Total Observations = 5
Avg. time per observation 3206 seconds (approximately 53 minutes)
Avg. ratio = boys : girls = 1 : 1.04

Average Time Spent Giving Attention During Large Group Instruction
Boys: 28 interactions lasting 206 sec. total = 7.36 sec. average/interaction
Girls: 30 interactions lasting 222 sec. total = 7.4 sec. average/interaction

Average Time Spent Giving Attention During Independent/Small Group Work
Boys: 54 interactions lasting 1,178 sec. total = 21.81 sec. average/interaction
Girls: 27 interactions lasting 371 sec. total = 13.74 sec. average/interaction

5th Grade Math

Total Observations = 5
Avg. time per observation 2948 seconds (approximately 49 minutes)
Avg. ratio = boys : girls = 1 : 1.08

Average Time Spent Giving Attention During Large Group Instruction
Boys: 27 interactions lasting 211 sec. total = 7.81 sec. average/interaction
Girls: 26 interactions lasting 159 sec. total = 6.11 sec. average/interaction

Average Time Spent Giving Attention During Independent/Small Group Work
Boys: 28 interactions lasting 759 sec. total = 27.11 sec. average/interaction
Girls: 18 interactions lasting 263 sec. total = 14.61 sec. average/interaction

5th Grade Language Arts
Total Observations = 5 Avg. time per observation 3001 seconds (approximately 50 minutes) Avg. ratio = boys : girls = 1 : 1.05 *Average Time Spent Giving Attention During Large Group Instruction* Boys: 20 interactions lasting 150 sec. total = 7.5 sec. average/interaction Girls: 22 interactions lasting 174 sec. total = 7.91 sec. average/interaction *Average Time Spent Giving Attention During Independent/Small Group Work* Boys: 39 interactions lasting 756 sec. total = 19.38 sec. average/interaction Girls: 22 interactions lasting 271 sec. total = 12.32 sec. average/interaction

BIBLIOGRAPHY

Adams, Glenn, Donna M. Garcia, Valeria Purdie-Vaughns and Claude M. Steele. "The Detrimental Effects of a Suggestion of Sexism in an Instruction Situation." *Journal of Experimental Social Psychology*, 42, no. 5 (2006): 602–615.

Adams, William and Sasha Baron Cohen. *I Like to Move It*. By Erick Morillo and Mark Quashie for "Madagascar." Dreamworks, 2005.

Adichie, Chimamanda Ngozi. "We Should All be Feminists." Presented at TEDxEuston, December, 2012.

Ali, Suki. "To be a 'Girl': Culture and Class in Schools." *Gender and Education* 15, no. 3 (September, 2003): 165–182.

American Montessori Society. "Introduction to Montessori," accessed January 3, 2015, http://amshq.org/Montessori-Education/Introduction-to-Montessori.

Ashley, Martin and John Lee. *Women Teaching Boys: Caring and Working in the Primary School.* Saffordshire: Trentham Books, 2003.

Association of Waldorf Schools of North America. "Waldorf Education: An Introduction," accessed January 2, 2015, http://www.whywaldorfworks.org/02_w_education/

Barker, Irena. "Society – Could Equality be as Simple as ABCD?" *tesconnect.* October, 18, 2013, https://www.tes.co.uk/article.aspx?storycode=6367563

Bartkowski, John R. *Remaking the Godly Marriage: Gender Negotiation in Evangelical Families.* New Brunswick, NJ: Rutgers University Press, 2001.

Bartkowski, John and Xu Xiaohe, "Religion and Family Values Reconsidered: Gender Traditionalism Among Conservative Protestants." In *Religion, Familes, and Health: Population-Based Research in the United States*, edited by Christopher G. Ellison and Robert A. Hummer. New Brunswick, NJ: Rutgers University Press, 2010.

Barnes, Henry. "Learning That Grows with the Learner: An Introduction to Waldorf Education." *Educational Leadership*, 49, no. 2 (October 1991): 54.

Bennis, Dana. "What is Democratic Education?" *Institute for Democratic Education in America,* accessed January 3, 2015, http://democraticeducation.org/index.php/features/what-is-democratic-education/

Biblarz, Timothy J. and Judith Stacey. "(How) Does the Sexual Orientation of Parents Matter?" *American Sociological Review*, 66, no. 2 (Apr., 2001): 159–183.

Bigler, Audrey. "On Language: You Guys." In *Bitchfest: Ten Years of Cultural Criticism from the Pages of Bitch Magazine*, edited by Lisa Jervis and Andi Zeisler, 76–80. New York, NY: Farrar, Straus and Giroux, 2006.

Blacker, David J. *Dying to Teach: The Educators Search for Immortality.* New York, NY: Teachers College Press, 1997.

Bricheno, Patricia and Mary Thorton. "Role Model, Hero, or Champion?: Children's Views Concerning Role Models." *Educational Research,* 49 , no. 4 (2007): 383–396.

Bridges, Ruby. "Untitled," Paper presented at the MLK Day Celebration Keynote Address, Millersville, Pennsylvania, February 6, 2013.

Butler, Judith. *Gender Trouble: Feminism and the Subversion of Identity.* New York, NY: Routledge, 2006.

Carrington, Bruce, Peter Tymms and Christine Merrell. "Role Models, School Improvement and the 'Gender Gap'—Do Men Bring Out the Best in Boys and Women the Best in Girls?" *British Educational Research Journal*, 34, no. 3 (2008): 315–327.

Chase, Sarah A. *Perfectly Prep: Gender Extremes at a New England Prep School.* New York, NY: Oxford University Press; 2008.

Clandinin, D. Jean. "Mapping a Landscape of Narrative Inquiry." In *Handbook of Narrative Inquiry: Mapping a Methodology,* edited by D. Jean Clandinin, 35–77. Thousand Oaks, CA: Sage, 2007.

Clandinin, D. Jean and F. Michael Connelly. *Narrative Inquiry Experience and Story in Qualitative Research.* San Francisco, CA: Josey-Bass, 2000.

Collins, Patricia Hill. "Toward a New Vision: Race, Class, and Gender as Categories of Analysis and Connection." In *Privilege: A Reader,* edited by Michael Kimmel and Abby Ferber, 233–250. Boulder, CO: Westview Press, 2010.

Connell, R. W. *Masculinities.* Berkeley, CA: University of California Press, 1995.

Crosby, Bing. *You Must Have Been a Beautiful Baby.* By Harry Warren and Johnny Mercer, 1938, Record.

Danaher, Kelly and Christen S. Crandall. "Stereotype Threat in Applied Settings Re-examined." *Journal of Applied Social Psychology*, 38, no. 6 (2008): 1639–1655.

Davies, Bronwyn. *Frogs, Tails and Feminist Tales: Pre-school Children and Gender.* Sydney: AU, Allen and Unwin, 1989.

———— *Shards of Glass: Children Reading and Writing Beyond Gendered Identities, Revised edition.* New York, NY: Hampton 2003.

Davies, Paul G., Steven J. Spencer, Diane M. Quinn and Rebecca Gerhardstein. "Consuming Images: Howe Television Commercials that Elicit Stereotype Threat Can Restrain Women Academically and Professionally." *Personality and Social Psychgology Bulletin*, 28, no. 12 (2002): 1615–1628.

Driessen, Geert. "The Feminization of Primary Education: Effects of Teachers' Sex on Pupil Achievement, Attitudes and Behavior." *Review of Education*, 53 (2007): 183–203.

Dewey, John. *Experience and Education.* New York, NY: Touchstone, 1938.

Easton, Freda. "Educating the Whole Child, 'Head, Heart, and Hands': Learning From the Waldorf Experience." *Theory into Practice* 36, no. 2 (Spring, 1997): 87–94.

Eckert, Penelope. *Jocks & Burnouts: Social Categories and Identity in the High School.* New York, NY: Teachers College Press, 1989.

Edwards, Carolyn Pope. "Three Approaches from Europe: Waldorf, Montessori, and Reggio Emilia." *Early Childhood Research and Practice*, 4, no. 1 (2002).

Eliot, Lise. *Pink Brain, Blue Brain: How Small Differences Grow into Troublesome Gaps—and What We Can Do About It.* New York, NY: Houghton Mifflin Harcourt Publishing, 2009.

Esco, Lina, Hunter Richards and Sarabeth Stroller. *Free the Nipple.* Directed by Lina Esco. Paris, France: Bethsabee Mucho, 2014. Film.

Fine, Cordelia. *Delusions of Gender: How Our Minds, Society, and Neurosexism Create Difference.* New York, NY: W. W. Norton & Company, 2010.

Flanagan, Caitlin. *Girl Land.* New York, NY: Little, Brown and Company, 2012.

Fletcher, Ralph. *Guy-Write: What Every Guy Writer Needs to Know.* New York, NY: Square Fish, 2014.

Francis, Becky. "Discussing Discrimination: Children's Construction of Sexism Between Pupils in Primary School." *British Journal of Sociology of Education* 8, no. 4 (1997): 519–32.

Francis, Becky and Christine Skelton. *Reassessing Gender and Achievement: Questioning Contemporary Key Debates.* New York, NY: Routledge, 2005.

Freire, Paulo. *Pedagogy of the Oppressed.* New York, NY: Continuum, 1986.

"Girls on the Run." Girls on the Run. Accessed October 4, 2014, GirlsOnTheRun.com

GLSEN. "The 2013 National School Climate Survey." Accessed November 20, 2014, http://www.glsen.org/sites/default/files/NSCS_ExecSumm_2013_DESIGN_FINAL.pdf

Good, Catherine, Joshua Aronson and Jayne Ann Harder. "Problems in the Pipeline: Stereotype Threat and Women's Achievement in High-Level Math Courses." *Journal of Developmental Psychology* 24, no. 6 (2008): 17–28.

Graves, Isaac. "What is Democratic Education? Sure, We Teach Democracy in our Schools—But We Need to Practice it There, Too," March 9, 2011, http://www.yesmagazine.org/happiness/what-is-democratic-education

Greenberg, Daniel. "R-E-S-P-E-C-T: What Children Get in Democratic Schools." *Mothering Magazine*, 103 (2000): 66.

Grumet, Madeline. *Bitter Milk: Women and Teaching.* Amherst, MA: University of Massachusetts, 1988.

Halberstam, Judith. *Female Masculinity.* Durham, NC: Duke University Press, 1998.

Halberstam, J. Jack. *Gaga Feminism: Sex, Gender, and the End of Normal.* Boston, MA: Beacon, 2012.

Hale, Shannon. *Princess Academy: Palace of Stone.* New York, NY: Bloomsbury, 2012.

Hey, Valerie. *The Company She Keeps: An Ethnography of Girls' Friendships.* Buckingham, UK: Open University Press, 2003.

Hickling-Hudson, Anne R. and Roberta Ahlquist. "Contesting the Curriculum in the Schooling of Indigenous Children in Australia and the United States: From Eurocentrism to Culturally Powerful Pedagogies." *Comparative Education Review* 47, no. 1 (2003): 64–89.

Hoffman, John P. and John P. Bartowski. "Sex, Religious Tradition, and Biblical Literalism." *Social Forces* 86, no. 3 (2008): 1245–1272.

hooks, bell. *Ain't I A Woman: Black Women and Feminism.* Boston, MA: South End Press, 1981.

——— *The Will to Change: Men, Masculinity, and Love.* New York, NY: Harper, 2004.

Inzlicht, Michael and Talia Ben-Zeev. "A Threatening Intellectual Environment: Why Females are Susceptible to Experiencing Problem-Solving Deficits in the presence of Males." *Psychological Science*, 11, no. 5 (2000): 365–371.

Jagose, Annamarie. *Queer Theory: An Introduction.* New York: New York University Press, 1996.

James, Allen and Alan Prout editors. *Constructing and Reconstructing Childhood: Contemporary Issues in the Sociological Study of Childhood, 2nd edition.* London, UK: The Falmer Press, 1998.

Jones, Alison. "Becoming a 'Girl': Poststructuralist Suggestions for Educational Research." *Gender and Education* 5, no. 2 (1993): 157–167.

Jones, Diane, Jodi Newman, and Sheena Bautista. "A Three-Factor Model of Teasing: The Influence of Friendship, Gender, and Topic on Expected Emotional Reactions to Teasing During Early Adolescence." *Social Development* 14, no. 3 (2005): 421–439.

Keltner, Dacher, Lisa Capps, Ann M. Kring, Randall C. Young, and Erin A. Heerey. "Just Teasing: A Conceptual Analysis and Empirical Review." *Psychological Bulletin* 127, no. 2 (2001): 229–248.

Kendall, Diana. "Class: Still Alive and Reproducing in the United States." In *Privilege: A Reader,* edited by Michael S. Kimmel and Abby L. Ferber, 145-152. Boulder, CO: Westview Press, 2010.

Kidder, Tracey. *Among School.* Boston, MA: Houghton Mifflin Harcourt, 1989.

Kiesling, Scott Fabius. "Homosocial Desire in Men's Talk: Balancing and Re-creating Cultural Discourses of Masculinity." *Language in Society* 34, no. 5. (November, 2005): 695–726.

Kimmel, Michael. *Angry White Men: American Masculinity at the End of an Era.* New York, NY: Nation Books.

———— *Manhood in America: A Cultural History.* Washington, DC: 1996.

———— *Misframing Men: The Politics of Contemporary Masculinities.* New Brunswick, NJ: Rutgers University Press, 2010.

———— "Solving the 'Boy Crisis' in Schools." *Huff Post Parents.* Accessed November 20, 2014, http://www.huffingtonpost.com/michael-kimmel/solving-the-boy-crisis-in_b_3126379.html

———— *The Politics of Manhood.* Philadelphia, PA: Temple University Press, 1995.

Kleinfeld, Judith and Suzanne Yerian. *Gender Tales: Tensions in the Schools.* New York, NY: St. Martin's Press, 1995.

Knowles-Carter, Beyoncé. *Flawless.* With Terius Nash, Chauncey Hollis and Rey Reel. March, 2013 by Columbia, digital release.

Kohn, Alfie. "Fighting the Tests: A Practical Guide to Rescuing Our Schools." *Phi Delta Kappan* 82, no. 5. (January, 2001): 349–357.

Krishnamurti, Jiddu. *3rd Public Talk.* Accessed November 14, 2014, http://www.jiddu-krishnamurti.net/en/1966/1966-11-05-jiddu-krishnamurti-3nd-public-talk.

Ladson-Billings, Gloria. "Toward a Theory of Culturally Relevant Pedagogy." *American Educational Research Journal* 32, no. 3. (Fall, 1995): 465–491.

Lahelma, Elina. "Lack of Male Teachers: A Problem for Students or Teachers?" *Pedagogy, Culture & Society*, 8, no. 2 (Dec. 2006): 173–185.

Lampert, Martin D. and Susan M. Ervin-Tripp. "Structured Coding for the Study of Language and Social Interaction." In *Talking Data:*

Transcription and Coding in Discourse Research, edited by Jane Edwards and Martin Lampert, 169-206. Hillsdale, NJ: Lawrence Erlbaum Associates, 1993.

Land, Deborah. "Teasing Apart Secondary Students' Conceptualizations of Peer Teasing, Bullying and Sexual Harassment." *School Psychology International* 24, no. 2 (2003): 147–165.

Logel, Christine, Gregory M. Walton, Steven J. Spencer, Emma C. Isserman, William W. von Hippel, and Amy Bell. "Interacting with Sexist Men Triggers Social Identity Threat Among Female Engineers." *Journal of Personality and Social* Psychology, 96, no. 6 (2009): 1089–1103.

Lombardi, Kate. *The Mama's Boy Myth: Why Keeping Our Sons Close Makes Them Stronger.* New York, NY: Avery, 2010.

Lowen, Cynthia and Lee Hirsch. *Bully* Directed by Lee Hirsch. New York, NY: The Bully Project, 2012.

Mac an Ghaill, Mairtin. *The Making of Men.* Buckingham: Open University Press, 1994.

Marston, Susan H. "Why Do They Teach? A Comparison of Elementary, High School, and College Teachers." *Education* 131, no. 2 (2010): 437–454.

Martin, Andrew J. and Herb W. Marsh. "Motivating Boys and Motivating Girls: Does Teacher Gender Really Matter?" *Australian Journal of Education*, 49, no. 3 (2005): 320–334.

Martino, Wayne. "Cool Boys, Party Animals, Squids and Poofters: Interrogating the Dynamics and Politics of Adolescent Masculinities in School." *The British Journal of the Sociology of Education*, 20, no. 2 (1999): 239–263.

Mee, Molly, Heather Haverback and Jeff Passe. "For the Love of the Middle: A Glimpse Into Why One Group of Preservice Teachers Chose Middle Grades Education." *Middle Grades Research Journal* 7, no. 4 (2012): 1–14.

Meiners, Erica, "Remember When All the Cars Were Fords and All the Lesbians Were Women? Some Notes on Identity, Mobility, and Capital." In *Queer Theory in Education*, ed. William F. Pinar, 121–141. (Mahwah, NJ: Lawrence Erlbaum Associates, INc., 1998).

Melvin, Joshua. "Government Slammed for Equality Classes U-Turn." *The Local*, July 1, 2014, http://www.thelocal.fr/20140701/french-leaders-slammed-for-u-turn-on-equality

Messner, Michael A. "Barbie Girls Versus Sea Monsters: Children Constructing Gender." *Gender & Society* 14, no. 6 (December, 2000): 765–784.

———— "Gender Ideologies, Youth Sports, and the Production of Soft Essentialism." *Sociology of Sport Journal* 28, no. 2 (June, 2011): 151–170.

Meyer, Elizabeth J. *Gender and Sexual Diversity in Schools.* New York, NY: Springer, 2011.

Minaj, Nicki. *Anaconda.* 2014 by Young Money Entertainment, Cash Money Records and Republic Records, CD.

Murnane, Richard, J. and Stephen L. Hoffman. "Graduations on the Rise," *Education Next* (Fall, 2013); 59–65.

Musen, Paul. "Early Sex-Role Development." In *Handbook on Socialization Theory and Research,* edited by David A. Goslin. Chicago, IL: Rand McNally and Co., 1965.

National Center for Education Statistics. "Degrees Conferred by Sex and Race." *Institute of Education Sciences*. Accessed December 10, 2014, http://nces.ed.gov/fastfacts/display.asp?id=72

National Center for Education Statistics. "Public High School Four-Year On-Time Graduation Rates and Event Dropout Rates: School Years 2010-11 and 2011-12." *Institute of Education Sciences.* Accessed December 10, 2014, http://nces.ed.gov/pubsearch/pubsinfo.asp?pubid=2014391

National Committee on Pay Equity. "Wage Gap Narrows Slightly but Statistically Unchanged." *National Committee on Pay Equity.* Accessed December 14, 2014, http://www.pay-equity.org/

Niccol, Andrew. *The Truman Show.* Directed by Peter Weir. Universal City, CA: Universal Studios, 1998.

Nissley, Charles, Ella West and Madison Grey. "*Queer* on Campus," *Vitae Scholasticae* 30, no. 2 (2013): 66–89.

Noddings, Nel. *The Challenge to Care in Schools: An Alternative Approach to Education.* New York, NY: Teachers College Press, 2005.

Nordic Council of Ministers. "Gender Equality in the Nordic Countries," accessed January 3, 2015, http://www.norden.org/en/om-samarbejdet-1/areas-of-co-operation/gender-equality/gender-equality-in-the-nordic-countries.

Oberski, Iddo. "Rudolf Steiner's Philosophy of Freedom as a Basis for Spiritual Education?" *International Journal of Children's Spirituality*, 16, no. 1 (February 2011): 14.

Oppenheimer, Todd. "Schooling the Imagination." *Atlantic Monthly*, 284, no. 3 (1999): 71–83.

Organization for Economic Co-operation and Development. "PISA 2012 Results in Focus: What 15-year-olds Know and What They Can Do With What They Know," OECD, (2014).

Ornstein, Peggy. *Cinderella Ate My Daughter: Dispatches From the Front Lines of the New Girlie-Girl Culture.* New York: NY: Harper Collins, 2011.

———— *Schoolgirls: Young Women, Self-Esteem, and the Confidence Gap.* New York, NY: Anchor Books, 1994.

Parliamentary Assembly. "Obligatory Deconstruction of 'Gender Stereotypes' and Violation of Parents' Rights." June 4, 2013, http://assembly.coe.int/ASP/Doc/XrefViewPDF.asp?FileID=19774&Language=EN

Pascoe, C. J. *Dude You're a Fag: Masculinity and Sexuality in High School.* Berkeley, CA: University of California Press, 2007.

Peek, Charles W., George D. Lowe, and Susan L. Williams. "Gender and God's Word: Another Look at Religious Fundamentalism and Sexism." *Social Forces* 69, no. 4 (1991): 1205–1221.

Pinar, William F. *Educational Experience as Lived: Knowledge, History, Alterity.* New York, NY: Routledge, 2015.

———— *What is Curriculum Theory? 2nd Edition.* New York, NY: Routledge, 2011.

Pinar, William F., William M. Reynolds, Patrick Slattery and Peter M. Taubman. *Understanding Curriculum.* New York, NY: Peter Lang, 2004.

Powell, Mark. "Gender Play and Good Governance." *Montessori Life*, no. 1 (2008): 26–29.

Prima, Louis. *Jump, Jive and Wail*. 1956, record. Quart, Alissa. "The Age of Hipster Sexism." *The Cut*. Accessed November 24, 2014, http://nymag.com/thecut/2012/10/age-of-hipster-sexism.html.

Queen, Carol and Lawrence Schimel. *Pomosexuals: Challenging Assumptions About Gender and Sexuality*. San Francisco, CA: Cleis Press, 1997.

Radcliffe, Rich A. and Thomas F. Mandeville. "Teacher Preferences for Middle Grades: Insights into Attracting Teacher Candidates." *The Clearing House: A Journal of Educational Strategies, Issues and Ideas* 80, no. 6 (2007): 261–266.

Reay, Diane. "The Paradox of Contemporary Femininities in Education: Combining Fluidity with Fixity." In *Investigating Gender,* edited by Becky Francis and Christine.

Renold, Emma. *Girls, Boys and Junior Sexualities: Exploring Children's Gender and Sexual Relations in the Primary School*. New York, NY: Routledge, 2005.

——— "'Square-girls', Femininity and the Negotiation of Academic Success in the Primary School." *British Education Research Journal* 27, no. 5 (2001): 577–588.

Renold, Emma and Alexandra Allan, "Bright and Beautiful: High Achieving Girls, Ambivalent Femininities, and the Feminization of Success in the Primary School," *Discourse: Studies in the Cultural Politics of Education* 27, no. 4. (December, 2006).

République Française. "Increasing Action for Equality Between Girls and Boys in Schools." June 30, 2004, http://www.gouvernement.fr/en/increasing-action-for-equality-between-girls-and-boys-in-schools

Richardson, Scott. "Blurred Lines of a Different Kind: Sex, Media and Kids." In *Gender & Pop Culture: A Text-Reader*, edited by Adrienne Trier-Bieniek and Patricia Leavy, 27–52. Boston, MA: Sense Publishers, 2014.

——— *eleMENtary School: (Hyper)Masculinity in a Feminized Context*. Boston, MA: Sense Publishers, 2012.

——— "Girls on the Run: When Efforts to 'Empower' Girls Go Wrong." *Sociological Images: Inspiring Sociological*

Imaginations Everywhere. Accessed November 20, 2014, http://thesocietypages.org/socimages/2014/07/30/girls-deserve-better-than-girls-on-the-run/

Ridgeway, Cecilia L., "Framed Before We Know It: How Gender Shapes Social Relations." *Gender & Society* 23 (2009): 145–160.

Rosin, Hanna. *The End of Men and the Rise of Women.* New York, NY: Riverhead, 2012.

Ruffner, Cristina L. and Emily C. Graybill. "Teachers' Perceptions of Teasing in Schools." *Journal of School Violence* 9, no. 2 (2010): 2–22.

Sadker, Myra and David Sadker. *Failing at Fairness: How Our Schools Cheat Girls.* New York, NY: Touchstone.

Schmidt, Amy. *Dog-Gone School.* New York, NY: Random House, 2013.

Sears, Pauline and David Feldman. "Teacher Interactions with Boys and With Girls." In *And Jill Came Tumbling After: Sexism in American Education,* edited by Judith Stacey, 147–158. New York, NY: Dell, 1974.

Shelton, Blake, Pistol Annies and Friends. *Boys 'Round Here.* By Rhett Akins, Dallas Davidson and Craig Wiseman. March 26, 2013 by Warner Bros., digital release.

Shih, Margaret J., Todd L. Pittinsky, and Geoffrey C. Ho. "Stereotype Boost: Positive Outcomes from the Activation of Positive Stereotypes." In *Stereotype Threat: Theory, Process, and Application,* edited by Michael Inzlicht and Toni Schmader, 141–156. New York, NY: Oxford University Press, 2011, 141–158.

Sigelman, Carol K. and Elizabeth A. Rider. *Life-Span: Human Development.* Belmont, CA: Wadsworth, 2011.

Sizer, Theodore R. *Horace's Compromise: The Dilemma of the American High School.* Boston, MA: Mariner Books; 1984.

Skelton, Christine. *Schooling the Boys.* Buckingham: Open University Press, 2001.

Sokal, Laura and Herb Katz. "Effects of Technology and Male Teachers on Boys' Reading." *Australian Journal of Education,* 52, no. 1 (2008): 81–94.

217

Soslau, Elizabeth. "Opportunities to Develop Adaptive Teaching Expertise During Supervisory Conferences." *Teaching and Teacher Education*, 28, no. 5 (July 2012): 768–779.

Stake, Robert E. "Case Studies." In *The Handbook of Qualitative Research, 2ⁿᵈ Edition,* edited by Norman K. Denzin and Yvonna S. Lincoln, 435-454. Thousand Oaks, CA: Sage, 2000.

Stetsenko, Anna, Todd D. Little, Tamara Gordeeva, Matthias Grasshof and Gabriele Oettingen. "Gender Effects in Children's Beliefs about School Performance: A Cross-Cultural Study." *Child Development* 71, no. 2. (March/April, 2000): 517–527.

Summers, Christina Hoff. *The War Against Boys: How Misguided Feminism Is Harming Our Young Men.* New York, NY: Simon & Schuster, 2000.

"The International Baccalaureate," accessed November 25, 2014, http://www.ibo.org/

Thorne, Barrie. *Gender Play: Girls and Boys in School.* New Brunswick, NJ: Rutgers University Press; 1993.

Tobin, Joseph, Yeh Hsueh and Mayumi Karasawa. *Preschool in Three Cultures Revisited: China, Japan, and the United States.* Chicago, IL: The University of Chicago Press, 2009.

Tolman, Deborah L. *Dilemmas of Desire: Teenage Girls Talk about Sexuality.* Cambridge, MA: Harvard University Press, 2005.

Traywick, Catherine. "Beyoncé's New Album Got FP Global Thinker Chimamanda Adichie All Wrong." *Foreign Policy.* (December 13, 2013).

Tyack, David and Elizabeth Hansot. *Learning Together: A History of Coeducation in American Public Schools.* New Haven, CT: Yale University Press, 1990.

U.S. Census Bureau. "Degrees Earned by Level and Sex: 1960 to 2009." *Statistical Abstract of the United States.* Accessed December 10m, 2014, https://www.census.gov/compendia/statab/2012/tables/12s0299.pdf.

Viefhues-Bailey, Ludger H. *Gender, Theory, and Religion.* New York, NY: Columbia University Press, 2010.

Walkerdine, Valerie. "Femininity as Performance." *Oxford Review of Education* 15, no. 3. (1989): 267–279.

Walkerdine, Valerie. *Schoolgirl Fictions.* London, UK: Verso, 1990.

Walkerdine, Valerie, Helen Lucey, and June Melody. *Growing Up Girl: Psycho-Social Explorations of Gender and Class.* London, UK: Macmillian, 2001.

Warrington, Molly and Michael Younger. "The Other Side of the Gender Gap." *Gender and Education,* 12, no. 4 (2000): p. 493–507.

Weis, Lois. *Class, Race, & Gender in American Education.* New York, NY: SUNY Press, 1988.

Wepner, Shelley B., JoAnne G. Ferrara, Kristin N. Rainville, Diane W. Gomez, Diane E. Lang, and Laura A. Bigouette. *Changing Suburbs, Changing Students: Helping School Leaders Face the Challenges.* Thousand Oaks, CA: Corwin, 2012.

World Economic Forum. "The Global Gender Gap Report 2014," accessed January 3, 2015, http://reports.weforum.org/global-gender-gap-report-2014/

Printed in the United States
By Bookmasters